LUCAS
ON
BASS
FISHING

by

JASON LUCAS

With illustrations and diagrams

NEWLY REVISED EDITION
A Family Weekly Edition

DODD, MEAD & COMPANY

NEW YORK

CONTENTS

PART I
FISHING METHODS

PART II

TACKLE

Selecting—Correct Use—Repairing

PART III

MISCELLANEOUS

PART III

MISCELLANEOUS

LIST OF ILLUSTRATIONS

(See Photo Section, facing page 96)

ix

DIAGRAMS

Introduction to Lucas

ALL editors are by nature skeptical. The editor of a magazine having to do with stories about hunting and fishing becomes exceedingly so. When I first heard about a fisherman by the name of Jason Lucas, I put him down as another of those piscatorial experts who are handier with conversation in a barroom than they are with a casting rod in a boat. People were just not catching their limit of bass each day in a lake only twelve miles from one of our largest cities, which everyone knew had been fished out years ago. Nor did they catch walleyed pike in that same lake which had not yielded a single walleye since it did briefly after the state conservation department stocked it ten years earlier.

Then one day an associate of mine asked Lucas to write an article on bass. I read it and was amazed. This man really knew something about fishing. The article had none of the old hackneyed dope that had been published in every outdoor magazine for the past fifty years. The information was new and came from first-hand experience. My appraisal of the man changed abruptly and I asked him to do a series of six articles on his new angling technique. That series is now a part of sportsmen's magazine history. The response from readers was immediate. They had been starving for fresh information on bass fishing for years, and mail poured in daily demanding more. I invited Lucas to become angling editor for *Sports Afield*.

No editor could ask for a finer staff member. Not only is

Lucas's angling department bringing in loads of mail, his copy good and strong and in on time each month, but best of all he has the delightful habit of dropping in with a nice catch of bass at the right time.

Jason Lucas has the enviable record of having fished eight hours a day for 365 consecutive days. He even has the best excuse we've ever heard for spending so much of his time fishing —he claims he works out the plots for short stories while tempting bass with an assortment of plugs and flies. No one but Jay could go out on a frigid November day in Minnesota and catch his limit just to oblige a photographer who needed pictures for an early spring issue that was ready for press. Nor would anyone but Lucas play a 36-pound salmon on sewing thread for 14 hours, and land him, just to prove it could be done.

In reading this book you won't find many things that have appeared in previous volumes on bass-fishing techniques. Some of his advice will be radically different from what you have read before. If you happen to disagree with some of his theories, I suggest you try them out before raising hell with the publisher. Jay has a very disarming habit of being right with some of his most outlandish claims.

TED KESTING

Introduction to the Book

THIS book is written mainly to help a man catch more bass in hard-fished water. Anyone can get plenty of fish in a wilderness lake, where they are so plentiful that they never find nearly enough food to go round, and consequently are ready to grab at anything, no matter how crudely presented. Such fishing is dub stuff, calling for no skill, and is boring to the expert angler.

To save much useless repetition, I shall speak mainly of lake fishing, and of the casting rod; in the second part of this book I shall deal with the fly rod for bass.

This, because what I am attempting is to give the reader the *feel* of bass fishing, and a thorough knowledge of its basic principles, which is a thousand times more useful than telling him minutely what to do under hypothetical conditions which he may never encounter. Where I do, rarely, give specific instances, it is purely to illustrate general principles.

I do not treat river fishing separately to any great extent, because bass, unlike trout, have practically the same habits in a river that they have along the shoreline of a lake, and are found in places of about the same kind. Fishing in a lake is by far the more difficult of the two, simply because there bass can get much farther from the shoreline, so it is harder to find where they are. A good lake fisherman has no difficulty in changing to river fishing; but a river fisherman almost has to learn all over again when he seeks bass in a lake. Here, of course, I am speaking of rivers of ordinary size; as we work up to the few very wide ones, river fishing comes more and more to resemble lake fishing.

Nor would it be at all useful to deal separately with different parts of the country, for no change of consequence in one's methods or equipment is necessary for different districts. Here, again, bass are completely unlike trout. The trout fly most successful on one stream may be very poor on another not ten miles off, for different stream bottoms breed different insects and their nymphs, and a trout can be peculiarly choosy about sticking to morsels of the type to which he is accustomed. Bass can be choosy too, but in a different way; their food is much the same wherever they are found.

I know that in some districts certain lures are regarded as "the best," and others as "no good here." I could never find that to be more than local notions. Naturally, if everybody in a district sticks almost exclusively to the Wheezy Geezer, that will be what nearly all the bass are taken on. They'll be caught only when they're in a mood for the Wheezy Geezer, and striking at the depth at which it runs; the rest of the time, they're "just not striking." At such times, I have made catches of the finest kind on, say, the Flopping Floozie. But try to change the local boys from their adherence to the Wheezy Geezer—just try it!

Naturally, when I speak of fishing in twenty feet of water, I know that a man cannot very well do that in a Southern lake only six feet deep. But he can seek the deepest place there is—he may find one as deep as ten feet—and see what luck he has there, when they're not in the shallow water.

In other words, a man must use his head a little sometimes, and adapt what I say to local conditions. If he refuses to use his head—well, he'd better give up bass fishing and make kelly pool his lifetime hobby. But probably he wouldn't get far at that either.

I stick mainly to the casting rod, because that is what at least nineteen men out of twenty use for bass. And, taking the season through, I consider the casting rod as by far the more productive for bass, in nearly all parts of the country. I know that some authorities disagree with me here and, as in all other things that I say, I am not insisting that I am right; I merely give my views for what they are worth. But the huge preponderance of casting rods used for bass seems to prove that most bass anglers do agree with me.

I am not counting the much greater number of very small bass that can unquestionably be taken, anywhere, on a fly rod. The fly-rod man will nearly always be safe in betting that he can get more bass than the man with the casting rod—if there's no limit on the size to be counted. My saying these things does not mean that I am opposed to the fly rod, or dislike it. As a matter of fact, when bass fishing from a boat, I usually keep both a fly rod and a casting rod rigged up, and use them alternately. But I do get most of my larger ones on the casting rod. And as to the common notion that a fly rod is more sport, or more sportsmanlike: I think it pure nonsense, for reasons that I shall explain in the second part of this book.

All of which is leading up to this: If bass are in a certain place, obviously they are there whether one is using a fly rod or a casting rod. And they will be taking a lure at the same depth, with about the same retrieve, whichever rod one is using. Therefore extensive separate treatment of each would be entirely useless.

Nor do I differentiate much between the smallmouth and the largemouth, for they are so much alike that many have difficulty telling which is which, especially since both, like all other fishes, vary a good deal in color in different places. It might be well to comment that neither is, strictly speaking, a true bass at all; they belong to the sunfish family. And that is exactly why they are so game. If bluegills grew to large size, they'd probably wreck all our tackle, for they're the gamest, toughest, scrappiest little beggars in existence— try them on suitably light fly tackle and see if they're not.

There are, however, three points of difference between the smallmouth and the largemouth: the smallmouth chooses more open, weed-free spots; he is generally caught deeper, where there is deep water; and he prefers a faster river, and will be found more out in the current there.

As to the notion that the smallmouth is gamer than the largemouth: Doctor Henshall, the father of bass fishing, who had caught thousands of both kinds all over North America, said emphatically that he could not find one iota of difference in their gameness, when both were caught in similar water. I agree with him. It is unfair to compare the battle of a hard, streamlined smallmouth from cold northern water with that of a largemouth taken in lukewarm water much farther south.

It is still more unfair to compare the fight of a small-mouth from a fast river with that of a largemouth caught in still water; an old shoe fastened to a line could give one a fine battle in a swift current. Only yesterday, I hooked a good-sized rainbow trout in a Western river which I am now fishing. He took my fly in one of the rare large, still pools. He put up a very disappointing fight, swimming around languidly, sulking. Until, by accident it seemed, he got into the rapids below the pool; then I found that I had a real battle on my hands—he was a very game fish indeed, and it was only by doing some gymnastics in heavy waders that I avoided breaking my fine leader. But which was doing the fighting, the fish or the current? His actions in the pool suggested that it was not the fish.

So, as I see it, only a smallmouth plus a current can give

one a better fight than a largemouth in still water. Indeed,
I am inclined to consider the largemouth the more sporting
fish of the two, because he will take a surface or shallow-
running lure more readily, and will do more of his fighting on
the surface.

I make no pretensions to telling "all about bass." I do
not know all about them, by any means. For instance, one of
the oddest things connected with fishing is that all the bass
in a large lake, or even in a whole district, can change their
notions almost at the same instant—their notions not only
as to what lures they want, but as to whether they will feed
freely or hardly at all. The thing sounds unbelievable, even
ridiculous; but all of us with much fishing experience have
seen it happen over and over again. I am still testing the many
theories put forward to account for this strange phenomenon,
but so far I have not found one which gave sufficiently consistent results for me to feel justified in becoming its proponent. For that reason I discuss none of these theories in
this book, but of course I reserve the right to do so later if
further experiments make me think that I have found something worth reporting.

Men of our race have been fishing for trout, and studying
their ways, since cave-man times; and during the past half-
century or so some men of brilliantly analytical minds—Hal-
ford, in England, was about the first of these—have devoted
practically their whole lives to truly scientific research in all
matters pertaining to the trout. Not until Doctor Henshall
began writing about him did white men really make the acquaintance of the American black bass. But great a debt as we
owe to Henshall as the evangelist of bass fishing, we must admit that he was more their inspired press agent than a student
of their ways; his original researches into their habits were

few, desultory, and of little value. But if any writer of equal merit on the subject has appeared since his day, I am not familiar with his work.

In short, we have had almost a plethora of trout study, but practically no real study of the bass, which now towers high above the trout as *the* American game fish. Why? Perhaps because solid foundations of trout study having been laid so long ago, it is easier for our contemporaries to build on them than to do original spadework, always a far more difficult thing than using foundations laid by others.

Some may ask if a book can teach anything about fishing. As well inquire whether a surgeon should invent all the operations he performs, completely ignoring the research of others, accounts of which he can find only in books and journals. As a matter of fact, the more advanced a fisherman or a surgeon is, the more assiduously he reads the literature of his subject, knowing that it is a poor book or periodical indeed from which he cannot glean at least some scraps of information which he might never stumble onto by himself—information which, in the fisherman's case, must, of course, lead to his catching at least a few more fish.

But it would be foolish to think that reading alone could make a good angler of anybody. Similarly, the cleverest man in the world could memorize all the best surgical textbooks there are, but unless he had practical experience—well, I shouldn't want him messing around with my duodenum.

If I were not angling editor of *Sports Afield*, I should not feel nearly as fitted as I do to write this book. Since it has by far the largest circulation of any sportsmen's magazine in the world, I receive a great volume of mail from anglers not only all over this country but in many others, from Finnish

Lapland to Korea and New Zealand. Therefore I am fully acquainted with the problems of the average angler, and of the pure novice.

I receive letters, too, from many of the finest anglers in North America, some of them well-known angling writers, asking me to help them with some problem or other. And I not infrequently call upon these same men to assist me in solving things which I do not seem able to figure out for myself.

From this it will be seen that I am not so foolish as to claim infallibility in fishing matters. Since I was practically an infant, fishing has been no less than a mania with me; I have actually spent over 3,000 hours in a single year fishing, and studying fish. But I make no more pretense to brilliance than I do to omniscience, and I doubt if I have learned a fourth of what I should have learned from all this fishing, and the many thousands of fish which I have caught; no, there is no doubt—I am sure I haven't.

So I am writing this book chiefly for the benefit of those who haven't found time to fish or to experiment with various methods as much as I have, hoping that it will help them get more bass. Indeed, I can promise that it will help them, for some of this, although now rewritten and expanded, has appeared in *Sports Afield* and I receive numerous letters from anglers giving actual instances in which methods I advised, previously unknown to them, have helped them get many more bass, and much larger ones, than they would have got otherwise.

Yes, one can deliberately go seeking lunkers, and get a lot more of them than if fishing for bass in general. I shall devote a special chapter to that.

I might add that whatever faults this book may have—and I know they will be many—no armchair theories will be found in it, for I have subjected all methods and theories which I mention to the most exacting tests, in much actual fishing, and find that they really lead to catching many bass.

On the other hand, I shall make no apologies whatever if in a later edition of this book—or next month in a magazine article—I contradict flatly something which I say here; those already familiar with my writing will know that I have more than once flatly, deliberately contradicted a previous statement of mine, when further research proved me wrong in my former opinion. "A foolish consistency is the hobgoblin of little minds."

This, of course, is but another way of saying that I am still learning about fishing, and I hope to continue doing so as long as I live. I am always trying to disprove my own most strongly held theories, to find better ones; and when I do, the old ones promptly are thrown out the window. If that sad day should ever come when I think that I know all of it and have no more to learn, I trust that I may have intelligence enough left to know that I am through forever, and grace enough to disappear quietly from the pages of sportsmen's publications. But I am hoping that this very spirit of humility, of willingness to learn, will sustain me a long time.

So here's hoping this book will help you get more bass, and larger bass, and more sport from those you do get.

Good fishing!

JASON LUCAS

PART I

Fishing Methods

Up to the Minute

Few additional remarks on fishing methods are needed for this Third Edition, because the things I said about them are as true now as when I first wrote them. This is because fish probably haven't changed their instincts or habits noticably in a million years—since long before there were men to catch them.

Therefore, this is to deal chiefly with the most recent development in tackle—rods, reels, lines, lures. And with changes in fishermen's habits!

In my Introduction to the book I served notice that I reserved a right to contradict anything I said about fishing, when further fishing experiments warranted that. So I make no apology here for contradicting a thing or two that I previously wrote.

Spinning, including spincasting—The spincast reel is also called a push-button reel and by other names; one maker lists his as a casting reel, which of course it isn't. It's sometimes known as "the American-type spinning reel." It's not that either, for reels of this enclosed type were tried, and rejected, perhaps sixty years ago in Europe.

The reason for the very high popularity of the spincast reel is purely that anybody can learn to use it quite well in half an hour or so. It calls for practically no development of skill to make long (and generally trouble-free) casts; of course it takes more time to develop reasonable accuracy.

When I did the last revision of this book, anybody who said that spinning (or its form called spincasting) wasn't the full answer to a maiden's prayer, a fishing method to end all other fishing methods, was howled down as an old fogey, a stick-in-the-mud too stupid to realize that fly and casting tackle were as out of date as the horse and buggy. So I was temerarious, indeed, to make the somewhat humorous remarks about spinning that you'll find in Chapter XXXII.

A great change has taken place since that chapter was written. Nearly all the large companies that then sold, and recommended, only spinning tackle now also sell—and boost! —casting and fly tackle; indeed, some of them say that spinning is to be regarded as an introductory method, to use before one advances to fly and casting tackle. And in their advertising matter they seem to agree fully with a veteran guide I was talking to only yesterday in Arkansas (I fish all over the country) who is one of the very best bass fishermen I ever met, and particularly noted for finding really big bass for his guests.

He said that he had kept accurate track of several thousand bass caught last season in the various lakes where he guides; that perhaps 90 per cent of those he saw fishing used some sort of spinning tackle—but that close to 95 per cent of the really worth-while bass were landed by that small minority using casting tackle.

I think the present status of the various ways of fishing might well be put thus:

The cane pole and bobber, with live bait, always has been, and probably always will be, the favorite of children and of some who merely hope to kill some fish (and time), anyhow, with no thought of the word "sport," or of studying fishing.

The spincast reel is a stage higher and will no doubt continue to have very great popularity, since its use calls for so little knowledge or practice. But note that all other things called participant sports (as for instance golf, bowling, tennis and kelly pool) are called sports purely because they do necessitate a good deal of study and development of skill.

The open-faced, under-rod spinning reel requires a shade more practice. It has a legitimate and useful place in fishing since it is best to handle lures too light for casting or spincast tackle, but too heavy for a fly rod. This, as I point out later, makes it about ideal for some smaller fish, such as crappies, that can be taken with real success only on a very small lure. With heavier lures, it gives more distance than a spincast reel.

But in spite of a common belief contest records seem to prove that a good casting reel can give more distance and accuracy than an open spinning reel, *for the few who learn to use it properly.* We have been told that spinning reels permit most distance because the line is so easily pulled off over the end of the stationary spool. But with a casting reel it isn't pulled off! It's shot off by the revolving spool—so fast, indeed, that some braking is needed to prevent overruns, "backlashes." Furthermore, it's shot straight toward the first guide, without the wild, energy-wasting, whirling thrashing of the spinning line—which is hampered much more in those of the enclosed, spincast type by restriction of the thrashing to within a small cone.

Not long ago it seemed that casting reels were about to vanish, and some fine ones indeed were taken off the market because of poor sales. Now there are many new and high priced ones appearing—certainly a whole lot of straws to show how the wind is blowing.

Proper use of fly tackle is regarded as the mark of the most advanced angler. In some places at about all times, and ın all places at many times, it will catch more bass than tackle of any other type—and always gives much the most sport with each one hooked. But it will not do the job always, everywhere, so most who use it should also have casting or spinning tackle.

I think the great majority of anglers are right in sticking to spincast (or spinning) tackle, since they don't take fishing as a serious or regular sport and wouldn't learn to use the more advanced forms with reasonable ease.

Contrary to a popular notion, it's almost as easy to learn to use fly tackle as spinning tackle—if one goes about it with the right, matching outfit, and learns correct casting technique. But since most don't do this, they can dub around for years and still not be really casting with their fly tackle.

Selection of casting tackle that will give satisfaction also calls for advice—either written, as here, or oral—from a thoroughly experienced angler; the average tackle clerk, in spite of his omniscient air, knows nothing whatever about more advanced fishing methods. While comfortable use of good casting tackle does call for some thought and practice, it can't be called really difficult.

The newer, imported, high-priced casting reels work very well, but most of them are much heavier than American reels. This doesn't matter too much, the weight being so near one's hand. Still, many experts prefer the lighter, narrow-frame American reels, costing a lot less, for practical fishing purposes.

* * *

Rods—The spinning rod with parabolic action has become obsolete in this country, though it is still popular in Europe. Americans much prefer one with faster action—the type of action, or bend in casting, I'll now describe particularly for fly rods:

It's a rod with, on a cast, noticable but rather slight bend up to somewhere around the middle, and from there on to the tip a bend that increases gradually but isn't very marked in any one short strip. In fly rods this used to be called "dry-fly action," until it was realized that it's also by far the best with wet flies, too. Now in a store you're unlikely to find a rod with the old "wet-fly action," so weak and sloppy as to be good for little except still-fishing for sunfish with worms. If a rod is not otherwise described, it will have this standard (formerly called dry-fly) action.

There have been strong attempts to boost rods with a "new" type of action—very stiff all the way up, except for a very pronounced bend in a short piece near the tip; they are called by various names implying that they are super-dooper. This is but an attempt to revive an identical action which was boosted, and flopped, around the turn of the century. The real truth is that it would be just too painful for sales managers to admit that the best action for rods was known at least 75 years ago—by a few advanced anglers who had expensive rods made to order.

Strangely, the companies most highly boosting this "new" action (and some other freak actions) are those that, in my opinion, have for many years made the very best rods in the world, with standard action. So, regardless of what the salesman says, get a rod with standard action.

Some rods are advertised as designed especially for spincasting. A spincast rod and a casting rod are identical; so if you have a good casting rod don't let some tackle salesman talk you into buying another and unnecessary one to go with a spincast reel.

Since I originally wrote this book, I have completely decided (and have been saying in magazine articles) that the long, heavy fly rod with "bass action" is but a crude, clumsy, tiring thing. For bass bugs, I now strongly recommend a rod not over eight feet, and perhaps three inches or so shorter, with *trout* action, to be used for anything from small sunfish to large salmon and tarpon. When I first wrote this in magazine articles, I brought howls of rage from some veteran anglers *who had never tried these lighter rods for bass*. Now I find a large majority of fly-rod bass anglers using such shorter, lighter rods.

With these rods, you shouldn't attempt to cast the huge, air-resisting bugs that most inexpert anglers think necessary for bass, and that won't cast reasonably well even on the heaviest rod. The best bass popper is of roughly the diameter of an average fountain (not ball-point) pen and perhaps three fourths inch long, with very little fluffy, air-resisting stuff sticking out. It will catch a lot more bass than the bulky ones because it can be cast much farther and more accurately—and is less tiring to use, so you'll keep it in the water more. Unfortunately, most who fish know so little about fishing that a great majority of bass bugs seen in stores are of the wrong, too-bulky type, since there's most demand for these. You may have to look in several stores to find some of the best size.

What I say further on about avoiding cheap rods does not hold so true any more. Production-line methods have permitted turning out glass rods of low price that have surprisingly good action, and will do nicely for one who can't afford better; but a higher priced one is advisable if you can get it. I refer to tubular glass rods; solid-glass rods have poor action but are very strong—they are suitable mainly for rough work, or for the fisherman who won't learn to handle better tackle.

*　　　*　　　*

Casting and Spinning Lines—A great blunder now is to confuse spinning with casting lines. Monofilament is much the best for spinning reels of any type—but braided line is far better with a casting reel.

Really, the usual stiff, wiry "casting line" is little better than soft monofilament on a casting reel; it is full of built-in backlashes and trouble. Much the best is a soft braided, coreless, non-waterproofed nylon line, which after a little use flattens out to resemble a ribbon. (Silk lines, now rarely seen, cast just a shade better, but they go bad so soon, unless given great care, that few want to be bothered with them now.)

This soft-braid line, with its splendid casting qualities, will not wear as long as hard-braid or monofilament—but it will hardly cost the average angler fifty cents a year extra to use it, a small price to pay for the fine, trouble-free casting it will let him do. Just now, I know of only two companies making this soft-braid line. Casting lines I've tried made of synthetic materials other than nylon were so wiry as not to be worth discussing.

Then how about casting reels advertised as "made especially for monofilament"? So long as many insist on using monofilament on casting reels, makers will advertise some thus —after all, it's their business to sell customers what they want, right or wrong, not to tell them how to fish properly. Use soft-braid on those "monofilament" reels.

I've been referring to lines for fishing. I don't pretend to advise the very small number of tournament casters what to use; much of their tackle is suited purely to stunting, not to fishing.

* * *

Fly Lines—A line must be of right weight to suit your fly rod or you practically can't learn to cast with it. But knowing what size to get is now difficult. Send for some line companies' catalogs. If one says that his lines are listed by *letters of the alphabet* to represent *weight*, not *diameter*—or if he'll tell you so in reply to a letter from you—the thing is pretty simple.

For a perfect fit on a rod of the type I recommended, get a C level (cheapest but rather crude), an HCH doubletaper (mainly for dry flies), or best of all, a GBF—called torpedo, three-diameter or weight-forward. For bass, that last should have a front taper not over six feet, usually called a bug taper or some such thing, and, to bring out the action of the rod, a belly (heaviest part) not less than twenty feet or so. This bug-taper line will work fine for all-around use; it will even serve with dry flies by using a long, tapered leader.

Be sure to get nothing but a line of *floating* type, which, in spite of the advertisements, is far better with wet flies than the sinking line advertised for wet-fly fishing—as well as being the only kind that's good with dries and bugs. There are exceptions to this, but hardly one per cent of the readers will ever engage in the specialized types of fishing for which a sinking line is really best. I regard the "intermediate"—sinking-floating—as an unfortunate hermaphrodite that has no real place in modern fishing.

That boiled things down for simplicity. The rest of this section will be a somewhat technical discussion of the matter that all but more advanced or serious anglers may skip.

The old system of listing fly-line sizes by letters designating diameters simply doesn't make sense with modern lines of widely varying specific gravities. The diameter of a fly line is of no interest to anglers; it's purely the *weight* of a given length that determines whether it will work with one's rod.

A newly devised system using letters and numbers (for instance, WF-8-F) is just as bad, since it includes weight of the forward taper, regardless of how long it may be. But this forward taper is not a "working part" of the line and has no bearing whatever on how it fits a rod! This should be obvious —for instance, if the G part of a GBF line had any bearing on fitting the rod, then a sufficient length (therefore weight) of G level should cast fine on that rod. But we all know that on any practical rod it would be as impossible to cast with the very light G level as with sewing thread. It would be just as sensible to include weight of the tapered leader, which may be twenty feet or longer—so none whatever of the heavy belly, the true working part, of the line would be considered!

Many letters from readers have shown me that they want no dealings with this new method, and consider it utterly worthless and confusing; they feel that a small number of line makers are trying to ram it down their throats whether they want it or not. Some tournament casters seem to favor it; but, as I said, the number of tournament casters is utterly inconsequential compared to that of anglers.

This now gives us two nonsensical methods of listing fly-line sizes, instead of just one, as formerly.

But there's still another method, which I have been suggesting in print, and in letters to makers, for at least fifteen years. And let me add hastily that I don't favor it so highly because I regard it as "my baby"; I read of it so very long ago that I forget who first recommended it.

It's simply to retain the old letters with which everybody is familiar, but use them to represent *weight*, not diameter, of any agreed-upon length of line. Some companies have used this system for years, and more are turning to it annually. They generally use as standard a weight that would be average for the silk lines for which the letter system was devised—about the same as that of the present "intermediate." Of course only the heaviest part of a line should be considered.

With this system, all you'd need to remember, or mark near your rod butt, is a single letter, the lowest letter of the alphabet found in the description of any line that fits your rod. So if your rod works fine with an HCH, it would work identically well with a C level or HCF—regardless of whether the line you're changing to is a floater or even the heaviest lead-cored sinker of very small diameter, and regardless of who made the line; you *couldn't* go wrong. What system could be simpler or less confusing?

I recommended a size larger (GBF) in forward-taper lines because the bellies of these are almost always much shorter than the pick-up of an angler of only very moderate skill; therefore, in an HCF, the belly wouldn't have weight enough to bring out the action of the rod—and, to repeat, tapers and levels before and behind the bellies have no bearing on the matter. The correct thing, of course, would be to make the bellies longer, and of size C, so that in buying a new line of any type or make one could stick completely to that "lowest-letter" rule.

* * *

Lures—Of the huge number of new lures that have come on the market, nearly all are but modifications or adaptations of old ones, so it would be waste of time to discuss them. And those that have been on the market for a generation or two will usually get considerably more bass than the new, highly touted ones—simply because, since they proved very effective, they're the tiny few still left of the many that came out at the same time. Of the hundreds of highly vaunted ones coming out recently, it's entirely safe to say that nearly all will be forgotten in a few years—because they're not particularly good fish-getters.

Pork-chunk black eels, plastic worms and jigs really do embody new principles—for fresh-water fishermen. They are excellent at many times. But the really experienced bass angler knows that no one type of lure can always be best, that he usually has to experiment with many lures to find what the temperamental critters want right at the moment. With fish of nearly any other species, one good lure is very likely to work well at any time.

The more advanced angler, who fishes for sport rather than just for dead fish, usually dislikes using black eels, plastic worms or jigs, since they must be fished slowly, much like live bait. But there are few with such high sportsmanlike feelings that they won't fall back on these lures when all else fails.

The beginner usually thinks that a natural imitation of something bass feed on should catch most. But owing to the sort of vision fish have (rather poor) the exact contrary is true, for it's purely the size, action and color of a lure that matter —and something with no resemblance whatever to any natural food nearly always has best action and will produce most fish.

Ignore a guarantee that some lure will catch fish. Any experienced angler will absolutely guarantee to catch fish on his ball-point pen, his pipe, his false teeth (if he has store teeth) or anything else of comparable size to which he can tie a hook and his line. But he also knows that he can get a whole lot more fish on a good, standard lure.

It's impossible to judge the merits of a lure from looking at it, or seeing its action in the water. Fish have such totally different minds from ours that we can never hope to understand them. There's but one good way to find out how well they'll take a certain lure—try it on them!

Toward the end of the book, I say that walleyes can be caught better on live bait than on artificials. I take that all back! I've since found that more can almost invariably be caught on artificials, fished at the bottom in deep water, by the method I describe in Chapter II for big bass.

When I first wrote this book, fishermen were inclined to use too-heavy, unsportsmanlike tackle, so I strongly recommended lighter lines, especially. The opposite is now true; most use lines so light that they have no chance at all to land their better bass among the weeds or brush in which they're nearly always found. The same is even more true of such big fish as pike and muskellunge.

* * *

Since the essence of anything to be called a sport is that both contestants have roughly an equal chance to win, it is not sportsmanship, but plain foolishness, to use tackle so light that you have practically no chance. This foolishness has been greatly aggravated by advertisements of tackle companies trying to sell "ultra light" tackle to those who know no better than to use it for larger fish in weeds or such.

It leaves one with the unworthy suspicion that some tackle companies are more interested in selling you just any fool thing they can talk you into buying than in giving you sound advice. And—it's an awful secret for me to divulge!—some tackle companies have officials who are very experienced anglers; but some others haven't a single official who knows much more about practical fishing than does my Siamese cat. Perhaps—just perhaps—these latter are so dumb about fishing that they really think ultra-light tackle practical where its use is plain silly.

There's but one sound rule in the matter: use tackle that will give you and the fish you may hook, in the places where you may hook them, something resembling an even chance to win.

*   *   *

Here's about the best counsel in this book: if you want to be a consistently (not just occasionally) successful bass fisherman, by far the most important item of your equipment is—your head! The average piece of advice I give here will no doubt work fine at least nine times in ten. But when fishing according to the rules won't get you bass, you must be ready to do some hard thinking and experimenting, to find out what will get them at that certain time and place. One who always fishes "according to the book"—this book or any other—can never become a top-notch bass angler.

CHAPTER I

Finding the Bass—Spring

How do we go about the practical business of catching bass, especially in hard-fished water, and preferably lots of them?

The first thing, naturally, is to find where they are. Without that, all else is useless, but having got where they are, at least some will generally be caught even when using the wrong lure and retrieve. Generally, but by no means always.

The first few times on a lake or river are always difficult; they should be regarded as dedicated mainly to learning the water, though with luck some fish should be caught. Remember that even the most skillful guide will not show to advantage on unfamiliar water. Remember, too, that you have all the opportunity in the world to learn a lake near you; it is not as it would be at some fishing resort where you might spend a few days a year, some years. The thing is to learn, and to learn as fast as possible, not potter around, hoping, as so many do.

Some parts of a lake are consistently better than others; some are so poor that it is best to avoid them entirely, though an occasional fish may be caught there. From the beginning, it is well to start sorting out the water of fishing depth into three categories: good, fair and bad. Stick almost exclusively to the "good," with, especially at first, occasional trips to the

3

"fair," and even to the "bad," to see if the classification should be moved up a grade.

To complicate matters, all sections of the water may have to be completely reclassified for each season, spring, summer, and fall. From this it will be seen that it takes a man several years to know a lake so well that, when he has not fished it for some time, he can go directly to a certain spot and be pretty sure to find it good then. But such intimate knowledge of the water is by no means necessary to successful fishing. A really good, experienced angler can size up a pretty large lake in a general way in three or four days, by swinging rapidly around it, trying the most promising spots—which, of course, he can recognize quickly. By the end of that time, he should be getting as many fish as any of the local men except the very few real experts.

Fishermen run to two types. One likes to learn a single lake so thoroughly that he almost knows every fish in it by its first name. The other prefers to try strange water—he has more of the explorer in him. Personally, I rank somewhere between the two. Fishing water which I know thoroughly is apt to grow monotonous to me, and even a trifle boring; there is no sense of novelty. On the other hand, I do not particularly care to fish at a place which I know I shall see only for a day or two, since I shall have no time to learn it, and learning the water is at least half the fun of the thing for me. In this I refer strictly to lakes; a river being much easier to learn, I can enjoy my first day's fishing on it, even when I think that I shall probably never see it again.

On a strange lake, the logical way to start finding spots best at the time is to ask somebody who should know—the man from whom you rent a boat, for instance. But remember that he himself has little time to fish—fishing season is his harvest, when he must garner his year's income—so his answers

are apt to be pretty vague, but accurate enough to start you on the right track.

If you borrow a friend's boat, don't take his advice too seriously unless you know him to be a fairly good fisherman. Moreover, he is almost sure to send you chasing miles off, when fishing may be much better in front of his house. Good fishing spots are like prophets; they rarely are given due credit by those most familiar with them. Far pastures look greener.

Out on the water, watch for that fairly rare man who is casting smoothly and effortlessly, for it is safe to assume that he is an experienced angler. Get near him, but not close enough to disturb his fishing, nor ahead of him, where he is going to fish. This above all: Courtesy and good manners go as far with fishermen as with other civilized human beings—perhaps further than with most.

Strike up a conversation with him, but wait until he sees that you are acting like a gentleman and a sportsman before you begin to ask questions; then he's practically sure to answer you to the best of his ability. Remember that there's a free-masonry among sportsmanlike anglers, wherever they are found, stronger than among Masons themselves. I know whereof I speak, for though I call the West my home, I know the East too, and I have found the same strong sense of brotherhood among fishermen all over the country. And, by the way, some of my own strongest and most lasting friendships have begun with the call to a stranger, "What luck are you having?"

Don't waste an instant on the man whose casting resembles shot-putting; he won't know much. And don't bother with a man who is using a long cane pole and frogs or minnows; he will probably resent anybody else being on the lake, and he may either answer you gruffly or be very foxy and send you widely astray, perhaps afraid you'll catch something when he's getting none. There are exceptions to this, of course, but few will disagree when I say that men using artificial lures are by far the most likely to be sportsmen, not mere fish-catchers. And a good sportsman is a good sport too, willing to see the other fellow have some fun.

It is fairly easy, by asking questions, to find the best parts of a lake in a general way. And don't get the notion that asking them will make you look green at the game; it is the experienced angler who questions others most minutely. But finding the exact good spots is a very different matter, and far from easy, partly because even the most generous of anglers is reluctant to point out those which he knows, and risk seeing them overfished. Usually, you will have to discover them for yourself. Tips on how to do that will be found scattered all through this book, for brief instructions in the matter cannot all be set down neatly here under one heading.

You must now begin prospecting for fish, as it were, along those stretches of shoreline which you were told are good. And here is where the novice goes completely wrong, wasting half or even all his time on water unlikely to contain any bass whatever. This is because he does not understand the most elementary principles of a bass's feeding habits.

Smallmouths may be found on open, gravelly bottoms, but largemouths rarely are. It is the largemouth's nature to hide, and dart out on his prey like a cat; he never chases it far, as do so many other fishes. So if a largemouth is seen lying on an open bottom, he probably is not feeding and cannot be tempted with any lure. The fact that there are occasional exceptions to this rule, as to most others, does not prove that it is not a good one; so do not waste much time trying to catch the largemouth which you can see.

His hiding place is generally among weeds; but under low bushes, under a log, even in stone crevices will suit him quite well. And he likes some open water in which to see his prey approach, and for his short chase. This open water may be either level with him or above him, over deep weeds often not visible from the surface.

Therefore the outside edge of surface weeds, or lily pads or such, is always an excellent place when bass are in shallower water. It should be tried with casts about six feet apart all along the edge, giving particular attention to little bays running into it, and to points of it sticking out. Open spots back in the weeds are also good. This is the kind of fishing where being able to place one's lure neatly and accurately is a great advantage—indeed it is almost imperative. And reasonable accuracy is not nearly so hard to achieve as most imagine; in fact, it is easy, *if* one uses correct tackle and casting form, which I shall deal with in their places.

The second great mistake which beginners make—and many of them never outgrow it—is in thinking that bass are always found in such places as I have just described, even when they can find deeper water. Perhaps it is because deeper fishing is unquestionably more difficult than shallow-water fishing that so many never attempt it. Later on, I shall show how to go about it.

The old general rule is that bass are in shallow water in spring and fall, in deep water during the hot weather of mid-summer. This is far from holding true invariably, especially on a hard-fished lake.

Certainly it is a bass's nature to stay mainly in shallow water during the first part of the fishing season. But that is when many more anglers are out than at any other time, and their continual whipping of the shallows and splashing around drive most of the bass to deeper water. Rather, I should say, they drive the larger and warier ones there, leaving the foolish youngsters near shore.

So, even in the earliest fishing, try farther out—in ten to

twenty feet of water. It is there that one is most likely to pick up the old granddaddies who were annoyed by all the hulla-baloo inshore and went out seeking peace and quiet. I might amplify this by saying that, in a hard-fished lake, shallow fish-ing is only for the man who is out there by the first gray of dawn, before others have had time to disturb things for the day. That early, even a comparatively poor lake will sometimes furnish superbly good fishing; it is only on extremely rare occa-sions that late evening fishing can at all compare with it.

There is one great advantage about spring fishing: if you can't find big ones in deeper spots, you can nearly always get in toward shore and pick up some smaller ones—"just right eating size," as we say when we can't get big ones. As a matter of fact, smaller bass are much better to eat than aged lunkers. But I'll take the excitement of landing the lunkers!

It is during this early-season fishing, in shallow water, that either casting or fly-rod surface lures are in their glory. They are especially good just after daybreak. As the season advances, their usefulness begins to drop off in most places, and one must go farther and farther out to find many bass—or any at all.

Always be on the lookout for exceptionally good spots, and remember them when you find them. Reasoning or obser-vation will rarely find these for you. When you catch an unusu-ally large bass, or a number of bass, at one spot, there was some definite reason why that large bass, or several smaller bass, were there, and others are likely to move in when you catch these out. There is always the possibility of finding a small good spot in the middle of a poor stretch; if you find such a spot, it is likely that nobody else knows about it. Later, I shall tell how to return infallibly to such places, no matter how far out.

Some will hold that a bass, like gold, is where you find it.

Certainly. But the "dude" prospector will waste weeks digging around in a limestone formation that an experienced man would turn away from with a single glance and a shrug, knowing that it takes igneous rock to produce gold *in situ.*

The shoreline will often, but not always, tell one what depth of water to expect near it. Low, flat land usually means a shallow bar running out for a good distance. At the foot of a steep ridge, there is commonly a sharp drop-off, most often a short way out, because stuff falling down from the ridge will have been leveled off by the waves to form a narrow bench.

On a wilder lake, such a drop-off is the ideal place to fish, for by casting in a circle from one spot you can fish from the shallow shoreline to outside the deepest weeds; and bass, both largemouths and smallmouths, do like to congregate along those underwater banks. The best and most deadly method is to stay just inside the edge, cast out, let your lure sink clear to the bottom, and then draw it up the steep bank.

This, as I have said, is on a wilder, little fished lake. On one which is fished hard, such a place is likely to prove poor— because it is so easy to fish that everybody works it to death. At that, it is worth trying, if too much time is not lost in doing so. If you find a shallow underwater point running out some distance from the bench, it is likely to prove especially good, particularly off its tip.

As the season advances, one must work out more and more onto the fairly deep bars. On a much fished lake, these bars are likely to be by far the most productive, even in the earliest fishing, because they are almost never worked thoroughly.

To fish them properly, begin near the shore and keep on out to where the deepest weeds end, down where they can't be seen—it's because they can't be seen from a boat that these bars are fished so little. Having found the outer edge of the weeds, follow along it, for during most of the season it is a splendid place for large bass.

I have heard men comment with awe on the uncanny skill of some old Indian guide who could follow the edge of deep weeds in all its convolutions; it would seem as if it might take a lifetime to learn how. I use a method so simple that anybody can do it easily the first time he tries:

As you go out, use any plug you choose until you get to where the weeds are down out of sight. Then change to a sinking lure; personally, I prefer one with a single hook, so that it won't tangle up too much. Cast ahead, letting the lure sink to the bottom, and reel in; you'll feel the weeds down there. When a cast ahead shows bare bottom, you're at the edge—unless you've found a deep hole in the bar, an excellent place for bass. Now follow the edge of the bar by casting to the bare bottom, but being sure that your lure drags through weeds before reaching the boat. It's just outside the weeds that you'll get most of your strikes, and sometimes you'll turn up an astonishing number of lunkers there, even on a completely "fished-out" lake.

Especially if you catch a really big one, anchor immediately, so you will not lose the exact spot, since these whoppers very often run in pairs. And you may pick up four or five big fellows there; if so, you've been fortunate enough to have discovered one of those spots—perhaps a spring-hole—where big ones frequently congregate, and you're entitled to feel pretty happy about it. Indeed, using this method, you're certain to discover some good holes, probably known to nobody else. Take careful bearings in the manner which I shall explain later on—there's but one way to do it—so that you can find the exact spot next time. I've known good holes that were no larger than a bathroom floor, with all the territory around them very poor fishing.

"How long," I have been asked, "is a stretch of good bass fishing?" It is, naturally, anywhere from a few feet to several miles; rarely the latter, fairly often the former. And another question frequently asked me shows still more aversion to even rudimentary thinking on the part of my interrogator.

He will begin with a sensible query as to the depth at which he is likely to get most bass then. I'll say, for instance, about eight feet. He'll stare at me a few seconds, his puzzled face showing plainly that he wonders how I can be so stupid as to give such a vague, meaningless answer. And then it comes:

"But how far from shore is that?"

It speaks well for my self-control that I can act patient with a man who asks that. I explain that it may be a yard, or it may be a mile; and, so far as I know, somewhere right in the middle of Lake Superior there may be a bar eight feet below the surface, and if so it is probably a fine place for bass just then.

No, the man isn't stupid; he is probably very clever in his own line of endeavor. It just goes to show that when it comes to fishing matters, a man seems all too often to have left his common sense at home in the pocket of his other pants.

However, I should remark that, as angling editor of the largest sportsmen's magazine, I receive a great volume of mail from anglers—and I answer every letter; I like those friendly letters, most of them sounding as though they came from old fishing pals. It is well known that most magazines get a continuous stream of "crank" and foolish letters; but the odd thing is that I get one of that kind so rarely that it is a welcome novelty. My prize, to date, is the one from the man who asked where he could find pedigreed angleworms, so that he could raise really good sunfish bait! True, often a correspondent will apologize for the foolish question he asks. But it won't be foolish at all. It may be elementary; but we all had to learn the rudiments of fishing at some time or other.

Which goes to prove what I have always staunchly maintained: that we fishermen are high above the average in intelligence, in spite of our occasional mental aberrations. After all, who is really the more intelligent—the man who puts in most of his life at a fine outdoor sport like fishing, which can bring nothing but pleasure to humanity, or he who toils day and night inventing an atomic bomb, to blow up himself and everybody else?

But just the same, I don't like to be asked how long is a good fishing stretch, or how far from shore is eight feet deep— or how high is up. I've answered the first two questions here, once for all, I hope. The third could, I feel sure, be more competently handled by some professor of mathematics who can explain why parallel lines meet at infinity though, being still parallel, they must be, say, a foot apart. Me, I'm only an angling editor, and I don't deal with the various aspects of relativity in my correspondence column.

CHAPTER II

Finding the Bass—Summer

MIDSUMMER bass fishing is undeniably the most difficult of all, for not only are the fish out in the deepest water, where they are hard to find, but they are not feeding much; and when a bass isn't feeding, there is no use trying to tempt him. Really, it would be about as well if the average angler, who has a limit to his patience and endurance, gave up bass fishing entirely during this period, saving his enthusiasm for a new start when fall fishing, the very best of the year, sets in. The real fanatic at the game will, of course, keep right on; he'd make Job seem like a flighty person.

Still, this is when summer resorts and lake cottages are jammed with people trying to escape the heat of the cities. If that is all they want to do—fine!

Have you ever noticed that nearly all resort owners are gray or bald, with distraught, hopeless expressions on their faces? That is from lying awake worrying because they can't coax fish to bite for their guests during the worst part of the season. I have met some very persuasive resort owners, but never one enough so to have a noticeable influence on what the fish out in the lake would do. Adding to the poor man's cares, there is the knowledge that later on the fish—not only bass, but everything from punkinseeds to muskies—will practically be flopping up to the cabins seeking lures. And the cabins all standing empty! If a midsummer guest would return then, the resort owner would almost let him have his best cottage for nothing, just to show him that there are fish in Lake Whatsit—that it's actually crawling with huge ones, all willing to die gamely for the furtherance of sport.

So my advice to the man who plans a vacation, and wants it to be fishing, is this: If you don't get away in spring—which, incidentally, is when mosquitoes and such creatures have their open season on fishermen—try to stick it out on the job during the hot weather, and take your vacation later. You'll find fishing!

Exactly when, one may ask, is this dullest period? That is almost like asking how far out is eight feet deep. It varies, naturally, according to latitude. And a shallow lake warms and cools much more rapidly than a deep one. And summers vary in length, if one goes by the temperature and not by what astronomers say; I recall one year in the north when there was practically no summer, when it remained cold and dreary and rainy all through—I never heard the weather so heartily cussed. Perhaps it was fiendish of me, and certainly selfish, but I was delighted with it and kept hoping it would stay that way; and it did. It was the grandest fishing I ever saw, with no slump whatever.

Of course what counts is the temperature of the water, not of the air. There will be a good deal of hot weather before the water warms up—the exact length of time varying with the depth of the lake, some very deep ones hardly warming at all. And in fall the water lags behind the air in cooling. So there is but one thing for the man planning a fishing trip to do: have the resort owner write and tell him how fishing is at the time. At a near-home lake, the angler will know all too well when fishing falls off for the summer. When it picks up again, he'll hear about it; or he can take an occasional exploratory trip to find out for himself what's doing.

However, if the angling virus has its full grip on a man, he'll keep right on fishing all through the summer. In most places, he will rarely be completely skunked. Some years, on some lakes, he'll get a lot, and many big ones. So how does one go about hot-weather bass fishing?

There is an incident which, though it occurred more than twenty years ago, sticks in my mind as the aptest possible illustration of right and wrong midsummer methods—of the only right method, I might almost say, and of one of the innumerable wrong ones. The right brought a phenomenal catch; the wrong, in exactly the same spot and with the same lure, failed to produce even a weak strike. The fact that I'd slipped a joker into the deck detracts in no way from the merits of the thing as an object lesson.

I was spending that summer fishing the many lakes and rivers of northern Wisconsin. One day, about noon, I decided to try a small lake which I had fished several times before, located not many miles from my cabin. Conditions were what a Bostonian might have called exceedingly unpropitious; it was around the middle of August, with a blazing hot sun reflected from warm, glassy water. A less fanatical angler than I would have regarded it as a good time for a snooze, with faint hopes of catching a small bass or two toward dusk.

I planned tactics as I drove over there. It would, of course, be deep holes or nothing. I decided to begin with a small bar rising sharply almost in the middle of the lake, about half a mile from shore. But when I arrived there I saw a boat already approaching that bar, one which I recognized as belonging to a man whom I shall call Nate Dowley—he might shoot me, next time I'm up that way, if I showed him up by telling his real name.

This Nate was a professional guide who had lived on that lake for almost forty years. He had been a very good guide at one time—when the lake was swarming with green bass that anybody could find, and that would bite on anything. But the bass had been learning, and Nate hadn't. He was a cranky, grouchy old chap, though in the presence of some city sportsman who regarded him with proper awe as a modern Leatherstocking he could expand and become quite genial, seeing that his piscatorial omniscience was at last being appreciated.

When I can avoid it, I will not fish close to another man, both for his sake and my own, and the good end of that bar was really only large enough for one fisherman. So, waiting to see if Nate would leave, I sat down under a tree and rolled a brown cigarette—a relic of my cowboy days; I just cannot learn to like "tailor-mades" or white papers.

Watching Nate, I soon was struck by an astonishing fact: he could not find the little bar, the tallest weeds of which could be seen only by looking straight down from a boat on a calm day; he was pottering around without method, seeking it. A notion came to me, and I strolled over to ask the boat-house man a question. Yes, Nate had been there a long time before I arrived, rowing around and around. And I had to wait a full half-hour until he gave up and headed back toward shore.

I went out there, using the crude but very exact triangulation method, without instruments, which I shall later describe. I followed directly along one of my lines until I came to the intersecting one, and slipped my anchor out. Only then did it occur to me to glance over the side as a check; yes, there was that one little visible patch of weeds, under me and on my left, where they should be. The good deep hole was fifty feet from the other side of my boat; I had anchored far enough off not to scare any fish in it, and to make a comfortable cast.

I might add here that I had discovered the bar by the

none too original method of seeing others fishing there, and rowing out. But I had found that particularly good spot by the method which I described in the last chapter, casting to a clear bottom, and seeing to it that my lure came back through weeds. The surprising thing was that none of the natives around seemed to know of that especially good little hole—perhaps because they were not familiar with the triangulation method of anchoring in an exact spot every time.

I have always been very methodical, perhaps even fussy, in my fishing; I think it pays to be, in number of fish caught. Now, I carry a tackle box so large and heavy that it makes me lopsided getting it to the boat and back; but when I lay it in the bottom of my boat and swing its ten cantilever trays open, I have everything arranged perfectly under my hand without further trouble. Then, I carried one of more moderate size, and pretty badly cluttered up, so I began operations by spending some time hanging lures and things in their exact places around the boat. I oiled my reel, a free-spool tournament one, which had to be adjusted just right—at least to suit me. I was using a line so light that pulling it with my hands would break it without telling me much about its strength; so I kept testing the worn end with a scales until I came to a part that held. All this somewhat lengthy ritual concluded, I was at last ready to fish.

My first cast into that hole produced a four-pound bass which seemed to be a star fish-school athlete. He had strong opinions, not coinciding with mine, as to where he should go. But I won the dispute, and at last I was able to run my thumb into his mouth, a finger under his lower jaw, and lift him in. I carefully disengaged the hook and dropped him back into the water.

Then came the surprise; a grumpy voice near me: "How're they hittin'?"

It was old Nate—and his tone implied that he hadn't been out near that bar for a month at least. Of course he couldn't admit that he'd had to rely on one whom he probably regarded as a "sport" and a mere boy to find the place for him. He eased his anchor out not twenty feet from me. Naturally, I was somewhat annoyed, after waiting half an hour for him to get out of there so that I would not interfere with him.

His face showed that he had seen me put that nice one back, and also that he had decided opinions of darned fools who would catch fish like that, only to let them go again. However, I noticed that he was digging hastily into his tackle box to find a lure just like mine—a small red-and-white casting spoon.

I thought to myself: "Very well, Mister Nate! I know you're a foxy old duck—and you know it too. But let's see how this works." And I slipped the joker into the deck.

I made a cast, and when my lure struck the water I immediately began to turn the reel handle quite fast. Nate probably did not notice that after a few seconds I swung my body partly away from him so that he could not see my hands, nor that I held the rod tip close to the water so the movement of the line wasn't plain.

Whup! Another on—a brute, this time. For Nate's edification, I deliberately made that the wildest, splashiest fight I could—with the bass cooperating wonderfully. And with a big bass on such a light line as I was using, it's always going to be a wild, splashy fight; there's no hauling one straight in, fins-over-tail. As I released him, I turned so that Nate could get a good look at him.

A third cast—to bring in another one, big and belligerent. Three lunkers on my first three casts! I was pretty excited, of course, and felt like whooping; but I tried to look very bored,

as if I could do that every day—which, of course, was far, far
from fact.

Within fifteen minutes or so, I had landed and liberated
six bass, the smallest of which would have run three and a half
pounds—and that's a good big bass any day on a cold northern
lake.

And how was Nate doing meanwhile? He wasn't. He was
beginning to show marked symptoms of approaching apoplexy.
He kept casting furiously into the exact spot where I was casting—very bad manners. And when his spoon struck the water,
he'd begin to reel in immediately at the exact speed he saw me
reeling. But he hadn't had even a sign of a strike—and I could
safely have bet my pet rod that he wouldn't get one.

Finally he could stand it no longer. He yanked up his anchor and rowed over until his boat bumped mine. "Lemme see
that spoon!" he demanded irately.

I could afford to diffuse sweetness and light. "Surely,
Nate," I said, in my most courteous and dulcet tones, and held
it out to him on the tip of my rod.

He fingered it, turned it over, examined even the hooks,
trying—if I may be permitted a mild pun—to find where the
catch lay.

"Why," he said at last, "it's just like mine."

"Exactly like it," I agreed pleasantly. "Want to swap,
Nate?"

He glared at me, and answered only by snorting like a
porpoise. He backed off, and anchored where he could get an
even better cast into the spot I was fishing. Evidently he had
never heard about fishing manners.

Not much over an hour went by, and I had landed eighteen lunkers, that three-and-a-half pounder still the smallest,
and the largest slightly over five—no giant, but a fine bass for

northern Wisconsin's cold water. I kept that largest one to bake next day. And all out of a spot no larger than a living-room floor.

Still, Nate, using the same lure and copying every move I made—so far as he saw—had not had a ghost of a strike. He was squirming wild-eyed in his boat, and the term "fit to be tied" nicely expresses how he looked. If he hadn't been such a completely ornery old cuss I'd have felt sorry for him and told him what to do. But then he'd probably have thought being advised by a "sport" even more infuriating than getting no fish; for to him I was a dude of some sort—even if I had put in a big part of my life as an open-range cowpuncher, a trapper, and a professional mountain-lion and bear hunter, which isn't exactly dude stuff.

At last a few unproductive casts convinced me that I'd cleaned out that hole, so I pulled up my anchor and left. Possibly I shouldn't confess to being so unfeeling, but I winked solemnly at Nate as I passed him. He sat glaring after me, mumbling bad words into his long stubble of beard. Watching from shore, I soon saw him row off—evidence that he had got nothing there.

It might amuse the reader, before proceeding further, to try to figure out for himself where the joker lay. It strikes me that I have, by chance, written the thing with the technique of a mystery story, clues and all. . . . Give up?

I was, as I said, using a free-spool tournament reel, a thing Nate had probably never seen before. When my lure would strike the water, I'd begin to turn the reel handle pretty fast—but I would not have thrown the lever to put the gears in mesh. So while I seemed to be reeling in, the spool was revolving the other way and letting the lure sink. In fact, I was fishing the very bottom, thirty feet down, while Nate was fishing close to the surface—and only rarely will a bass come up that

far after a lure. I was also using a certain peculiar retrieve—
which was why I turned to hide my hands from Nate—but I'd
probably have got most of those fish even without that, so I'll
let a description of it go until I can deal more fully with the
matter of retrieves.

I have related this incident at some length because I am
attempting the almost hopeless task of getting the average user
of artificial lures to fish deep water, and fish the bottom of
deep water. Having observed innumerable anglers, I will say
that certainly not one in a hundred does the latter. And usually, during the middle of summer, it is by getting down there,
and only by getting down there, that one can catch bass of a
number or size worth considering—or any at all.

Even in my earliest spring fishing, I have got many of my
largest ones from these deep holes. Some of the biggest lunkers
seem to spawn early, and take to deep water immediately;
probably, as I have said, because in shallow water they are disturbed too often to suit them, by the many anglers there—the
younger and more scatterbrained bass don't seem to mind so
much. Or perhaps some of the smarter young ones do mind,
and get out, and so live to become granddaddies; maybe that is
the only reason why we find really large bass in a hard-fished
lake—a few were born with more sense than the rest.

Not one day in thirty, I should say, will many bass come
up near the surface, from deep water, after a plug. Why expect
them to? After all, the angler isn't doing a fish any favor by
pulling him from his native element and baking him. Perhaps
he is doing him a favor by catching him and letting him go
again, with no worse than a pin prick on the lip, thereby in-
structing him in how to live to a ripe old age and leave many
offspring. But try to convince a fish of that!

No—it's much better to drag the lure right under a fish's
nose, slowly, with a nice, enticing wiggle—or one of the re-

trieves which I shall describe later—so that he can yawn and reach out for it lazily without inconveniencing himself in the least. When it's that easy, I've found that even a Socrates among bass has not the strength of mind to resist temptation—unless, of course, the angler has been splashing around to let him know he's there and put him on his guard.

I freely admit that there is no thrill for an angler like that of seeing a big bass take a surface lure with a mighty, explosive splash, which always, somehow, comes unexpectedly. But when they will not take on the surface, or even near the surface, isn't it much better to fish deep for them than to go home empty-handed?

Finding and fishing these mysterious deep holes has a peculiar fascination of its own—for me, at least. I cannot say whether I like surface or deep fishing better; they are entirely different things, and sometimes I prefer one, sometimes the other. But most certainly, taking the season through, I have caught a large majority of my really big bass by this "deep stuff."

How about night fishing in midsummer? In a few places it is quite productive, but in most parts of the country I have found it far from what it's cracked up to be. I have done quite a bit of it, but I never could work up much enthusiasm for it; I like to see what I'm doing, and to see the scenery around—and mosquitoes and their kin are pestiferous enough in daylight, without letting them sneak up on one in the dark. In other words, hoot-owl fishing is fine for those who like it, but I don't happen to be one of them, and a big majority of the anglers I know feel as I do about it; they'll take theirs in daytime.

Which, for most men, leaves but one profitable form of bass fishing in midsummer—deep stuff.

CHAPTER III

Finding the Bass—Fall

THIS is the chapter in which I debunk myself.

When I first became its angling editor, *Sports Afield* printed an item about me which stirred up quite a little excitement in bass-fishing circles. So that the story of it may be fully understood, I'll begin at the beginning:

Ted Kesting, the editorial director, who offered me the post, is a big, genial young man with out-size shoulders that I always envy—I myself exemplify the beanpole school of architecture. He has a quiet sense of humor that always catches me off guard, accustomed as I have been all my life to the cowboys' sad-faced joking. When, unexpectedly, he put the proposition to me, my immediate reaction was a cry of alarm—"What! *I* stick in an office!"

From Ted's slight smile, I guessed he'd been waiting for that. He gravely explained that he wouldn't give me an office, or even a corner of a desk, for he firmly believed that an angling editor's place was living within sight of fishing, all the year round, in different parts of the country, and experimenting with different types of fishing for the benefit of his readers. I would not, Ted warned me soberly, be considered as doing my duty to the magazine unless I fished more or less practically every day in the year—the more the better. Nor could I expect many salary raises unless I did that.

Afterward, Ted assured me that before he finished speaking I had a grin stretching from ear to ear, so he knew he'd hired an angling editor. I insist that I was keeping a poker face, waiting to see what salary he'd offer me—even if I did feel like Jesse James practicing his profession. And of course there was one serious drawback to the position: I'd have to stop fishing long enough every month to do an article for the magazine. But, then, what job is perfect? If they'd only let me be angling editor and not make me write anything. . . .

That was in late fall, and my first departmental article, for January, had to reach him in November. During the last days of November, the office called me long-distance at the lake where I was.

"We like that stuff you sent in, but we need photos of you with bass, to run with it."

I said, "Well, I'll try to catch some tomorrow or next day, if the lake isn't frozen up. I'll phone you if I get 'em."

"We'll be out in about an hour," came the voice.

I emitted such a howl that the long-distance wires were hardly necessary. That, I said, just wasn't how fishing was done. They couldn't do me that way!

The voice at the other end of the wire was soothing. "Sure you can do it—we must have those pictures. Oh, by the way—you know that in a photo a bass looks only about half as big as he really is. So be sure they're real lunkers that'll show up well."

I argued, coaxed; I used strong language. I broke out in a cold sweat, the only kind of sweat one can work up toward the last of a Minnesota November.

It ended with that voice saying patiently, as though arguing with a stubborn child who refuses to do something very easy, "Well, we'll be out in an hour; we're starting now. Do the best you can."

They certainly had a lot more confidence in my fishing ability than I had! Or—the thought came to me—could it be that they were testing me the hard way, to see if I was really fitted for the post of angling editor? And why wasn't there a Society for the Prevention of Cruelty to Angling Editors?

I grabbed up my rod and tackle box, and hurried to the boat. Fortunately, there was not much ice on that shore, for the wind had been blowing in there; some other bays were already frozen up.

With the outboard wide open, I raced out through cold, choppy waves of the dull, leaden color they get to be at that time of year. I was doing some fast thinking. The north shore of the next bay, if it wasn't frozen up, might produce some good bass; I'd try it first. There would be little time to try a second place, for it would take me almost fifteen minutes each way to and from the spot I'd picked. Which left me only about half an hour to get those lunkers—they had to be lunkers; better nothing than smaller ones, to bring snorts of scorn from those fellows. Br-r-r—it was cold, heading into those waves!

I got there, and luckily it wasn't frozen up, though thin sheets of ice floated all around. I shut off the motor and started to cast. Immediately, icicles began to form on the guides of my rod. When I paused, the line froze to the spool, and I had to strip it off and dabble it in the water to limber it up enough to cast again. What a day for fishing!

Curtain.

Scene two: A quiet cottage by a northern lake. A car stopping. Shivering men climbing out, bundled in overcoats and mufflers. A long, lanky cuss (me) leading them proudly to the back porch, where lay a limit of flopping bass, the smallest over four pounds, the largest nearly six.

The photographer stood goggle-eyed, his mouth open.

The other two from the office looked quietly smug, with an I-told-you-so air—I wondered afterward if maybe they hadn't made some bets with the photographer.

"Nice ones. Let's hurry down to the lake and shoot some pictures before it gets too dark." No praise; no back slaps; no medals pinned on me. No—their new angling editor had done only what was expected of him, so let's get this job done.

And next day the whole lake was frozen over.

They ran a short account of this in the magazine. Immediately, letters came pouring in. Was it true? And if so, why did all the angling authorities say that bass are dormant when water temperature gets below fifty-five or so? When I was in the office next, they asked me about that. I didn't know; I didn't pretend to be an angling expert—just a fellow who caught a few fish once in a while.

I went to the public library and looked over every book on bass that was there. Not a word could I find about this late fishing, not even a mention of it. Nor did anybody whom I questioned later know a thing about it. So the following are purely my own observations, and an account of how I get bass in the fall. Naturally, no one man's observations should be regarded as the last word, so I shall be glad to hear from others who really experiment with the thing, and to pass on any information that I get from them.

Of course, all fall fishing isn't that late—nor that chilly. The point I am trying to emphasize is that there *is* fall fishing, though hardly anybody seems to realize it; and that it's far and away the best fishing of the year, and that it lasts right until the freeze-up in the North. In the South, there's fine bass fishing all winter, except in rivers which grow too muddy then.

Here is the usual pattern of the year's fishing, as it strikes me:

Comes opening day in spring, with everybody out, after

pawing eagerly, like racehorses waiting for the start. They get bass, quite a few of them—simply because many bass are then in shallow water, and a great majority of anglers fish for bass in shallow water only, and just refuse to try farther out, with deep-running lures.

But what sort of bass? Few really big ones—mostly good eating size, no more. True, it's fun getting them on surface lures, and shallow-running lures, and casting accurately into little pockets in bushes or lily pads. But the fact remains that most of them are not very large bass; nor do they always put up the terrific scrap that a bass can put up. It's fun mainly because we've been so long without fishing of any kind and we're easily satisfied. And this, too, is the time when the fly rod is at its best for bass, so he who prefers the fly rod is happy.

We could go out to deeper water and get larger fish. But they're a lot harder to find out there, and we're having sport anyhow, so generally we don't go out.

Then the water begins to get pretty warm. The bass, even the smaller ones, move farther out. Mornings and evenings we may catch some in the shallows—or may not. Since the average angler refuses to get away from the shallows, his interest in bass wanes rapidly, for he's getting none to amount to anything. As he sees it, bass fishing is almost over for the year; he'll make a few more half-hearted trips out, expecting little or nothing, and getting just what he expects.

The hot weather of midsummer arrives. The really good angler is getting bass, and perhaps a few very nice ones, from deep spots. But even the most expert is working hard for them —working his head, thinking, and his arm, casting. Now is when the average man quits cold; he must see some bushes or surface weeds to cast to, or he'll think he can't get bass.

Labor Day comes, with everybody moving away from the resorts and summer cottages. The very next day, so it seems, bass fishing begins to pick up, partly from natural causes, partly because the bass are not disturbed so much as before by fishermen—hardly at all.

I've been speaking, obviously, mostly of the northern tier of states, from Maine through Michigan and Minnesota. The dates will, of course, have to be modified for other districts— and from year to year for the northern border districts—according to when the freeze-up comes. When one gets so far south that there is no freeze-up, one still gets the largest bass, and finds the best bass fishing in every way, after the first really hard frost.

In the north, that first hard frost will come toward, say, the end of September. Out on the big lake is a solitary boat, looking very lonesome when seen from shore, and many wonder what poor fool is trying to fish at that time of year. But the man in it (generally myself) has a happy grin on his face. He's catching bass—big ones! And they fight like wildcats. They don't just "stand on their tails"—they leap high out of the water like muskellunge, but shake themselves in a savage way that no musky could imitate. And can they sling plugs a mile when they do that!

But, believe it or not, sometimes one of them, after slinging a plug at the angler's left eye, will strike again on the very next cast. And perhaps throw the plug again, and strike a third time, to be brought in. He doesn't seem to do it from stupidity, like a northern pike; he does it from sheer savagery. And the man who uses light tackle is getting gray hairs, wondering what those rampaging brutes are going to bust. But is he having sport!

From now on until near the freeze-up is by far the best bass fishing of the whole year. Really, the very best begins when the maples around the shore have turned to their amazing, unbelievable fall colors, after the first hard frost. The sight of them is so beautiful that it will almost make a man stop fishing to enjoy it. Almost—but not quite; no real angler will stop fishing for any reason when bass are acting that way.

No mosquitoes, no gnats—nothing to bother one. No sudden storms even, such as one gets during the hotter weather. And there, all over the North Country, are resorts standing empty, where would-be guests had been unable to secure accommodations a couple of months before. Most of them even offer cabins now at bargain rates.

While this book is about bass, we might here say a word on other fish found with them in northern lakes—chiefly pike, walleyes and muskellunge. This is when practically all the really large ones are caught—caught by the very few who fish now. The members of the *esocidae* family—the true pikes, such as the "northern" pike and musky, as distinct from the walleye, which is a perch, and related to the real pikes in no way—feed actively all winter, as everybody knows; catching them through the ice is a common northern sport—if one wants to call it sport. But why they run so much larger in late fall, nobody knows.

Isn't it cold, fishing then? Though no one can guess what fall weather is going to be, normally it's by far the best time of the year, the pleasantest, in the northern parts. There are many days when, outside of the good fishing, it's a sheer joy to be out on a northern lake, and to be alive. Now is when the loons are calling, and a strange beauty and peace settles down on the North.

Sometimes, especially as winter comes closer, it can be cold, dreary, rainy. But is the angler willing to confess himself made of weaker stuff than is the duck hunter, who will sit shivering in a blind hour after hour? And one can always be as warm as he wants, simply by bundling up in enough clothes.

Some to whom I've said this answer that they cannot cast

when hampered by a lot of heavy clothes. They are really confessing that they cannot cast—period. They are trying to heave a lure by a swing of the arm, instead of with a flip of the wrist. Perhaps, as I shall point out more fully later, that is because they have never learned what correct casting tackle is.

The man going on a fishing trip then should have a long slicker and some sort of rainproof hat; on some days, at least, he will need them. Also overshoes and heavy wool socks; the bottom of a boat can get mighty cold, against that icy water.

The one thing that may give real trouble is the hands, for if they are stiff with cold one cannot cast. But they can easily be made accustomed to staying flexible in the cold; the man figuring on a late fall fishing trip should go without gloves, and expose his hands to as much weather as possible for some time before setting out. Washing them in ice-cold water, soaking them in it, helps toughen them; such a soaking immediately before starting out to fish helps a great deal. Of course, the few of us who fish hours practically every day through approaching fall, good weather or bad, will have little trouble casting even in freezing weather, if there is no wind.

And there's a little trick which even I, tough though my hands are, resort to during the very last days of fishing—gloves. How, one may ask, can one cast in gloves? The thing to do is to buy a pair of heavy cotton work gloves with knitted wrists, getting them of as good a fit as possible; for a man whose hands are not very large, women's work gloves may be best. Cut off the fingers and the thumb a half inch or so above where they join the palm. Now cut the palm out, leaving the wrist and that half inch of fingers; in fishing, the strip left will soon roll into a sort of string, but that does no harm. It is really surprising how warm these, with so much gone, will keep the hands—perhaps because the large veins on the backs are protected. These gloves look clumsy but do not feel that way; they do not hamper one's casting in the least.

It has often struck me that such gloves, but made of buckskin or something else that would look neat, would be good even in summer for a surgeon, a musician, a watchmaker, a man who uses a typewriter a good deal, or anybody else who should keep his hands as flexible as possible. There is no question, I think, but that much exposure to the weather has a stiffening effect on the hands. Would wearing them in summer look queer? Well, a man can wear gloves golfing in the warmest weather, and nobody pays any attention to it.

Now, what peculiar tricks are there to this late fishing, what great secrets that I alone have discovered? No very great ones, I must confess; I can soon tell all I know about it. But I shall begin by saying that generally the shallow-water man might as well stay at home at this season. Nor, for some reason, have I found many bass in very deep water at this time of year —fewer than at any other. I have seldom found them at a depth of less than six feet, and still more rarely as deep as fifteen. Naturally, conditions vary in different lakes, according to vegetation, oxygen content, and so on, but in most places around eight or ten feet of water seems to be a favorite place for bass at this time.

They are far more likely to be in groups now than at any other time of year—often groups of great lunkers, with the small ones seeming to have vanished mysteriously from the lake. Perhaps the younger ones do hibernate; I don't know, but it looks suspiciously like it. The way to locate the groups is to swing rapidly along the shoreline in one's boat, casting, and not to waste much time at any one spot; now, bass are practically never found scattered all over, as sometimes earlier in the year. Swing in and out in a long zigzag, to try water of different appropriate depths.

When a strike comes, work the vicinity thoroughly for more; they are practically sure to be there, but perhaps that first one was a straggler on the extreme outside edge of the school. If there is any wind, it is best to anchor, so as not to lose the spot. But don't stay pottering in one place; it might have been a stray.

What plugs? Surface lures are nearly useless now. Use those that run at least four feet under the surface—oddly, I have not found bottom fishing at all productive in most places during the latest fishing, though often very good indeed earlier in fall. Keep changing lures; there will be some days when bass insist on one thing, and that only, though usually they are not that finicky.

Color of plugs? Generally a bass likes plugs pretty highly colored and contrasty. But toward the end of fishing, I seem to have done best on dull ones, and at the last I will about have standardized on a dull bronze-scale finish—that seems to be what they want mostly then. But it is almost imperative to have at least one black plug, for there will be days when it, and it alone, will get them.

Some time in November one can notice a change in the actions of the bass—and even in lakes normally full of vegetable matter one will find the water crystal clear now, so that it is possible to see a bass take a lure if one is looking down. (Such beautifully clear water, by the way, adds considerably to the pleasure of this late fishing.) The change is this: Your lure is coming in, and you are watching it wriggle along slowly four or five feet down. A bass rises to it. But not with his usual flash; the whole thing reminds one of a slow-motion picture, though of course not quite that slow. Keep reeling; perhaps give the plug a little short twitch or two, with brief pauses between, to add more life to its action, but do not rush it away from him—earlier, making him think it was trying to escape might be a good thing, but not now. You see him open his mouth, and if he's one of the great lunkers one frequently gets at this time of year, you may open your own mouth as wide, wondering if he'll really take it. His head blends with the plug, and you feel it stop gently. You strike and set the hooks— which, as I shall point out, distinctly does not mean trying to yank his head loose from his body.

You may have a disappointment here. He won't fight as a bass usually does; his battle, too, is in slow motion. There will not be much excitement to getting him in, and you must get your main pleasure from showing such a whopper—very likely a string of whoppers—when most people think that bass can't be caught at all. Or perhaps you'll get your chief enjoyment from eating him next day; for he is now food for a true epicure, with a delicate flavor entirely unknown to those who have eaten only bass caught earlier in the year, and never a trace of that weedy tang so often found in them during midsummer.

When they act in this sluggish way, the freeze-up is near at hand; you expect it, perhaps prematurely, on the first dead-calm day. If it stays windy, to keep the surface broken, there may still be a couple of weeks or so of fishing. But bass fishing does unquestionably get worse now in nearly all places; fewer bass, and poorer fights from those you catch. Still, the really fanatical angler—or the epicure—is out there, working hard and shivering, hoping to get one or two more lunkers before the ice.

How late can they be caught? I have often got them, as in the incident which I related, when the smaller and more sheltered bays were frozen over, and when there were sheets of thin ice floating on the larger ones. I have taken an ax and chopped a lane through a hundred feet or more of heavy ice, to get my boat out to open, windswept water, and caught bass. Indeed, I have known of their being caught by fishing through thick northern ice in January and February.

I recall one evening, twenty years ago or more, when a dead calm fell suddenly, after a long period of steady winds. Immediately, crystals of ice began to form all over the lake on which I was fishing—it was weird-looking—and before I knew it these were making a solid thin sheet. I rowed madly for shore, before the ice got heavy enough to cut and damage my boat. Looking back I saw that the freeze-up was there, having come with astonishing suddenness, almost instantly. But in my hand was a stringer with my limit of fine bass.

Should I confess the rest of it? I spent most of the night packing, and long before daylight I was headed rapidly south— for some fishing! And, as I recall it, I bought six non-resident licenses before I reached my destination; I just did not have the strength of mind to drive past a likely looking lake or river without trying it.

All this disproves the commonly held theory that all bass hibernate; whether any of them are completely dormant in winter I do not know. They are sluggish, yes; but some are still moving around and feeding at least a little through the very coldest weather.

Old-timers have explained the excellence of fall fishing to me by saying that after a hard frost the bass have no bugs or frogs to feed on. But I have found it equally good in large lakes where stuff from land or from the air would constitute only a negligible portion of the bass's diet. My explanation—my guess, rather—is that a bass's instinct makes him try to fatten up, as a bear does in fall, before his winter of comparative inactivity. Still, this does not explain the preponderance of large bass, and the practically total absence of small ones, unless, as I have suggested, the small ones do go into pretty complete hibernation.

So my getting those lunkers for the photos wasn't so astonishing after all. True, I was lucky in getting them so quickly; in fact, I was lucky in getting more than one or two, on the day before freeze-up—a couple of weeks earlier I should have regarded it as just an ordinary good day's catch. And some more of my "miraculous" catches would have as simple explanations: some knowledge of bass and their ways, and quite a bit of luck mixed in; naturally, it's the man who knows bass pretty well who will have the luck—for luck needs helping along.

So, resisting the temptation to pose as a miracle-man of fishing, I have debunked myself. Anybody could have got those pre-freeze-up bass as well as I, once he knew the few simple facts which I have written here.

CHAPTER IV

Plugs in General—Depth

Is it really necessary to carry a lot of plugs? Won't one really good one get as many bass? My unequivocal answer is this: It is absolutely necessary to have quite a selection if one is to have consistent, not occasional, success.

I can hear some grizzled old-timer snort at this as sheer nonsense. He says firmly, "Just keep on casting—casting anything—and if they're hitting you'll get 'em. It's all luck."

But he'll invariably add mournfully that he himself generally doesn't have much luck; he's hoodooed, when it comes to fishing. "Young Jim Jones over there has all the luck; he always brings 'em in. And he's fished only this one season and knows nothing at all about it. That proves it's luck!"

If this old-timer is loquacious, he may add a remark that will throw a good deal of light on why Jim gets fish so consistently.

"To show you how darned little Jim does know about fishing, he's always trying to learn about it from books and magazines. And he has a whole big box of crazy plugs that I wouldn't be caught dead with. Danged if *I* see how he has all the luck he has, messing around with all that foolish stuff."

Get talking to Jim, and he'll probably have read this too, and he'll be ready to discuss it at the drop of a size twenty-two hook, which is so small that one almost has difficulty seeing it.

He may not agree with everything I say—there's no reason why he should, for when disagreement among anglers stops, it will mean that progress has stopped—but he's a real student of angling, and is not overlooking anything that may help him. In short, he has learned more about the fine points of the game in one season than the old-timer has in perhaps fifty.

Here's what's wrong with the old-timer: He can't forget the days when lakes and rivers were full of hungry bass ready to grab anything one might throw to them. But that kind of fishing is gone forever, except for a few spots in the northern wilderness. And good riddance to it—it would bore a skilled modern angler to death.

Nowadays, if one is to do well, one *must* study fishing in all its phases; and that is exactly what makes it so interesting to anybody beyond the beginner stage. And the proper selection and use of plugs constitutes a big part of what we must study—perhaps the biggest part, now that fish don't gather in schools any more, but in colleges.

Possibly the thing I'm most frequently asked by correspondents is to recommend, by name, some of my favorite lures. This I never do. In Chapter IX I will mention some *representative* lures, but they are not necessarily favorites. It's partly that I don't want to be suspected of being subsidized by any lure maker—it would be very easy to find one to do it. Anyhow, before you finish what I have to say on plugs, you should know how to choose your own.

At best, my list is little more than a matter of random choice. And hardly two other experienced anglers would agree with me—or with each other—on a selection. This very diversity of opinion shows how inconclusive such a list must necessarily be. It is used solely for purposes of illustration.

But here's the most important reason of all: I always hold

that a man should try with all his might to resist the natural temptation to have one or two pet plugs. If he has such pets, he will keep on using them far too long, when bass just won't take them, but seem to be waiting eagerly for something else.

I must admit that, being human, in spite of all my fishing I haven't yet quite broken myself of the pet-plug vice. And sometimes I run into a new one—or an old one which I've overlooked before—with which I immediately get tremendous results.

So here at last is the wonderful lure I'd always been searching for, the one that always gets 'em. Result? In a few days the bass change their notions and decide it is just exactly what they don't want. And I, like a rank amateur, keep on casting it steadily for hours, instead of finding out as promptly as possible what they do want now.

Let me hasten to add that this doesn't happen to me once in two seasons, on the average. But some—such as my "grizzled old-timer"—will stick to one or two plugs day after day, week after week—yes, even season after season! I've seen them do it. And when such a man chances to make a big catch, he points to it with pride. "There—didn't I tell you! If they're hitting at all, they'll take my Snodgrass Double-Action Galumpher." In his joy, he forgets that young Jim Jones has been getting them every day.

All of which doesn't mean that the Snodgrass Double-Action Galumpher isn't a whale of a good plug—for perhaps one day in ten during the season. Which means that you've got to have it along if you happen to be out that day, or the old-timer would show you up properly. Or maybe you'd better leave it at home; it's so seldom the poor old fellow gets to crow and strut, and he's so happy when he can. If he'd only use his Galumpher *in the right places* . . . but we'll come to that later on.

Of course, the raw beginner, buying his first casting outfit, must have certain lures recommended to him, since the very number of them strung in rows in a store makes him dizzy. We'll give him his advice in a hurry, and get on to the more advanced angler.

Any experienced tackle clerk can tell him better than I can which are the most popular, and these are what he wants, to begin. Fishermen are a peculiarly hard-headed crowd when it comes to lures, and I've never yet seen a single lure get any reputation whatever on advertising alone. The most popular plugs are that solely because they're good; they land plenty of bass.

There's a catch to picking plugs that way: If the clerk is green, he won't know which to recommend; and if he is experienced, he may want to pawn off on you some things that aren't selling well, to get rid of them. So have some friend who's a good bass fisherman tell you just what store to go to, and what clerk to consult there. And tell the clerk the name of the friend who sent you and told you that you could rely on him; that puts the clerk on his mettle to do a good job of advising you.

Now for the man who has fished, and who has some of these best-known plugs in his tackle box, but who isn't getting nearly as many bass as he should. There will almost invariably be two reasons for his failure: he won't have plugs enough, and he won't be using those that he has in the right places. Or rather, he may have a larger number than is necessary, but they're badly chosen; they won't be the proper assortment for various conditions.

And that is exactly the man for whom I'm writing this. Maybe I'm unduly sanguine, but I don't see how he can help getting a lot more bass after he reads what I have to say.

There are four principal things to be considered in buying

plugs—running depth, size, color and action. I shall take them up in that order.

I am putting running depth first purposely, because I think it the most important. I know that this will seem revolutionary to most anglers, who never think of it at all. But frequently bass are feeding at a certain definite depth only, and if a lure is too high or too low, it makes no difference what size, color or action it may have—one will get few or no strikes. Recently I had a fine example of this when I was fishing in a boat with a friend. It's worth relating briefly, to emphasize my point.

I was using a scale finish and he a red-head. I picked up bass after bass, but he did not get even a single strike. Of course he thought it was all in the color or action of my lure— and another time it might have been, but not then.

Since I get more pleasure from experimenting with fish than from actually catching them, I changed to a red-head just like his, to see what would happen. And I went on catching them as fast as before, though he still didn't have even a bunt. I even exchanged lures with him, and I still got them and he didn't. He was completely mystified; it must have looked like magic to him.

Of course, after a little kidding, I let him in on the secret, which was this: I had slipped on a small sinker a foot or so ahead of my lure. When I'd cast, and before retrieving, I'd let the thing go down to the depth at which the pike finish plug had been running. There, they grabbed it viciously, but they simply would not come up nearer the surface for it. When he put a sinker on too, he did just as well as I.

This, nearly always, will explain why the old, skinned-up wooden plug often proves such a wonder, in comparison to the new one just like it. It's simply that, the paint being gone in spots, it has become waterlogged, and so goes much deeper than a new one. If it were refinished, and still as heavy as before, it would be even better.

It's worth mentioning that there are days when bass in very deep water won't take a plug sent down to them, but will come up near the surface to strike readily. But it's worth no more than a bare mention, for I have found such times extremely rare. However, as I have said before—and will repeat often, trying to make it sink in—the greatest blunder the average bass angler makes is sticking almost entirely to surface and shallow-running lures.

I have no quarrel whatever with the occasional man who gets no pleasure from catching bass unless they strike on the surface, and so will stick to surface plugs when he knows very well that he'd get many more, and larger ones, by fishing deeper. He's a good sportsman—indeed, I must admit that possibly he should be called a better pure sportsman than I, and it hurts me to admit that of anybody. I'm too fond of my tussles with bass, and of seeing them come in—even if I do turn nearly all of them loose immediately—to stick to any one type of fishing.

Some object very much to casting with a weight ahead of the plug: the double weight goes out whirling around somewhat like a South American gaucho's bolas that he uses to catch cattle. And of course neither maximum distance nor accuracy can be attained with a weight ahead. But there are lures made to run at every depth. For fishing the very bottom in deep water, a metal lure is generally the most convenient, simply because one doesn't have to wait so long for it to sink.

But for this bottom fishing, by no means overlook the sinking plugs of wood or plastic—as nearly everybody does. Frequently they will get more fish than the metal ones, so it will be well worth while to give them the time necessary to go clear down. The man using a fly rod will have to wait a long time for his lure to sink, for, if he is experienced, he will object strenuously to adding even a tiny grain of split shot more than is necessary, to give weight; it makes for disagreeable casting.

In fishing deep, but not on the very bottom, any sinking lure can be used. Begin by dropping it overboard in clear water, holding the line six feet, say, away from it, and counting slowly until it has gone down the six feet. Then when you cast you can count at the same speed and so determine very accurately how deep it is going to run. If you get strikes when it is back near you, and so coming up, you will know that you had been letting it sink too far in the first place.

There are also plugs which pull down a long way of their own accord even when you start to reel as soon as one strikes the water. The deepest of these generally have long metal scoops under the heads. These will often be more effective for smallmouths than for largemouths—though they have their place for largemouths too. Unfortunately, some plugs of this type do not seem to have very desirable action, from a bass's point of view, though the action appears all right to a man—I have found this out simply because of not getting as many bass on them as I should have got: I'd do better by changing to a slow-sinking plug. But these same deep-diving plugs are often very effective for walleyes, nearly always deep feeders in daylight.

The proper thing to do, except during midday in hot weather—when bass are always far down—is to try all depths. And having found the right depth for the time, stick to it. True, there are rare days when bass strike savagely at almost any depth, and at any lure. These are field days for the beginner, who suddenly discovers that he's a simply wonderful angler, and knows all about it. (Alas, how he'll be disillusioned next time he goes out!) But seldom are bass feeding at different depths at the same time.

CHAPTER V

Plug Size Is Important!

Now for the size of plugs. Here again I shall probably seem no less than revolutionary, for I put size of lure next to running depth in importance. Generally I favor the smallest that one can cast comfortably with one's outfit. My main reason for doing so is this: I contend that a small lure will invariably hook a much higher percentage of strikes than a large one.

Nowadays, in most places, one cannot afford to miss many strikes—each one missed is a fish that you don't carry home, but very likely could have landed had you managed things right. Frequently the angler's day on the water produces nothing but the strikes which he missed—say, six of them—and perhaps barely felt. These missed strikes mean nothing, except possible irritation, and a grim decision (highly impermanent) to quit fishing forever. With smaller lures—and really sharp hooks, which few men have—the chances are very good indeed that he'd have gone home with six fine bass, and a healthy pride.

The ideal must be to hook every bass that strikes. This, needless to say, is impossible. But I have often gone days in a row without failing to land a single bass that struck. I attribute practically all this success in hooking them, not to any particular dexterity on my part in setting the hook, but to the small lures which I almost invariably use.

I am often asked if these little lures won't get too many small bass, and not so many large ones as a bigger lure. One does get a good number of undersized bass on a small plug— but more big ones too. Perhaps I get more *strikes* from big ones on a large plug; I don't know, since a fish striking under water does not announce his weight. But a strike rolled in cracker crumbs and fried would be mighty poor eating for a hungry man.

Let me say here, parenthetically, that since the man using small lures does get so many undersized bass (as well as more large ones), it most certainly is incumbent on him as a sportsman to be very careful to release those little fellows uninjured —if he wants good fishing next year, for himself and for others. And I would strongly suggest that if he fishes a lot, and so doesn't mind losing one occasionally, he might try my own method; using mostly hooks with the barbs filed off or flattened down with pliers.

Just exactly how much greater percentage of bass will one lose from barbless hooks than from barbed? My opinion on this will be regarded as radical, for I am going to say—perhaps no greater; perhaps one may land *more* on the barbless hooks. This, because one unquestionably hooks a good many more fish on the barbless, especially where the barb is filed carefully off instead of being squeezed down, and the point made very slim and sharp, like a needle. This will penetrate easily where a broad barb would not hook the fish at all. Striking with it, and what a bass does in the first second or so after being hooked, has a completely different feel from setting a barbed hook and what happens then. That feel is hard to describe; I can only call it easier. I intend to compile figures on the percentage I hook with and without barbs, when I can get around to it among the many experiments with fish which I have in mind.

I will go even further and say outright that in open water one will always land more fish on barbless hooks, if one plays them at all properly; and I mean just straight barbless points, not those of the "hump" type. So I shall have to keep tabs only on the number landed each way in weeds and snags counting, of course, proportion landed to number of strikes, which is really what matters, and not only those lost while playing them. I should appreciate it if anglers in different parts of the country would help me with this experiment, and let me know how it turns out for them.

I will also say this positively: The man changing to barbless hooks will get a satisfaction from his fishing that he never knew before; he will find a new pleasure in it. A twist of two fingers instantly releases a small fish with only a tiny puncture in his lip, and no lacerations whatever. And when he brings a big one in, he knows that he has played him skillfully, and has given him more of a break than usual. In that—giving one's opponent a good break—lies the essence of sportsmanship. And the exact opposite of sportsmanship lies in taking every possible advantage, and insisting on always winning or refusing to play a game.

So, for the man who wishes to get the maximum of sport, pleasure or whatever one cares to call it, out of his fishing, I recommend that he at least try small lures and barbless hooks thoroughly.

There is one important point, in connection with small lures, which seems obvious, but should be mentioned. A bass, leaping or otherwise, cannot throw a small plug nearly as easily as he can a large, heavy one. Which means just that many more landed.

So much for my actual experience with small lures. What is the theory behind it? I must touch upon that, because few anglers will blindly follow advice without having reasons explained to them—I certainly wouldn't.

I think it unquestionable that most bass barely pluck at a large plug, lightly, to test it before going further. How else explain all the missed strikes in bass fishing? Or the fact that only rarely does one land a bass with a plug in his mouth? It is generally dangling outside, with one hook through a lip, except with an extremely large bass. For contrast, consider, for instance, the pike, frequently hooked by the gills inside; he really gobbles a lure.

Of course, with a surface plug, a bass can make a big splash without biting hard—mighty big! But in bass fishing one almost never feels that savage tug which a pike, and far more so a muskellunge, gives in striking. Indeed, one generally feels little or no pull from a bass for at least a second or two; he's that long waking up to the fact that something is wrong. I am not saying that a bass cannot immediately feel a pull from the man who tries to heave him back over his head, probably breaking something.

But a bass, if he's of any size worth keeping, won't bother to pluck thus at a small lure. He'll take the whole thing into his mouth, figuring on ejecting it again if it doesn't taste right. Naturally, if a bass takes the whole small lure well into his mouth, it makes hooking him pretty certain. And if the lure is in fairly deep water when he takes it, he may hang on a surprisingly long time, mouthing it, giving even the sleepy fisherman time enough to set the hook.

At or near the surface, things are different. Here, a bass seems afraid of some enemy from the air, and so is anxious to strike and whirl back down as soon as he can. Therefore it's much more of a hit-and-run affair. But even in surface fishing I hook a far greater percentage on small lures than on large ones.

This mouthing or "hanging-on" time varies greatly, not only according to depth, but according to the type of lure. If the lure feels soft or "crunchy"—a deer-hair mouse, for instance —bass will hang onto it considerably longer than if it is hard plastic, wood or metal, and so one can hook more of them. The trouble is that it's easier to get attractive action in the hard lures, which leads to more strikes.

All of this may sound like arguments for using small, soft fly-rod lures instead of plugs. But I personally consider these too small in most places, and at most times, for the best results with larger bass. Indeed, I have come to think that a three-eighths-ounce lure of average size will bring in more good bass almost anywhere than one noticeably larger or smaller, taking the season through. This, as I say, is purely a personal opinion, and I should certainly feel not the slightest antagonism toward the man who does not agree with me—it would be but another completely friendly disagreement between two anglers.

Unquestionably there are days—I have found them mostly in late fall—when a bass prefers a good-sized plug to a small one. But I believe that such times are uncommon, and therefore I consider the smaller plug as nearly always the better.

The reader may want to know definitely what I call a small plug. A few years ago—and even now by some more old-fashioned anglers—a five-eighths-ounce plug would have been regarded as small. Nowadays heavier ones are not often seen, and the bulky things of twenty or thirty years ago have about vanished. Half-ounce lures are gaining rapidly in favor, and we should scarcely call one of that size light now—but it is about as light as the average man's rod, reel and line will handle well. So I should apply the term "light" only to plugs of three-eighths ounce or less, which still are not seen nearly so much as I think they deserve, considering their efficiency and the great ease with which they can be cast on a suitable outfit.

This brings up a question which correspondents often ask me: "Can I cast three-eighths-ounce lures well with my outfit, which I've always used for five-eighths-ounce or heavier?" This is not as easy to answer as may appear, for I should have to go deeply into a man's method of handling a rod, his average casting distance and many other things. On a given rod, one man might have to use much heavier plugs than another man to get proper action, so I think a full discussion of the matter belongs properly in the second part of this book, dealing with tackle and casting methods.

However, some answer, even a loose one, may be desirable here. So I say that I think the average man's rod should handle many three-eighths-ounce lures in a satisfactory manner, provided he uses a line of not over twelve pounds test—nine is much better—and he has a sufficiently long rod and a reel of at least medium grade, in good condition, clean inside, and kept well oiled.

And now I hear someone ask, "Why did you say many three-eighths-ounce plugs? All three-eighths-ounce plugs weigh the same."

Here lies the catch in the thing, a point that few seem to think of. Light plugs vary immensely in the ease with which they can be cast with any given tackle. Some will handle easily on practically any outfit; and some won't cast well even on the best, made for light lures. And I should mention that the following will hold just as true for heavier plugs, when using a heavier rod and line and a less free-running reel.

A small, roundish plug, very heavy for its size, will shoot out like a bullet, pulling line from the reel so fast that a backlash can hardly result from anything but sheer clumsiness—

of which even the most experienced of us are sometimes guilty. Indeed, with the best plugs in that respect, the thumb can be entirely removed from the spool after the start, with no anti-backlash device used, and we can watch the thing sail 'way out.

Here the inexperienced angler nods gravely and says, "Fine! I'll use all little round, heavy ones."

That would do if one were interested only in easy and spectacular casting. But the trouble is that we want to catch fish, and preferably lots of them. So some inherent bad points of a plug of this kind must be considered.

The main one is that, the immutable laws of gravity being what they are, this small, heavy lure sinks rapidly. Reeling in very fast will prevent this with most of them—but it happens that a bass almost always prefers a slow retrieve, with frequent stops and starts. And these smallest bass lures are also excellent for crappies when they run any size; but a crappie likes an even slower retrieve than a bass.

And the longer the cast, the farther the heavy little plug can sink as it comes back, to hang on the bottom or in weeds. So, as one gets toward the shoreline, one must make shorter and shorter casts, until in the shallowest water such lures can hardly be used at all; you would be fishing so near the boat that bass would see you and refuse to strike. If you wade carefully, things are better in this respect, for your head is so close to the water that a bass cannot see you very far. On the other hand, if a lure does hang up when one is wading, it's much more likely to be lost than when one can row a boat over it.

From all this it will be seen that these small, heavy plugs are little short of ideal for deeper fishing in fairly weed-free water—but there their utility almost ends.

In the same class we can put small casting spoons of the

wabbling type. These vary, but an average one will cast very well, and has an advantage over the little plug in that it can be retrieved quite slowly without getting down too far. That is a general statement, but I cannot be more specific without giving separate treatment to each of the many casting spoons. And while on the subject of spoons, I should mention that I do not like the usual large spoon, with hooks behind the tail, for bass.

And by the way, here's a very interesting—and amusing —way of fishing with one of these little spoons, though I never heard of anyone else using it. Where there are fish of many varieties, remove the regular tail hooks and fit on a small single, say a size ten, with a ringed eye. When you cast, work it as slowly as possible and still get action out of it. This will take practically any of our fresh-water game fishes quite well; one cast may bring you a good bluegill, the next a muskellunge. And when you do get a big one on that frail little hook, you've got to be a real fisherman to tire him out and land him. Certainly it can be done, as any experienced angler knows; I've got some big brutes on that rig, and I can recall losing very few indeed from it. But remember that one sharp pull, or a split second's hesitation in giving line as a big one whirls back, and the little hook will break or straighten out and let him go. Using this little rig will make a really skillful fish-player of a person, if anything will.

At the other extreme of casting ease are plugs very large and air-resisting for their weight, and of non-streamlined shapes. These cast wretchedly; they slow down so rapidly in the air that the spool overruns unless one thumbs extremely hard during the whole cast. Even an expert may backlash a good deal when casting one of them, if he tries for even moderate distance. They can hardly be cast at all into even the slightest breeze, and they actually work well only with a howling wind at one's back to carry them out.

To add to the troubles, I've never found an anti-backlash device that would work satisfactorily for me with lures of this type, or allow even reasonable distance. Remember, I'm not saying there isn't one, but if there is I haven't run onto it—and I've used about all reels. This would pretty well preclude the use of such lures by the man who doesn't fish enough to learn how to thumb a free-running spool. Of course, the man who gets out a good deal rarely uses the anti-backlash device except for night fishing, when a chance backlash might be a calamity and stop his fishing.

"So," the novice will say, "if the darned things are so hard to cast, we just won't use 'em."

But there are times when we have to use them, if we want to get fish, for among them we find some fine fish-getters. Certain actions are possible in them that can't be obtained in heavier plugs—that's why they're made as they are. And we can forgive a lot of bad casting qualities in a plug on the day when it, and it alone, will bring in our limit of big, scrapping lunkers —and these days are quite frequent.

There is still another reason why many of us must carry these light, bulky plugs: There are, as I have said, undeniably days when bass prefer a big lure, and even if these days are somewhat rare we must be prepared for them if we want to be consistently successful—and I consider consistent, not occasional, success as the one true measure of an angler's skill. The man who uses lighter tackle cannot cast a big, heavy plug of the old-fashioned type without grave risk of ruining his rod promptly—besides which, a lighter rod has completely wrong action to handle such lures. But he can have half-ounce ones just about as large, for such times, and even the lightest casting rod will handle a half-ounce plug nicely if very long casts are not attempted. Indeed, there are even some three-eighths-ounce plugs that are quite bulky.

It might be well to mention here that these light, bulky lures of half-ounce weight handle moderately well on the average casting outfit, if it's in good shape, and the rod not too short—it should be at least five and a half feet for them, though five feet will work, after a fashion. When one gets down to the three-eighths-ounce, one runs into trouble, and quarter-ounce lures just cannot be cast except on a special light outfit, with, preferably, a rod six feet long or even more—I myself like one of six feet six for these, with, of course, extra light action. Casting with such an outfit is the last word in artistic fishing, and for that reason many top-rank experts use it. This, though they may believe, as I do, that a three-eighths-ounce lure is generally more efficient.

A point that should not be forgotten in connection with light lures, and especially light, bulky ones: Such a plug alights on the water with much less splash than a heavy one. On some days bass actually like a big splash of a lure striking the surface, and it attracts them. But when they are shy, as in a hard-fished lake—and almost always when they are in shallow water—the more quietly a lure comes down, the less likely it is to scare them away.

A few years ago, it was practically impossible for those of us who used them to find these smaller lures; they just weren't made. Most of us whittled out our own—a tedious and most unpromising task, for there is no way of designing a plug so that one will know what action it will have in the water; it must be trial and error. Many trials, mostly errors; fortunate was the whittler who found that one in two dozen had even reasonably good action after all his work; and luckier still the man who once in his lifetime devised a plug as good as some of the better ones on the market. There are still plug-whittlers;

my mail brings me quite a stream of new plugs made by anglers, for me to test. Alas! The merits of the things lie mostly in the fond imaginations of their inventors, who believe that their plugs are unique. Nearly all of them are poor, though of course with persistence, and knowledge of bass and their ways, one can catch fish on them.

No, plug-whittling is a thankless task, and I advise the angler to put in his spare time at something more promising. And there is no need for it nowadays, since practically all the better plugs are made in sizes ranging from great things for muskellunge, and even for large sea fish, down to the lightest that one would use on a fly rod. In some parts of the country, where old-fashioned notions about desirable plug size still prevail, these lighter ones will not be found stocked by dealers. They can, however, always be ordered for a customer—or an angler can send to a mail-order tackle house, the address of which can be found in any sportsmen's magazine, for what he wants.

CHAPTER VI

Color in Plugs

I SHOULD begin this chapter by saying that the old notion that all fish are color-blind has recently been about completely discredited by scientists, who seem to find that they distinguish not only colors, but fine shades of a single color, at least as well as does man. In another chapter, I shall go more deeply into this matter of color vision in fish, for I consider it of great importance to the angler.

The discussion of color in plugs must blend a good deal with that of action. That is the case in writing about many phases of fishing; it is impossible to keep each subject neatly in its place—they are bound to mix.

I know that I am controverting the theories of most anglers when I put color of a lure as, on the whole, of more importance than the action. I ask those readers who disagree with me to wait until they see what I have to say about action before writing to tell me that they think I may be in grave error.

I shall, for the moment, appear to contradict what I have just said when I say that, so far as I can judge, the color of a surface lure is of no importance. One could, if one wanted to, think up plausible arguments to prove why this is so—or is not so. I will only say that in actual bass fishing (but distinctly *not* in trout fishing) I find surface lures of black, white, and all colors in between equally efficient.

The point is that all plugs are not of the surface type, and as soon as you get only an inch or two under the surface, different conditions prevail. In quite shallow-running plugs, I must admit to finding red-and-white about as good as any under all conditions of light and water. I believe that if a bass won't take that, he is unlikely to be interested in anything offered. I do not mean only a red head and white body, but any plug that is mainly white with some brilliant red—for many occasions, I consider some other red-and-white pattern perhaps more effective than the red-head.

Now for color in plugs which run farther down, but excluding those fished practically on the bottom: these must be taken up separately, since they call for totally different treatment.

I believe that the man who would fish these middle depths exclusively—say, from eight to twenty feet of water— would get, on the average, at least twice as many bass as he who keeps entirely to shallow water—as so many do—and larger bass also. It is hardly necessary to compare him to one who fishes only near the bottom in deep water; I never heard of such a bass angler.

This most certainly is not counseling a man to stick to any one depth; that isn't how to fish. It is merely emphasizing the productiveness of deeper fishing. And I do not withdraw the statement when I recall that cold summer in the northern part of the country, mentioned in an earlier chapter, when the shallow-water man would have come out well ahead. I had never before seen such conditions, and I hardly expect to see them again.

Since these middle depths are so productive at most times, one certainly should have the right plugs to fish them properly. And it is here that almost the whole difficulty of selecting plugs, not only for color but for action, comes in, for it is at these depths that bass are far and away the most particular about both action and color.

Not only are these middle-depth bass particular at a given moment, but they are unpredictably temperamental. They will go along anywhere from an hour to as much as, though rarely, two or three weeks, favoring a certain lure. Then their preference changes so rapidly as to catch even the most expert angler napping, and leave him fishing away a long time with the wrong thing, believing that he just isn't finding the places where they are.

As a rule, a few bass will take almost any good lure worked at the right depth, but there probably always is some one thing that can get more than any other, if the angler can find out what it is. On some days this preference is far more strongly marked than on others. I have seen times—rare, thank goodness—when they absolutely insisted on a plug of a certain size, color and action. The brown trout is much more frequently this finicky; but in his case it is generally possible to explain why he is so, while with the bass it rarely or never is.

So it is for this middle-depth fishing, which should be, so to speak, the backbone of one's fishing in most places—that a large assortment of lures, in many colors, is necessary if one doesn't want to get skunked all too frequently.

However, I find that certain colors work well here more often than any others. These are the silver and bronze scales. I do not find that the exact shade matters much in these, and I would call them about equal in efficiency, bass sometimes preferring one, sometimes the other.

Perhaps I should promote orange to a full equality with the silver and bronze scale, for I certainly have got many fine bass on plugs of that color—why, I don't know, for it resembles no natural food of the bass. And here appears one of those strange quirks of middle-depth fishing; certain shades of orange seem to be much superior to others not very different.

When they do not want any of these three colors, what should one offer them? The only way I know of finding out is—keep on trying all of them until you chance on the proper thing. This is very indefinite advice, but I've spent thousands of hours trying to find some reason for their sudden switches of taste, and I'm no closer to an answer than on the first day I cast a plug. I have had men give me rules for determining the proper lure for given conditions, but I have found them so useless in actual fishing that I shall not trouble to repeat them. I am still working hard on the thing, and perhaps some day I shall be able to announce a solution—but I'd advise nobody to wait to go fishing until I do!

Trying different colors is simple, but at the same time one must experiment with different depths, and plugs of different actions. All this complicates matters so greatly that perhaps it's no wonder the average angler neglects these middle depths almost entirely; it would seem about hopeless to get everything right at once. But one can very soon fall into an almost mechanical routine for trying a given stretch of water quite thoroughly, without wasting too much time on it. On bad days, there's always the possibility that the next combination will start them striking furiously; it may be one of those times I just referred to when they want but one thing.

I should say that, roughly speaking, one of the three colors mentioned will work well about half the time. For the other half, the only suggestion I can honestly make is—try everything. Sometimes their preference will be some queer combination of colors which one would think no self-respecting bass would look at. And I have found an odd thing about a solid black lure when used for these depths: at most time it is a very poor producer; but when it works at all, it is wonderful—and when they prefer it they generally show little interest in other colors. Nor can I find that the brightness or darkness of the day, or the clarity of the water, has anything to do with the matter.

And now, finally, we're down on the very bottom of the lake, in deep water. It is down here that I get most of my real lunkers, and very few little ones. Not only will bass run much larger in the depths, but, the water being cooler down there, they likely will prove gamer than those from shallower, warmer water—and most of us would rather hook one furious, dynamite-packed scrapper than six that come in comparatively easily. Also, they will usually have a much better flavor than shallow-water fish.

Down here the matter of color returns to such beautiful simplicity that I can feel safe in giving definite advice. Yet, if few try the middle depths, almost none try this—except the Indian, or a professional guide when out alone, for fish to eat. Indeed, there is a superstition that for very deep bass fishing live bait is all that does any good, and artificial will not work. I believe this to be the exact opposite of the truth; it is down here, more than anywhere else, that I have seen artificial lures prove their superiority—and I consider them superior at almost any time or place if the right ones are used and they are worked properly.

The fact is that this bottom fishing is the easiest of all for the user of artificial lures. What leads him astray is the difficulty of middle-depth fishing; he thinks that deep bottom fishing, still farther out, must necessarily be harder.

It is not easy, we must admit, for beginners—or for those who refuse to learn—to find the good deep spots, but once one catches onto the thing it is fairly simple. And these productive deep spots stand up, year after year, in a manner unknown to good shallow spots, mostly because they are little affected by ordinary changes in the level of shore-line water. Greater variations of water level do, however, affect them, by causing a change in the kind and quantity of weeds that grow down there; this is caused mainly by the rapid decrease of actinic rays of sunlight with increasing depth. Sometimes, also, in a lake in which a thermocline forms, a previously good spot may find itself in the hypolimnion, and so perhaps totally devoid of oxygen; therefore if a bass were somehow forced down there he would be dead of asphyxiation within a few minutes. Nor can plants grow in such a hypolimnion. But so far as I know, a thermocline has never been observed to form at less depth than twenty-five feet. If some readers are not familiar with these technical terms, it is not worth while to explain them here, for this book deals exclusively with practical fishing and is not concerned with the science of lake dynamics and chemistry, though a slight knowledge of that would occasionally be of benefit to the fisherman.*

We shall come to the matter of action and retrieve later on, but as far as color goes, I find that down here two colors seem superior to all others, and one of these is just plain white. A slight amount of other color with it seems to do no particular harm, but neither does it seem to do any good.

The other color is almost never seen in use, for it is so drab and ugly that not many men would buy it, and therefore few tackle stores stock it. The plain fact is that most anglers buy plugs to suit their own aesthetic sense, with little or no regard for a bass's notions on the subject.

Nearly all of the bottom-feeding fish which bass eat are of a dirty-brown color, with dirty-white or dirty-yellowish bellies. So, as might be expected, a dirty-brown plug often seems to get them down here when nothing else will. But on most days

* The thermoline is discussed fully in Part III.

I have not found it as good as plain, clean white. Why this is, I cannot even guess; it is just one of the things I have discovered through years of experimenting, years of catching bass. And the fact that a proposed experiment looked illogical on the face of it never made me hesitate before trying it—one never can tell!

Do not be concerned if you cannot find a lure of that dirty-brown shade. Do as I do—it seems to work better anyhow than using a pretty plug. Pick out one of your old sinking plugs; I can't find that action matters very much in this particular instance, but here as elsewhere I generally prefer a small one. Get a ten-cent can of the dirtiest-looking, ugliest brown enamel you can find; or mix some left-over paints to get a tint that looks particularly bad. Now use this on your old plug.

Somehow it seems that, to use a Hibernicism, the worse job of painting you do, the better. Leave the bottom of the plug unpainted for the moment; later, mix a very little of your brown with some white for that, unless you have some yellow handy. Finish by blending the edges of the two together roughly with your brush.

Remember, if you're an inexperienced painter (and the more inexperienced the better, for this job) that two or three light coats make a far more durable finish than one heavy coat —and actually leave the plug ready for use in much less time. Also, if the plug is of wood it should be completely dry all through before painting, to give a permanent job.

There is one sure test of whether you've done good work on it: if it seems so awful that you want to hide it in the bottom of your tackle box when a friend comes around, so that he won't see it—then you've got a reliable fish-getter, and to a bass it will appear as something on the order of caviar.

Some time ago, in a magazine article, I first described this plug and the theory behind it, and I received many letters from men in various parts of the country who had tried it, with results that surprised them.

A warning: Except for bottom fishing in deeper water, I have found this to be one of the poorest colors I know of for bass.

CHAPTER VII

Plug Action, Including Retrieves

THERE were two reasons for my calling the matter of action perhaps the least important to the reader of the four headings under which I am discussing plugs, but these were not based on a foolish notion that action is of no consequence. If I had looked at it from another angle, I should have called action the most important of all, next to running depth.

The main reason was this: I take it for granted that a man will buy his plugs, instead of engaging in the tedious and generally unprofitable task of trying to devise good ones for himself; and I presume that he will purchase only those of standard makes.

One need never worry as to whether a lure of standard make has fish-getting action; they're all good in that respect. The competition between plug-makers is very strong, each trying to devise a better lure than the other. The result is that a plug with poor action has no long-range chance whatever on the market, no matter how much it is advertised; as I've said before, anglers are a peculiarly hard-headed crowd in this matter.

The older makers have learned from experience that, in the long run, it is throwing good money away to spend it in advertising lures that won't produce, and produce well. Some new tackle companies haven't learned this lesson; and they go on playing us anglers for suckers. The National Gadget & Widget Corporation, for instance, now turns out so-called bass plugs for the dime-store and cut-rate trade. The president of the company wouldn't use the things himself—if he ever fished. To the experienced angler they are rubbish; but too many anglers are not experienced, and the monstrosities sell by the carload.

This is by no means a blanket condemnation of all new tackle companies. A few of them—a very few—are completely sincere, and are turning out very fine products indeed, though some of these new products need further refinement. I number myself among the staunchest partisans of these few; we need them to keep the older companies on their toes.

It might amuse the reader if I recount here an incident that happened recently. A man traveled well over a thousand miles to consult me about a plug he had invented. I hated to tell him, but there was nothing particularly original about it, though it had some good points. He gravely told me that he had, on the advice of his fishermen friends, decided to make it only in ounce-and-a-half weight, and only in a bright yellow color—they had assured him that it would then catch bass at all times. He was a friendly, well-meaning chap, and I spent good parts of three days straightening him out, lecturing him on plugs, and practically redesigning the thing completely. Then it occurred to me to ask him how much he had fished. As a child, he had caught a few punkinseeds on worms, and that was all! He just thought plug manufacture an easy way to make a fortune. It isn't; it's a business with fierce competition and small profits. This incident will serve to show how many "bass lures" originate. Except that most of the originators would not think of consulting somebody who understood such things, before going into production.

Of course, any plug will catch an occasional bass; so would a pencil with hooks tied to it—I'll bet at long odds that I can get bass on one, though I've never tried. There are nitwits among bass as well as among men, but few of them among the former live to attain any size. The thing is that these off-brand plugs will not get even half as many bass as those properly made. This, although many of them—pure imitations—look so like certain standard lures that even close inspection will show no dissimilarity. But there will be some difference in balance and action to render them comparatively ineffective.

How do the standard makers get their plugs so good? Sometimes one of them will buy patents from an experimentally minded angler who has stumbled across something worth while. More often the plugs are devised by their own research men, who have spent years trying to figure out just why a bass will strike viciously at one plug and yawn at another. Not that they ever learn much about it—nobody knows much about it—but when such a man does design a lure he tests it thoroughly, by actual fishing in different parts of the country and under various conditions. Then he usually sends it out to experienced anglers for their opinions of it—I myself receive a good many such experimental lures. After all this, it will probably flop, before it has seen the light of an advertisement. Rarely will it be thought worth while to put one into production.

All this is not done from any altruistic desire to help us anglers to more sport—though the chief men of nearly all good tackle companies are among the most fanatically enthusiastic anglers in the world, and do like to see others have their sport. It is done simply to avoid wasting huge sums of good money advertising something that won't go over.

True, occasionally a lure put out only after all this testing does fail to produce expected results for the average angler—and therefore for the pocketbook of the company. But I, for one, am always ready to gamble on the new product of a good maker, hoping it may be that wonder-plug I've always been looking for, and knowing that if it doesn't work well he will stand to lose many thousand times as much as I. Barnum would not have taken so cynical an attitude toward human credulity if he had been dealing exclusively with bass fishermen; he would soon have learned that you can fool none of them very long.

A point worth remembering is that it is by no means the lure with the *most* action that has the *best* action—that most attractive to bass. Many anglers go wrong here. I know some excellent lures with a movement resembling that of a hula dancer who had just sat on a red-hot stove. On the other hand, the action of some of the others among the most deadly is hardly perceptible as one reels in—nevertheless, it's there, and the bass like it.

Boiled down, it comes to this: Buy plugs of standard brands and you can almost forget about action; it'll be there, and thinking much about it will do you no good, for after all you're no bass, and you can't judge things from a bass's viewpoint.

Here's my second reason for putting action last: No matter how much or how good action a plug may have, *it hasn't half enough*. By this I mean that, to be really and consistently successful, especially on hard-fished water where bass are shy, the angler must add the other half. The plain fact is that almost every angler cranks his reel as steadily as if he were turning a cream separator, which is wrong, and greatly reduces his catch, especially of large bass.

This means that we're getting into the matter of retrieves. But I regard the retrieve as no more than part of the action— the part the user must add. And I feel quite sure that changing from a steady retrieve to a proper one will alone almost double any man's catch, and get him much larger bass on the average. This is especially true where bass are shy. This change will seem difficult at first, and call for some slight concentration on the angler's part; but within a few days he will have the habit so firmly fixed that he will actually find it difficult to hold himself to a steady retrieve on those occasions when bass seem to prefer that—yes, there are such days, but I believe them to be very few indeed.

On the surface, again, it's simplest. I find that, for me at least, there is one retrieve that will almost always work, if anything will. Cast, and let the plug lie a few seconds—I see no point in the minutes which some recommend; in fact, I generally have less success after such long pauses.

Then, with your rod tip, give the plug a quick little movement of not over two or three inches. Pause somewhat longer than the first time, and do it again. If a bass doesn't strike by the third twitch, he has probably gone visiting friends in some other part of the lake, and you're unlikely to get one as you reel in for another try farther along—so it's as well to reel in fast, to save time.

There is a curious thing to be noted here. Sometimes a bass will strike as you reel your lure along the surface, slow or fast. I've had one strike furiously, with great splashes, five or six times or more before I got the plug to me. But I have hooked them comparatively rarely on this incoming plug. Why? I don't know. The thing is, with a surface lure, if you don't get a bass practically where the plug first struck the water, you are unlikely to get one at all. Missed strikes don't count.

There is another slightly modified form of this retrieve which often works well when nothing else will, especially on a dead-calm day, and where bass are exceptionally wary. This consists of barely moving the plug gently two or three times in succession, with fairly long pauses. It should do no more than throw out some small ripples which you can just see.

Generally, most of your surface strikes will come *while the plug is lying dead still*. I am emphasizing this because if one's mind is wandering the least bit, one will miss the strike; one must be, so to speak, on hair trigger, ready to set the hooks like a flash. There is no other retrieve which brings such a mighty, nerve-racking explosion, always unexpected. For this reason, a few enthusiasts use no other, thinking one bass caught this way better than ten hooked down out of sight. But, as I said before, I do not stick to any one method; I use whatever seems to get most fish at the time—anyhow, I like variety. That's purely a matter of taste, with no grounds for dispute.

It should be mentioned that there are occasionally days when a bass will not take a plug fished thus with his usual splash. He will suck it down almost imperceptibly, as a brown trout takes a dry fly. Then one must be watching the plug carefully, just as one does the fly.

Many anglers have the mistaken notion that the more rumpus a surface lure kicks up, the better. Sometimes this rumpus does get them to striking, but often, on hard-fished water, it puts them down so they won't strike at anything; while a quiet one does the trick—especially a small, light one that strikes the surface with little commotion. At such times, a fly rod and bug would be best, if one has them along; but after all there is little difference between the largest fly-rod bug and the smallest casting lure.

In shallow water, and especially, it seems, in a river, a big, heavy plug splashing down hard will nearly always scare bass away, and make it impossible to get them by any means for a long time. Yet there are rare days when the hard splash makes one strike instantly.

Perhaps the best way to learn how to use surface plugs correctly is to remember this: The plug is supposed to be some edible creature from the air or from the bank which has dropped, rather hard, onto the water. It lies partly stunned a few moments. Then it begins to struggle, but weakly, with many pauses to rest. Keeping that in mind, one is fairly sure to get bass-taking action.

Hardly anybody seems to realize that any floating sub-surface plug—the kind that goes under only when being retrieved—makes about as good a surface lure as any, but can do double duty. Merely let it lie and twitch it a little where it fell. If that does not work, it may pick up a bass as it comes back under water. Sometimes it would seem as if a bass had been watching it on the surface but refused to take it there, then hit it savagely when it had gone a short distance down.

Now for plugs worked entirely under the surface.

There is no difference in retrieve between those used in shallow water and those fished farther out, and so running deeper—though I find the same colors not desirable. No matter at what depth one is using these, a slow retrieve is almost invariably the best—and by that I mean the very slowest that will bring out the action of the particular plug one may be using. This varies greatly with different plugs, but it's easy to find what works by watching the lure as it is reeled in.

There's a little fly in this ointment: the slower the retrieve, the harder it becomes to hook one's strikes; on a fast retrieve, a bass generally hooks himself if he can be hooked at all. I think it is for this reason that the less experienced angler falls into the habit of reeling quite fast; he has not learned to hook fish on a slow retrieve—it's merely a matter of training oneself to strike instantly when one feels the least tug. And the great trouble is that as he gets experience he still keeps his old habit of reeling fast, though he would get many more fish if he'd change.

Rarely should it be a slow, steady retrieve. Flip the lure a little with the rod tip; slow it down; accelerate it. Make it seem like a minnow going slowly along by fits and starts, with hesitations; it is much more lifelike that way.

And the best movement of all for the big boys is, as I said before, none. By this I mean sometimes—fairly often—stopping the plug dead for a second or two in midwater, and then starting it off with a sudden, quick jerk. But not with too long and fast a sweep, whipping it away from a hesitant bass which has a halfway notion of striking, but is far from decided. And here the beginner at this method is due for a frequent surprise: he finds that what was meant for a tantalizing little twitch becomes the act of setting the hooks in a good fish; for again, as on the surface, a bass that will not touch a moving lure will often take one while it is perfectly still—provided, of course, that he had seen it move before, to give him the very natural notion that it's alive. It seems such easy prey, and is so long within his reach, that his laziness or reluctance breaks down and he cannot resist taking it.

A bass hardly ever follows a lure some distance, examining it, as do most other fish. But where the plug is moving very slowly, with pauses, he will frequently rise slowly to examine it at close range. He may be within inches of it, looking at it perhaps with a good deal of doubt as to its desirability. Suddenly it seems to see him and to realize its danger. It starts off in panic; that appears very plain to the big bass's mind—or, more properly speaking, to his reflexes. No predatory animal or fish can well resist something running from him, but within easy range. His reflexes work before he has time to stop them. He makes a short, quick dash, mouth open. Wham! He's got it!

If the dash had to be long, his few cells of higher brain might have halted him before he struck, or led to a weak strike without his being hooked, as he changed his mind.

For this sort of retrieve one usually uses a plug of such specific gravity that it barely floats, or barely sinks; then it will stay almost at one level in the water when stopped. But sometimes a light one, coming straight up, or a heavy one, going down fairly rapidly, will do the trick. This, on a hard-fished lake, may be because few bass there had ever seen a plug going straight up or down, and so are not suspicious of it—but I really do not credit the bass with this much intelligence, and I think there must be some other explanation.

To learn a really tantalizing retrieve, there is nothing an angler can do that could be better than this: Cast from some bank or bridge, into water clear enough so that you can see down well from your height. Watch the lure coming in, and try doing various things to it. Before you know it, you'll have worked out some retrieves that will really do wholesale business for you if you cultivate them. You'll learn far more that way than from anything I can write. This piece of advice is not original with me, and I should credit it to the proper source, but unfortunately I've forgotten what that is; I read it long ago in some book or magazine article on fishing. I've a notion my old friend Robert Page Lincoln is the one who wrote it; in his many years as an angling writer, he has given fishermen a great deal of sound advice, for he knows fish as few others do.

We're down on the bottom again, in deep water. And here retrieves, as colors, become quite simple. I have found one retrieve that seems to work here if anything will: Let the plug go all the way down and rest a few seconds on the bottom. Point your rod down the line, and reel in the slack. Then make a firm but not too fast sweep of the rod tip of, say, six feet or so. Let the lure go to the bottom again, and repeat.

Theoretically, I suppose, this would represent the movement of a crawfish, but I have had my best success with it in water where, so far as I know, the bass had never seen a crawfish. I cannot explain why it is so deadly at many times, especially to lunkers. I discovered it many years ago by experiment, and if all the big fellows I've taken with it were laid end to end, they'd stretch a long way. An odd thing about this retrieve is that, like a solid-black plug, at times when it works best almost any other attempt to lure bass is nearly useless.

Stones and weeds down there? Yes, you'll hook into them sometimes. But, so far at least as largemouths are concerned, if you never hook any weeds, neither will you hook many bass. The smallmouth will get you into stones more, for he is a deeper feeder and generally found in more weed-free, gravelly spots. If you do hook into a stone, and you're in a boat, there's but one thing to do: row straight across it and to some distance on the other side, when your lure will nearly always come loose by itself. When wading a river, you can usually get across to the other bank; if you can't—well, there's a good plug gone, if you're using a bass line and not a tarpon line, as some do for bass.

Of course, a single hook will hang up much less than multiple ones, and a small hook less than a large one. Sometimes, when there's a bad, stony bottom in a river, I purposely use a very light, weak hook that will straighten before the line breaks; such a hook is plenty strong to play a fish, if one really does play him, and not horse him in.

Aren't weedless hooks best for such fishing, the reader may ask. I have little confidence in most weedless lures—too many of them are also fishless. They vary greatly, however, in this respect. Some wonderful weedless contraptions I've seen, highly touted by their makers, were merely fit subjects for mirth; the bass that could manage to get himself hooked on one of them would indeed be a piscine genius. I've had some of this sort which I kept solely to amuse myself and my friends at times when I'd caught all the bass I cared to; our fun would come from watching bass after bass fail to hook on in spite of apparently mighty efforts to do so. A very few weedless lures seem to take almost as many fish as those with open hooks—but I fail to see how any can work quite as well, and hook as high a percentage of strikes. Still, weedless lures must be used in some places, if one would fish them at all.

And of course it makes a world of difference where one is fishing. In wilder country, one does not mind missing a good many strikes—as is said of women and streetcars, there'll be another along very soon. Where the place is fished hard and bass are scarce, it is a different matter; a missed strike is a serious matter.

CHAPTER VIII

Pork-Rind Lures

PORK-RIND lures are so different from all others, and so effective at times, especially for deeper fishing, that I am devoting a short chapter especially to them and their use. Oddly, they are not used nearly so much as they deserve; a majority of bass anglers do not seem to use them at all, though I think that he who is without at least one good one is incompletely equipped.

Lures of this type were originated in 1916 by Al Foss, who was equally enthusiastic and skillful as a fisherman and as a tournament caster. For a long time he himself manufactured them, until he sold out to a larger company so that he could retire to Florida and not have business affairs interrupt his fishing. Now many companies make pork-rind lures, of varying merits.

My favorite is no longer manufactured. It was no more than a small, roundish metal head, with a spinner blade ahead —one of the single-propeller type, sticking out permanently. This *single* spinner seems a desirable feature with a pork rind, for it starts a shimmying movement which travels down the rind. The head was nickel-plated, but I always used bright red enamel on mine—not, of course, on the spinner, which I kept highly polished. I believed that I had much better results with

73

the red head. What I liked about that lure was that it was the smallest possible, hardly more than a little weight to carry the rind out. I believe strongly that the smaller the head of a pork-rind lure, the better—especially, and oddly, for the largest bass.

Why do I describe so carefully, and praise, a lure no longer made? Because I am hoping this may induce somebody to turn out one of that sort again. Not, perhaps, that I consider it so superior to some pork-rind lures made now; perhaps just a shade so, and possibly it's all but a notion of mine; but I do want to be able to get lures of this type again. And many others would like them, especially those who prefer the lightest and smallest lures, and single hooks.

I have seen long periods when pork-rind lures were about the most ineffective things imaginable, almost useless. But there are many times when nothing else on earth seems quite as good; therefore I say that nobody can afford to be without one or more of them. Some complain that they are useless when fished near the surface. I do not find this to be the case; I have made many fine catches near the surface on them—but the times when they seem best for this are comparatively infrequent. The deeper one gets, the more often they work, and they are among the best of lures for bottom fishing in very deep water.

I do not at all like the sloppy trick some have of just hanging a pork rind onto anything—it will probably spoil the action of the other lure, and its own peculiar movement will not be brought out properly or at all. One should get lures especially designed for use with pork rind; they send currents back past the rind and give it that tantalizing wiggle in which about all its attraction lies.

The common notion seems to be that pork rind owes its merit to its taste or scent. It doesn't, at least so far as bass are concerned. A bass usually flashes in and strikes too fast to use either taste or scent—he does not hunt by scent anyhow, as his feeding methods plainly show. It's that little wiggle that gets bass; to a fish, it seems obviously the tail of something swimming very actively—perhaps nothing else used in artificial lures seems quite so lifelike. "Rubber pork rinds," more convenient to use, cannot compare with the real thing for action, and so are far inferior in fish-taking abilities. However, I should say here that there is one exception: a metal fly-rod lure with a rubber tail which flips around bravely; this is an excellent bass-getter.

The action varies greatly in rinds of different brands. Some of them are cut to a wrong thickness or shape or length; some are so impregnated with chemical preservatives that they are practically tanned, and remain stiff and lifeless in use. One should get the best obtainable, which are cut and treated just right for optimum action. This again brings us back to buying things of a well-known, standard brand, and avoiding those put out by the National Gadget & Widget Corporation and its kind, which also make fly swatters, mousetraps and general novelty goods. Even the best pork rind is so cheap that it certainly is not worth while to try to make one's own; one probably wouldn't get it right anyway.

Here are some more virtues of the pork rind:

A bass generally takes one deep into his mouth, which of course makes him easily hooked. And, having got a good bite on it, whether he tastes it or not it has somewhat the feel of a tough, thick-skinned little fish. So he'll hang onto it a fairly long time, mouthing it, giving you more time to set the hook.

If you find yourself missing strike after strike on a pork rind, you'll probably think I'm much mistaken in saying that. But it's practically sure to be pickerel or northern pike nipping at the tail end of it—even large ones will do that sometimes. Or it may be crappies or big bluegills; they, too, like to follow up and nip its tail. If all that is getting you down, merely fasten a small, light hook—I use a ten—to the rind, so that the rear part comes just even with the end, and those smart fellows down there will be due for a big surprise. Remember that trail hook must be small and light, so as not to disturb the action. And if a really big fish hangs onto that small hook, as one frequently will, it's going to be promptly proved whether you know how to play a fish or not—if you do, you're pretty sure to land him safely without straightening or breaking the hook; if you don't, you'll soon be sitting there red-faced and cursing me for recommending such an impractical device.

The usual pork-rind lure has but one hook, so it can be worked in pretty thick weeds without hanging up too often. Many of them come with wire weed guards, and these I promptly remove; it takes but a moment or two and a small screwdriver. However, I keep the weed guards in my tackle box, to put back on when occasion demands—but for me occasion seldom does demand it.

There is another great advantage to a lure of this type, but since it is common to all single-hook lures I am putting it last. When a fish tangles in weeds and is lost, it is rarely the line that tangles there, or tangles first. It is the extra triple hooks hanging outside his mouth. The man who uses a very light line will land a much larger percentage of his fish caught in thick weeds when he uses single-hook lures.

As I have intimated, large pork-rind lures do not seem nearly so efficient as small ones, and the very large ones formerly on the market have now practically disappeared—another case of bass fishermen soon finding out what is good and what isn't, in spite of all the makers may have to say. Small though some pork-rind lures look, they are very heavy for their size, and cast beautifully, even into a wind.

Here's a trick in using them which so far as I know has never been described by anybody else:

You are fishing the bottom in deep water, and make a long cast. You pause to let the pork-rind lure go all the way down. It stops, as your suddenly dead line shows. But quite often it isn't on the bottom; it's reposing in the mouth of a big bass which grabbed it as it sank. That was because the heavy head went down fast, with the flexible tail wriggling merrily behind —swimming, as the bass saw it.

Now, if you begin your retrieve gently, the bass has only to open his mouth and let it go out again, and you'll never know but that it really was on the bottom. So, when a sinking pork-rind lure stops, always start it off with a firm sweep of the rod tip. Not too strenuous a sweep; the hook may possibly be fast to a stone on the bottom, and if so you might break something. If it's a bass, you'll feel instant movement, and then is the time to strike and really set the hook, the point of which, if it is sharp, has been embedded sufficiently by that first pull to hold it in place temporarily. A bass's tendency to hang onto a pork-rind lure a moment or two is what makes catching him in this manner possible. I have got some very large bass in this way.

No piece of pork rind has the best action when first put on; it needs breaking in, to limber it up, and to wash some stiffening preservatives out of it. So, if you finish a day with one in good shape, save it for next day. Putting the old one back into the jar with the new ones eventually does something undesirable to them. It is much better to keep a separate little jar of plain water—or water with salt in it if you do not fish very often—for if it is allowed to dry once, it is never the same pork rind again. You will also need this second jar in fishing; when you decide to try something other than the pork-rind lure, drop the whole lure into that jar of water, to keep it soaked—of course do not leave it there overnight, to rust the hook. With care, a single pork rind may be used for some time, but I always discard one when it has lost its white color, and break in a fresh piece.

Sometimes, try splitting the rind up the middle, into two narrower strips. This gives a sort of double-wiggle effect often quite successful—but not, I believe, usually as good as the single strip with its minnow-like action. There would be no harm in keeping two lures, one with the single tail and one with the double, soaking in that little jar—I frequently do that; though perhaps that is getting down to unnecessarily fine points.

I have given considerable space to pork-rind lures, and it might be thought that I consider them something very superior—perhaps all that one needs in bass fishing. I by no means wish to imply that. I have treated them at some length because, with their peculiarities, they could not be handled properly lumped in with other lures. Certainly no fisherman should be without one of them, but, as I try to emphasize, there is no one lure that is best—or even good—under all conditions.

CHAPTER IX

Some Representative Lures

IN THIS chapter I am going to depart from tradition and mention some specific lures by name, though each is a patented article, owned by a certain company. I am prompted to do this for one reason only: I know that to do so will be of great assistance to the reader, especially to the reader who is a comparatively inexperienced bass angler.

I am by no means putting forward these lures as the best, nor am I recommending them above some other very fine ones which I omit. If I tried to discuss every bass lure made, the thing would run into a book longer than this one, and be dreary and monotonous reading. So I shall take a number of lures, more or less at random, each with an action different from the others mentioned here but fairly representative of a group, and comment on them. The reader can adapt my remarks on each to others with similar characteristics.

I can only hope that no maker will think me unfair, or that I am discriminating against his lure by omitting it—it may be one of my own favorites, which I did not think quite as representative of the group as one which I include.*

The River Runt

I am beginning with Heddon's River Runt because it is the most beautiful exemplification of something which I said a

* See Plate 14, Photo Section.

while back: that nobody knows why a certain lure may be very good for bass, while another, with better action as a man sees it, is among the poorest producers.

It might be interesting to go into the rather unusual history of the Heddon Company. Back in the 1890's a man named Jim Heddon carelessly tossed a piece of wood into Dowagiac Creek, in Michigan—and thus began the Heddon Company. A bass struck at the piece of wood. It gave Jim Heddon some notions, and that evening he whittled a length of stick to the shape of a cigar, cut a hole in the end of a pop-bottle cap, and forced the pointed end of his stick through that. The result was something on the order of the old Wood-pecker lure, the metal collar throwing up a spray when the lure was retrieved.

That was the little acorn from which Heddon grew. Soon his lures were so popular that—only the older anglers among us will remember this—"Dowagiac," often corrupted to "Wa-Jack," was for a long time commonly used as a generic term for all bass plugs of any make.

And now for the River Runt, one of the newer lures, which met with so much success that after the war it could be purchased only from "under the counter," and often at black-market prices (a thing which its makers, of course, fought strenuously) when there would be many other lures in plain sight.

Nothing could have appeared less inspired than the Runt; it had just a plain, medium-speed wriggle. There had been numerous plugs before it, differing from it hardly at all in appearance or action. There have been still more numerous imitations since, some of them looking actually better as they hang in a tackle shop. It differed from all these in but one slight particular—it would get perhaps three times as many fish as the best of the imitations. Why? Heaven—or a bass—only knows. Why did a few notes which Brahms put together, in the simplest way in the world, end up as his beautiful *Lullaby*? Certainly he could not explain it.

The Runt is made in floating and sinking types, in a wide selection of patterns, and in weights from the little two-fifths-ounce Midgit-Digit on up. Perhaps the most useful for the average man and his tackle are the floating one of three-fifths ounce, and the sinking model of half-ounce weight—one for shallower fishing, the other for deeper. If I were confined to one of these in a single finish, I think I should choose the Silver Shore-Minnow. I have made many good catches on this, and I find that it works well about as often as any lure and finish that I know of. Some would prefer the White and Red Shore, and some would have other choices. Then there is the Black and White Shore-Minnow, for those times when bass insist on a black lure. True, it is not all black, but I cannot see that the small amount of white on it does harm, and perhaps it does some good.

There is a slowly sinking model of three-eighths ounce, and this is my own favorite of the lot; it is easy to time this in sinking, and so run it at any desired depth, and it casts nicely on light tackle—though very light tackle is not necessary for it.

One may wonder why I, with my preference for light rods and lines, do not use mostly the Midgit-Digit, of only two-fifths ounce. This brings up a matter which applies to all lures, and is very important to remember, though I never saw it commented upon before:

The fact that a certain lure is very effective in one size by no means guarantees that it is equally so in another—sometimes a smaller or larger may be exceedingly poor. Some lures that I know, excellent in one weight, are among the worst producers in lighter or heavier.

So far as I can see, Runts of three-eighths ounce and heavier are all about equally effective. But, for me, the Midgit-Digit has proved somewhat inferior to the larger ones. This is not condemning it; I use it a good deal, and have caught some fine bass on it, but I think the larger ones better. One trouble was that the Midgit-Digits I used did not prove alike in action, as do the bigger ones. And it should be noted that a very slight twist of the eye to which the line is fastened may change the action of this little plug a great deal, making it better or worse. That will be found true also of some plugs of other makes.

This small plug sinks quite rapidly, making it most suitable for fairly deep water. Also, it must generally be reeled rather fast to bring out its action, a none too desirable feature, as I see it. In its favor, I should remark that a bass almost invariably takes it deeply into his mouth, and so is as good as landed, and that it is very useful for crappies where they run large.*

The naturally deepest running of the lot is the Go-Deeper River Runt, which had a long scoop under its nose to take it far down. I must confess that I have never had any particular success with this lure, though it has apparently good action, differing slightly from that of the other Runts. Perhaps it is only that I have not tried it enough, for the standard models which I used were too heavy for my bass rods. This is made in a "Midget" model, but I never happened to get hold of one, and so cannot comment on it.

There is also a jointed River Runt, a fairly fast sinker, which to the eye of a man has a much better and more lifelike action than the solid ones, and so should catch more fish. I have had some exciting half-hours with this, and made some fine catches on it, but I have not found it nearly as consistent a producer as the solid ones—it is one of those lures that remind me of the little girl in the old rhyme:

* This plug is now made of plastic, with superior and far more uniform action

When she was good she was very, very good,
And when she was bad, she was horrid.

I believe that the times are quite rare when one of the solid models cannot do as well as this one or better—but there are such times. For some reason unknown to me, I have had much the best success on this jointed model in the "Yellow Shore-Minnow" finish, though I have never found that color particularly good in the solid models.

I know that many prefer the red head and white body in the Runts, but it happens that I have never had any great success with it, though I like that pattern for certain other plugs. Of course, the Runt is made in many finishes, and I have no quarrel with the man who prefers colors different from those which I like.

And this brings us to something else which applies to plugs in general—just another of those unexplainable little things which one finds so often in bass fishing: The finish that seems most effective on one lure may be very poor on another.

Al Foss Pork-Rind Lures

I have devoted a special chapter to pork-rind lures, and since the Al Foss models, now made by True Temper Division of the American Fork & Hoe Company, may be taken as typical of these, there is no need to go further into the matter here.

The Bass-Oreno

This is a plug against which I have a real grudge—I hate the sight of the thing. Why? Because every novice I see using a roundhouse swing for casting, and backlashing two casts out of three, is using one, or an imitation. That has been going on for a generation or so. It would seem that any bass with a shred of self-respect would flip an indignant tail at such an overused lure; his grandfather would have been laughing at it before he was a week old.

And still it catches bass, and a good many of them. It's infuriating to the experienced angler to have to keep one in his tackle box—but how often does one see a tackle box without one?

And, almost invariably, the finish is the same red head and white body, for that's unquestionably the best color for it. Same plug, same color, through generations and generations of bass—and still they take it well. I wish they'd stop, and let some of us who are vain enough to think ourselves somewhat above the average as bass fishermen get our fish on more exclusive things. But they show no sign of doing so. Which, in my opinion, discredits the theory that bass learn to avoid much-used plugs.

This plug has a slow, long sweep from side to side as it is reeled in. That is, it is supposed to have. Occasionally, but not often, one gets a genuine Bass-Oreno that hasn't got it, or not to a marked extent; that is because it is made of wood, so the density and center of gravity necessarily vary. When one does happen to buy a Bass-Oreno which turns out to have poor action, it is better to discard it—and go right out and buy another. There is no getting away from death, taxes, or Bass-Orenos, it seems.

We have a Bass-Obite, which is nothing but a Bass-Oreno made of tenite. I find no difference in the fish-taking qualities of the two, but the action of all plastic lures will be found about uniform. Also, they are much more durable than the wood ones, and so to be preferred by the man who fishes a great deal. The larger Bass-Obite weighs five-eighths ounce, which makes it much more suitable for flexible rods than the wood one of three-fourths ounce, a weight going rapidly out of favor

It is also found in half ounce, which is fine for the man who likes smaller lures.

To show that even one who fishes as much as I, and makes such a study of the thing, cannot know all about lures: I never knew until just now, when I looked in the South Bend catalogue, that there is a wood Midg-Oreno of three-eighths-ounce size; I thought I knew that company's products too well to have to study its catalogue. If one of these little fellows is obtainable, I'm going to have it the next time I get on bass fishing; and if it's not a good producer, and pleasant to cast, I'm making a very bad guess indeed.

There is a wooden Babe-Oreno in half-ounce size. It is considerably stubbier than the larger wood one, or the half-ounce plastic one, with a noticeably different action from either, on the same order. I consider it a more effective fish-getter than the regular wood Bass-Oreno, and quite an efficient fish-hooker in spite of being rather bulky for its weight—but I prefer the plastic model in that weight. There are also some other models of the Orenos, and I consider them very uniform in productiveness.

As just intimated, I believe firmly that, in lures of a good size, a slender one will hook more of its strikes than a bulky one. As plug size decreases, this difference decreases too, until it vanishes in the small ones.

South Bend now makes a plug it calls the Two-Obite. The line can be fastened to an eye at either end, one way supposedly giving regular Bass-Oreno action, the other a much deeper-running lure. I must admit that I do not like this as well as the regular Bass-Orenos and Bass-Obites.

There are few plugs imitated more than the Orenos. I should guess that there are many more imitations sold than real ones, partly because they can be had for less, partly because it is almost impossible to tell them apart when examining them in a store; the purchaser generally thinks he's getting the real thing.

But I have not seen even one imitation that had the right action—and this is one of the few cases in which the difference in action is generally plainly visible. A great many of the imitations come in perfectly straight, or with very slight and ineffective side action. As bass-getters, they are infinitely inferior to the real thing, and are generally about worthless.

This holds true of all really successful lures and their imitations. Some of the imitations are particularly brazen. It would seem that the copyers are hoping to clean up a little money on other men's ingenuity, persistence and hard work before they are stopped by lengthy—and expensive—lawsuits. Naturally, men with consciences of that sort are not at all troubled by the fact that they are defrauding the public too, with ineffective lures.

The Pikie Minnow

This is another old-timer. In action, the head is almost stationary except for its forward movement, and the tail has a fast wriggle, none too noticeable. Really, it has very little action of any sort. But what little there is, a bass unquestionably likes. Northern pike strike it freely too, and I have got some good muskellunge on it—muskellunge can, of course, be taken on any bass lure.

This is most usually seen in the "Natural Pikie" finish, a sort of bronze scale. The votes of innumerable anglers have chosen that as the best color for this plug, and I have never found any reason to controvert them.

The size nearly always seen in use is the three-quarter ounce. It is one of the last of the heavier lures to retain popularity, and it takes a stiff rod to handle it properly; because of its weight, and the somewhat clumsy rod it takes to cast it, I rarely use this size for bass—I like it for muskies, instead of the still larger model made for them.

One rarely sees the jointed Pikie in use, but I have always preferred it in the larger size, especially for bass. It seems to me that a bass strikes the jointed model more savagely, and so is more likely to be hooked well.

There is a half-ounce model, but for some reason that I don't understand it is not often seen; it would be best for average bass tackle. My own favorite is the quarter-ounce size. This is a deadly little devil, pleasant to cast with very light tackle, and it hooks its strikes about as consistently as anything I know of. This smallest Pikie makes an effective, almost submerged surface lure, if you merely bob it very gently where it fell; I find it among the most dependable of surface lures for hooking its strikes. Some of these little fellows will not float; then, I exchange the hooks on them for smaller, lighter ones. The action of a Pikie is not so much affected by a change of hook size and weight as is that of most other lures. But it does take a long, light rod to handle this small plug effectively, and a free-running reel. It appears to me that there is room for a three-eighths-ounce model, which more men could handle on their tackle. This is another of the lures which seem to bring about equally good results in all sizes.

With the line attached to the ring on the metal gadget in front, the Pikie pulls down quite deeply on being retrieved. Lately it has been made with a ring on top of the head also, for the line, which sends it much deeper. This changes the action somewhat and, for me, makes it less effective. Though I like the jointed model in the three-fourths-ounce size, I much prefer the solid body in the quarter ounce, and even in the half ounce. I seem to get better results with the solid body in these—but there's no use trying to figure out an explanation.

Here is a matter which one should note carefully in connection with this lure and others of similar type. Sometimes one will find a Pikie, especially in the smallest size, which hasn't quite the proper tail action. A slight bending of the metal thing in front, up or down, will almost invariably remedy this. The only way to find the right angle for it is to bend it just a shade, cast, and watch it come in; a few bends and trials will get it right.

The Dardevle

This is another much imitated lure. Anybody can easily and at little expense have some heavy sheet metal stamped to this shape, and then paint stripes on it.

The real Dardevle is an excellent spoon, because of its peculiar rocking action. No imitation which I have ever tried, though it might look exactly like the real thing, had the same action. There would be a difference in the shape, the thickness of the metal, in something, which inspection in a store would not disclose. So, none of these imitations was nearly so efficient a fish-taker.

Theoretically, the Dardevle is not supposed to revolve in the water and twist one's line—a most undesirable thing. But one sometimes will do that if not reeled at the proper speed; the user must watch carefully for that. This holds true of about all casting spoons of the rocking type, in spite of what their makers say to the contrary. I know a quite popular spoon of this type so bad in this respect that I never found one that I would use. Most anglers do not seem to notice this, and let their lines get all twisted up; they take the maker's statements at face value.

The standard Dardevle, of full ounce weight, was formerly the choice of most bass fishermen, but preference is swinging rapidly to the smaller models, for it takes a stiff and powerful rod to handle a lure of this weight—what I should call a musky rod. In spite of its popularity for bass, I never considered this large one a true bass lure at all.

Why? Because it is a bass's nature to strike a lure from the side and pretty well forward, most of the time, so where the only hooks are dangling from the tail he will too often miss them. The only way one could call the larger Dardevle an efficient bass lure would be to argue that it gets so many more strikes than some others that it will hook more fish anyhow.

Too many lure makers overlook this manner in which a bass generally strikes, or do not seem aware of it; some even will put a spinner well ahead of a lure, on the leader—these spinners I promptly remove, and I find that it leads to far fewer missed strikes. Recently Lou Eppinger, maker of the real Dardevles, brought out a model with hooks in the middle too, but some do not regard this as quite as attractive to fish as the older model. There are so many bass lures on the market, and it takes such long testing to form an accurate judgment of the merits of any particular one, that I will frankly admit that I have not used this "Winged Dardevle" enough to care to express an opinion one way or the other.

The Dardevlet, of three-fifths ounce, is rapidly supplanting the larger one as the favorite of bass fishermen. Since it is smaller, a bass is much more likely, if he is of any size, to take the whole thing into his mouth, and so be caught by the tail hooks.

The smallest of the family is the "Imp," two-fifths ounce. A bass worth keeping rarely misses the hooks on this, and indeed the Imp usually hooks even the tiny fellows which nobody wants. I frequently use this with a single sunfish-size hook, in a manner which I described in Chapter V; there is no guessing what the next strike may bring, where fish of many varieties are present. This method is an interesting novelty to mix with one's more orthodox fishing. Instead of a bare hook, I have sometimes used a small fly at the rear, especially when I wanted to pick up crappies or large bluegills, among the others.

The Dardevle is one of the few lures not meant for a pork rind but with which one works very well—this is especially true of the Imp. An Imp and pork rind sometimes make an effective lure for bottom fishing in very deep water for bass, with the retrieve which I described as particularly useful for that.

It might be well to mention that the Dardevle is among the best lures ever devised for northern pike, pickerel and muskellunge. For the musky, I generally prefer the plain nickel finish, but I find solid copper or brass very good on occasion. I use the one-ounce model mostly for these large fish, though there is a still larger one made for them. For bass, and even for pike, the red with a wavy white stripe is the favorite, but the unpainted ones just mentioned are well worth trying. The other patterns have never attained much popularity.

The Hawaiian Wiggler

In action, this resembles a pork-rind lure so closely that I am somewhat doubtful whether it should be placed in a separate classification. But instead of a single strip of pork rind, there are a large number of thin strips of rubber—the "skirt." I have said that I do not consider the single strip of "rubber pork rind" very effective. That remark does not apply to this skirt, which has an attractive movement in the water when retrieved.

These skirts may be had in various solid and combined colors, the red-and-white seeming to be the most popular; one may quickly be slipped off the hook and another put on. By reversing the skirt, it bulks out larger and has a different action, often more effective. This lure is made in three types: Number 1, deep running; Number 1½, medium running; and Number 2, shallow running. Each of these may be had with either single or double spinner; for bass, I prefer the single spinner.

The Hawaiian Wiggler comes in the weedless type only, the weed guard consisting of two projecting wires which cause the point of the hook to ride over obstructions, and which flop forward out of the way. I consider this about the best form of weed guard, the one least likely to cause missed strikes. Still, since the wires cannot be detached and replaced, as on some lures, I recommend that one have a Hawaiian Wiggler or two with the wires entirely removed, for fishing in open water; this should mean hooking at least a few more bass.

Unfortunately, the Hawaiian Wiggler is now made only in quite heavy weights, which renders it undesirable for the users of light rods. Fred Arbogast & Co., the makers, tell me they are considering making some in lighter weights when conditions permit—it must be remembered that while lighter lures are rapidly gaining in favor, there is still a much larger market for quite heavy ones, which can be cast on cruder tackle. In the deep-running model, it is easy to file or whittle away some of the soft metal from the body to make the lure lighter, touching it up afterward with vermilion paint, but this cannot very well be done with the other two models.

One should avoid leaving this lure on a hot boat seat or exposed to the sun in a tackle box, for this causes the thin strips of rubber to stick together and lose their life.

The Cockatoush

One of the favorite lures of all really advanced and expert bass fishermen whom I know is a fly and spinner, with a small lead weight to carry them out. Hardly anything else can cast so far and so easily, even in a stiff wind, and it is also an excellent fish-getter. But, strangely, its use seems to be confined almost entirely to the few experts; the average bass angler almost never uses it.

One can make up any combination he wishes in this, but it would be hard to beat the Cockatoush, made by the Prescott Spinner Company of St. Paul, Minnesota. The fly is a special sort of woolly-worm thing, tied substantially to withstand the mauling that bass give a fly, and the spinner is of excellent quality; a small dipsey or keel sinker of appropriate weight for one's rod is used with it. My own favorite is the white with a gold spinner, and I have made some fine catches on this.

If I am devoting little space to this fly-and-spinner combination, it is because I can find only this to say about it: it is among the most useful of lures, and there is no reason that I can see why its use should be left to the experts. The amount of space given here to different lures has nothing to do with the merits of each; it depended solely on their peculiarities which I have thought it well to discuss fully. The fly-and-spinner has no noticeable peculiarities—but that does not keep it from catching bass.

The Flatfish

Charlie Helin, a mechanic in Detroit, lost his temper. Otherwise there probably would now be no Helin Tackle Company. He devised a spoon which he sold to some company on a royalty basis, but it was never manufactured, so Helin did not get a red cent from it. That made him mad.

Now that he has had business experience, he freely admits that that company, after studying the invention, and considering business conditions, probably decided that making the spoon would not prove profitable after all—and that perhaps it was not as good as he himself thought it was. Anyhow, when he invented the Flatfish he started making it in his basement in spare time, then full time; then he hired a man to help him, and soon more men to help them. . . .

He probably called the thing a Flatfish because it isn't particularly flat and bears no resemblance to a fish; that's his way of doing things. In fact, it looks like nothing that a bass ever ate—or didn't eat. Not satisfied with this, and in spite of the many standard patterns to choose from, he began mixing paints to try on it until he found some colors that were nightmarish. He finally decided to use mainly a shade of orange unlike anything a bass ever saw.

Incidentally, this lure had a peculiar swiveling motion from the middle, all its own, and certainly no fish's or frog's, or anything else's. So in color, shape and action it was a monstrosity at which any experienced angler could not help smiling.

There was but one thing to be said for it: the darned thing caught fish, and lots of them. Why? Nobody knows, not even Charlie Helin; he may think he knows, but I'm quite sure that he doesn't. In fact, one of the matters pertaining to fishing of which I feel most certain is that Charlie Helin's notions about a fish's color vision are completely wrong, and some of the most recent experiments of scientists in that matter back up my views, not his. But still his plugs catch fish.

Never willing to leave bad enough alone, he fits his lures with very small hooks—he has to, to get that somewhat delirious action. I don't see how the average fisherman, who, after all, is a fish-derricker, ever lands a big fish on one of the things—maybe he doesn't. It would seem that having those small hooks would be against the plugs, except for the more expert anglers who know how to play a fish, who would like them. It isn't; they sell about as fast as Helin can make them; and that's fast.

They're so light for the size, so hard to cast, that he recommends using a lead sinker a foot or more ahead, to take them out, and to take them down deep. Perhaps he doesn't realize it, but only a negligible number are used thus, as he means them to be used, for most anglers object to that double weight flying around, sun-and-planet style, making distance accuracy or casting ease difficult. So, the man who likes small lures will often use the big trolling model for casting—and that weighs only three-eighths ounce.

I found a way out of that lightness-and-bulk trouble—nothing very original; it goes back to the oldest plugs. I bore a little hole in the middle of the bottom of a Flatfish with a brace and bit, and fit in a disc of lead, then paint over it. This gives casting weight without a sinker, and takes them down, but since it merely forms a sort of frictionless pivot it does not interfere with the action. I thought myself mildly ingenious, until I found that many others were doing just the same thing with the Flatfish. I suggested to Charlie Helin that he make them that way as standard, and maybe he will some time; I won't guess.

I never saw an angler use a Flatfish without cursing it for being so hard to cast, and for the way the hooks tangle in each other and in everything else; but he'll keep on using it, because the darned contraption does catch fish, and there's no denying it. I never heard of a man who could be so completely wrong in everything as Charlie Helin—and still be so right. In short, the only good word to say for the Flatfish is that it does get bass, and plenty of them. It's almost as good as Helin thinks it is; nothing could be *quite* that good.

Unlike all the other lures discussed here, it is not typical of any class of lures. It won't fit into any of the other classes, but it can't be ignored. Or one might say that it is the type for its many imitators, whose chief habitat is the dime store. They look more or less like it, but not one of them that I ever saw was worth two whoops in a rain barrel for getting fish; they are completely worthless.

And here I make what is really an insert. Just as I was getting ready to mail the manuscript of this book to the publisher, I received a letter from Charlie Helin. He asks why I don't just clip on a couple of big buckshot to the middle bar, for casting weight, and to take it down. When a woman asked Doctor Johnson why, in his great dictionary, he called a whale a big fish, he answered, "Ignorance, madam—pure ignorance." So now I'll say, "Stupidity, Charlie—pure stupidity." I never thought of that.

But I want to find out now what effect such buckshot or lead wrapped on might have on the fish-taking qualities of the Flatfish. Maybe those hooks flipping around so freely on the bar, like legs or fins working, have a good deal to do with the effectiveness of the Flatfish; lead would slow that up a lot. And maybe it has nothing to do with it. More experiments for me! *

*   *   *

Why, some may ask, have I not included some typical surface plugs in this list? Simply because they do their work up in plain sight, and any man can see for himself what they are doing, so I do not think a discussion of their various actions is necessary. A man must use his own head and his own judgment a little.

Let me repeat: I by no means wish to imply that these specific lures which I have discussed are the best; I have taken

* Have tried it extensively since. Less action, but much easier to cast—and catches fish.

each only as representing a type, because I had to take something. If I were to write this over again, probably at least half of those which I have mentioned would be missing, and others would be described in their places. Therefore apologies to the makers of some splendid lures omitted should hardly be necessary.

I have little doubt that this chapter will prove valuable to the less experienced bass fisherman, in showing the peculiarities of lures of each type. And I have still less doubt on another matter: that no manufacturer whose plugs I have mentioned will like what I say; each will think either that I have not said enough about his product—or that I have said too much.

PHOTO SECTION

1.—Let's try this cove.

2.—Now, which plug will they take?

3.—Aim over rod tip.

4.—Back no farther than this.

5.—Out. Notice wrist action only.

6.—Play one thus.

7.—How to land a bass.

8.—"Good catch!" the pilot said.

9.—Begin pick-up here.

10.—Up, fast! And stop suddenly—

11.— . . . no farther back than this.

12.—Should be one there.

13.—There was—and a big one!

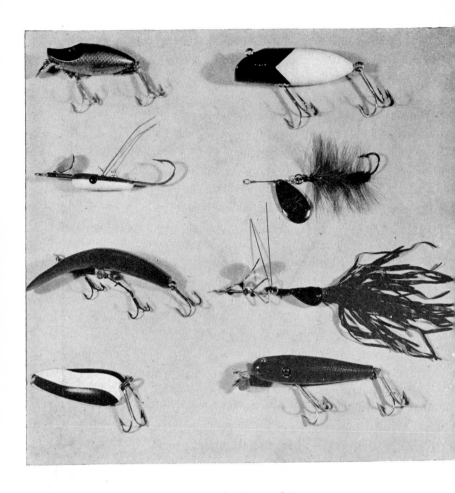

14.—Castings plugs.

River Runt.	Babe-Oreno.
Oriental Wiggler.	Cockatoush.
Flatfish.	Hawaiian Wiggler.
Dardevle's Imp.	Pikie Minnow.

15.—Nice ones from Lake Minnetonka.

Jason Lucas

CHAPTER X

Can a Fish See Colors?

I AM warning the average reader, the man without a scientific bent, that he may not care about this chapter. In this one chapter alone I depart from the strictly practical and delve into the purely theoretical; it is a discussion of a fish's vision, and especially of that much debated matter, the possible extent to which a fish can distinguish colors.

When a man buys plugs or bass flies, what is it that he should mainly consider? Unquestionably, it is exactly how a fish will see those flies or plugs. But this does not occur to one in a thousand; the rest take for granted that a fish will see them about as they themselves do. I believe there is not the faintest chance that this is so. Let us compare a bass's vision with a trout's, and both with a man's, and try to find out where they differ.

A fish's eye is constructed on a completely different optical principle from that of a man or any other mammal. In a man, change of focus is accomplished by flattening or rounding of the lens itself by the use of tiny muscles. In a fish, the lens is moved forward or backward in relation to the retina, as a camera lens is moved forward or backward in relation to the film, to focus on objects at various distances. But it is doubtful if that in itself would make an appreciable difference in what a fish sees. Substantially the same result is achieved, but by a different method.

More important is the fact that the structure of a fish's eye shows him to be very near-sighted. This is only what one would expect, for long-range vision would be useless in the dense medium of water, and it is against the laws of evolution for any living thing to acquire and retain completely useless characteristics.

It is well known that acuteness of vision varies widely in different fishes, all the way down to bullheads, for instance, which are mainly nocturnal and feed almost entirely by scent, and hence have very poor sight, and to some cave-dwellers, living in total darkness, which are completely blind, their eyes rudimentary. Fishes have the vision—or lack of it—that their habitats and feeding methods require.

But if a fish has the vision best adapted to his feeding habits, what should we expect in the trout? He feeds, at least during a large part of his life, mainly on flies and nymphs, tiny creatures, which he certainly should be able to distinguish one from another, to know what he is about to eat. Hence we should expect close-range vision little short of microscopic, and there is some reason to believe that he has acquired this to a certain extent.

A good reason why it is not perfect is that no members of the animal kingdom but men and monkeys have developed the *macula lutea*, that tiny yellow spot on the retina of the eye which alone permits one of the primates to concentrate his vision on a small object at some distance and see it very clearly, with all around it hardly seen at all. To a creature without the *macula lutea*, everything must appear at least slightly blurred at all times. Therefore, even if a dog—or even the lynx, famed for keen vision—were intelligent enough to read this page, he could never learn to do so, for the print would seem blurred to him.

That is what scientists say, and my own observations during years as a professional big-game hunter amply bear it out. A man has far better sight than any wild animal except those of the monkey family; and many, such as the bears, seem partially blind to an experienced hunter.

With this, undoubtedly, many sportsmen will be inclined to disagree, recalling incidents in some of their own deer and turkey hunts. The point to be remembered is that most wild animals have learned to use such vision as they have to the fullest extent possible; they had to, to survive. But even the most accomplished professional hunter, white or Indian, has not trained himself to use one-third of his; and a sportsman, an amateur hunter, is doing well indeed if he reaches one-tenth of his capabilities in this respect. During my own hunting days, when my eyes were kept in constant training, I often saw a deer standing perfectly still, among trees, at a distance of half a mile or more; indeed, I have many times walked onto open ground, seen one thus, and leaped back to cover without being observed, though the deer's head would be toward me. But I cannot recall once having had a deer see me, when I remained perfectly still, at fifty yards, if there was some background into which my body would blend to some extent.

So a fish, much lower in the evolutionary scale than any mammal, very likely sees a thing at any distance only as a vague blur. But a trout, which habitually feeds by sight, and on small objects, can undoubtedly examine a fly thoroughly as he rises slowly to it. This is particularly true of the brown trout, which is a true trout—as the brook trout, for instance, is not; he is a charr.

From this, what actions should we expect from a trout, when we go fishing for him? That sometimes, when he is hungry and feeding avidly, he may be pretty careless as to the fly he takes, but that at other times he may be extremely particular about its size and shape—we are not speaking of its color here. And that this holds true is borne out by the experience of every angler; sometimes a trifling difference in the size or shape of a fly can make a great difference in one's catch; two flies alike in color but varying in these other respects may vary widely in utility at a given time.

But how about the bass? It should be remembered that he is a very different fish from the trout. His pugnacity is greatly exaggerated, but he is certainly far more aggressive than the timid trout, except on comparatively rare occasions. And he can well be called almost omnivorous, for he will eat just about any living thing of suitable size, if he sees it move. This though his preferences certainly can change, especially when he finds more food than he requires, as in a hard-fished lake where bass are kept thinned out by anglers but the supply of food remains undiminished—increases, rather, for there will be more of these smaller creatures left uneaten by bass, to serve as breeding stock.

And the bass's feeding methods are very different from a trout's. They are more like a cat's, in that he prefers to hide and dart suddenly upon his prey from some distance—too great a distance for him to have been able to see it clearly, as a rising trout does a fly. Furthermore, he darts out and strikes so rapidly that he has no time to examine his prey at close range, as does a trout. Therefore one would be led to think that, according to the utilitarian laws of evolution, he could not have developed the more or less microscopic vision that a trout seems to have, since it would be about useless to him. Actual fishing experience confirms this, for some of the most successful bass lures bear no resemblance whatever to any natural food of the bass, or indeed to anything else in nature.

On the other hand—and again as one might expect—he is keenly conscious of size and movement in a lure, at some distance, though he sees it only in a blurred, indistinct way. This, as every fisherman knows, is amply proved by the fact that a slight difference in the "action" of two bass plugs, sometimes imperceptible to the human observer, will greatly influence their comparative bass-catching abilities.

All this is fairly well understood, though most often unconsciously, by the majority of anglers, and explains their great care in selecting plugs. No one holds that all lures of equal size and roughly similar shape are equally efficient for catching bass; the "action" of the different ones is always taken into account.

But our knowledge of the psychology of bass is rudimentary indeed. It must probably always remain so, because they are such totally different creatures from us, and from any other warm-blooded animal—from a dog, for instance, the psychology of which we understood quite well long before the investigations of Pavlov. So it is pretty safe to assume that even the inventors of the best bass plugs have little notion of why their lures are effective; they found, empirically, by making many lures and trying them in actual fishing, that those made in certain ways caught more bass than others. Nobody can sit down in an armchair, or at a drawing board, and devise a plug that he can guarantee will be good for bass; it is pure whittle-and-try until one stumbles, after innumerable failures, upon an efficient one.

This does not hold so true of flies for trout. Most of these are designed to represent flies or nymphs upon which trout feed. Sometimes the resemblance is pretty sketchy, but nevertheless it is there, and probably a trout's lack of the *macula lutea* covers its deficiencies.

In the "fancy" flies—those not pretending to copy nature

—it does hold true; they are devised by trial and error as much as bass lures are. Who can explain why the Royal Coachman, one of the oldest flies still to remain highly popular, takes trout so well, in about all parts of the world? Certainly the king's coachman who devised it long ago in England could not; he merely tied up a fanciful combination of peacock herl, red silk, and other things, peculiar not only in its colors but in its long, slim waist, and went to the river to try it, with not the slightest notion of whether it would catch trout well or not. Probably he was very much surprised to find it so effective.

It is the matter of a fish's color vision that is most baffling of all. Until a few years ago it was taken for granted that a fish saw all colors well. Then the theory became popular that all fish are completely color-blind, as are most mammals, including the dog, which can see things only as various shades of gray. Many anglers, not wishing to appear old-fashioned, gave lip-service to this theory; but a glance into their fly books or tackle boxes would have brought a smile at the discrepancy between practice and expressed belief, for there one would invariably find flies or plugs of all the hues of the rainbow. They had learned in actual fishing that this wide variety of colors was imperative for maximum success in the practical matter of catching fish.

Then the pendulum began to swing. The first really weighty statement I found expressing the other view was that of Professor Samuel Eddy of the University of Minnesota, whose researches were made in close cooperation with the well-known Thaddeus Surber, of the Minnesota Department of Conservation, co-author with him of the authoritative *Northern Fishes.* This is the flat statement: "Although it has been claimed that most fishes are color-blind, some, such as the bass, can distinguish certain bright colors like red."

Other scientists began to look into the matter, though it seems that none has found sufficient time to devote to it so that his researches could be called definitive. Some used test tubes filled with liquids the colors and shades of which could be changed easily: a tube of one tint would mean food for the fish; that of another, a mild but disturbing electric shock. The result of this seemed to prove that many fishes are perfectly aware not only of major colors, but of quite small differences in shades of one color—at least as much so as is a man.

In my desire to get to the bottom—or top—of the question, I consulted the man who is generally regarded as the most brilliant research worker in the field of optics, light and related subjects: Professor Brian O'Brien—the world-famous "Butch O'Butch" of the University of Rochester's Institute of Optics. The information he gave me stated, in part:

"The evidence reported by various investigators is somewhat conflicting, which is in part due to failure on the part of experimenters to control properly the brightness factor. However, in spite of this it seems probable that some color discrimination does occur in fishes, although more carefully controlled experiments are required to determine how extensive this color vision may be."

This might be called "the cautious language of science." But the language of science is necessarily cautious, for a scientist of Professor O'Brien's high standing is invariably characterized by a marked reluctance to accept any findings, including his own, as final. But it will be seen that he does favor the theory that fishes have color vision. If he himself could be induced to delve into the matter . . . But we don't want that; he might come up with some discovery that would make the catching of fish too easy to be any sport; the only thing one

can reasonably expect from that astonishing man is the unexpected, the apparently impossible.

One strong argument which I have never seen used, in
favor of a fish's having acute color vision—though probably
it has been—is this: The common sunfish, among many other
fishes, develops very bright and beautiful tints during the
mating season, the purpose of which can only be explained as
sex-attraction. Why should he develop them if his prospective
mate were color-blind and could not discern them? That would
be against the evolutionary law of development and retention
of biologically useful characteristics only. I give particularly
great weight to this matter because it is not dependent upon
the observation of a man—who can never see as does a fish—
but upon that of another fish.

It should be remembered that our "black bass" is not a
true bass at all, but a member of the sunfish family; therefore
similarity of his vision to that of the smaller sunfishes could
reasonably be expected. And from the feeding habits of the
trout, one should expect him to have more highly developed
color vision than the so-called bass. Practical experience in
fishing seems to confirm this.

Postulating, then, that our commonest game fishes are
not color-blind, there is a perplexing phase of the matter to
which, so far as I know, no attention has been given, beyond
my casually calling attention to it in a magazine article which
appeared in 1945. The thing which first turned my attention
to it was this:

At a fishing resort where I was staying, in Wisconsin, I
wanted to repaint an old bass plug that was much the worse
for many maulings not only by bass but by such sharp-toothed
fish as pike and muskellunge. Not having my own paints there,
I mixed some from partly empty cans that I chanced to find,

and wound up with a queer shade of yellow. Merely to preserve the plug from water, I used that. To my surprise, I
found that it took fish, bass especially, far better than it ever
had before.

Interested, I went to the nearest town and bought new
paint of what appeared to me as exactly the same color, and
put that on another and similar plug. It was no good, a very
poor fish-taker. Thinking the difference lay in some variance
in action of the two plugs—though I could observe none—I
tried switching the paints back and forth on them. Invariably,
the one bearing the original mixture caught far more fish.
Unfortunately, I had paid no attention either to the labels on
those cans or to the proportions of each which I had used, and
I had thrown the empty cans away.

Hesitantly, I published an account of this in that magazine article. And waited for the derisive comments to come
in many letters, waited meekly, wondering why I had been so
temerarious as to publish the thing. As much to my astonishment as to my relief, no one seemed to doubt it. A surprising
number of readers wrote me of having had parallel experiences
with various colors—two looking alike to them but having
widely different fish-taking abilities.

I had gone even further and commented diffidently that
unpainted metal spoons, apparently identical in color but of
different alloys, seemed to me to vary in effectiveness for
catching fish, especially muskellunge; I added hastily that it
must, of course, have been purely my imagination. Several
who wrote to me had observed the same thing but, like me,
were inclined to put it down to coincidence. One, a man who
was not only an ardent angler but a trained metallurgist, had
been so impressed by the matter that for some time he had
been experimenting with making and using spoons of various

alloys but identical appearance, though he professed himself to be completely at a loss for an explanation of their seeming diversity of effectiveness.

Only after a great deal of thought, a possible explanation came to me. And it was almost absurdly obvious: A fish's color vision should not be expected to embrace the same range of the spectrum as a man's, and only muddled thinking, or no thinking, could lead one to take it for granted that it does; indeed, it may, I think, be taken for granted that it does not.

This deduction, if original—which it is, so far as I know— would open up a new field of research into color vision of fishes, and it would explain as inevitable the discrepancies in findings of previous investigators. It would be a matter of great importance to the millions of anglers, to the manufacturers of plugs, spoons and flies, and to commercial fishermen.

If a fish's range of color vision should be more limited than ours, but contained within it, it seems probable that he would see the colors within his circumscribed range much as we see them, so the difference in color vision between him and us would be quantitative rather than qualitative, and so of no great moment. But what evidence have we that he cannot see beyond either end of our spectral range, or beyond both?

To us, the wave lengths lying beyond the red are "infra-red," or "black light," or "invisible light"; those lying beyond the other end of our spectrum are "ultra-violet." Really, to us they are nothing at all, for we can have no conception of colors which we have never seen. But who would be so presumptuous as to say that no other creature can see them? About as well argue that a dog cannot hear "ultra-high" sound waves, though thousands of dogs are called daily by means of whistles made to produce these sounds, inaudible to man.

To some creatures, undoubtedly, infra-red is as clear and distinct a color—or range of colors—as yellow, midway in our visible spectrum, is to us; these creatures could plainly see a landscape illuminated solely by that light, though we should think ourselves in total darkness. Of recent years, camera film has been introduced which will make clear pictures by infrared rays, invisible to us, and film of the older type was always sensitive—too sensitive—to ultra-violet.

During the Second World War, utilization of this "black light" enabled our soldiers to draw accurate beads on Japanese even on the blackest nights—to the Japanese, perhaps the greatest mystery of the war was that Americans could see, and shoot unerringly, in pitch darkness. But our men did not see those infra-red rays; they were, for their benefit alone, ingeniously transmuted, at the rifle sights, into visible colors. And who could have performed this apparent miracle but Professor Brian O'Brien—Butch O'Butch himself?

So who will say that certain fishes cannot see infra-red quite plainly? Or that ultra-violet is not a distinct color—or wide range of colors—to them?

This would explain quite simply why two specimens of paint, seeming exactly alike to us, might appear totally different to a fish. There would be a difference in the pigments of the two samples, one reflecting much more ultra-violet or infra-red than the other, perhaps even enough to drown out all the yellow, green or other color most visible to us. So of two flies or plugs seeming alike to our eyes, one might appear to a fish as of a color known to us, and the other of one totally unfamiliar; or perhaps both would be to them of colors that we cannot even imagine.

To some this may seem far-fetched, for we are used to our own little range of colors, and it may seem impossible that other clear and distinct colors could exist. But they do exist, as infra-red and ultra-violet photography—and those night-sights for rifles—plainly prove.

There seems to be corroboration of this in a matter that has puzzled trout fishermen for ages. Every experienced trout angler has long known that two flies tied exactly alike, one with natural feathers and the other with dyed, may have very different trout-taking abilities, though to a man they look identical in colors. But if my tentative theory is correct, it would be almost impossible that they could seem alike to the trout, for there most certainly would be a difference in the amount of infra-red and ultra-violet light reflected by each.

We must consider, too, the unlike refraction of different colors—light waves of different lengths—in passing from one medium to another. In any discussion of a fish's vision, this means from air to water, but in the case of air to glass it alone permits spectrum analysis; and it also causes the chromatic aberration of camera lenses, which has to be so painstakingly corrected, not only for color photography but to secure the sharpest possible delineation in black and white.

Even apart from color, the dry-fly man has another thing to consider: the formation of many diminutive lenses by the impinging of his hackle points upon the water; it is, of course, the rather odd phenomenon of surface tension which permits this. This matter has been treated many times in books and magazine articles.

And what, if any, polarizing effect has water upon light entering it, and then entering a fish's eye, and what effect might that have upon how a fish sees things?

"And what," the angler may ask, "has all that got to do with my catching bass? It sounds to me like what they call 'pure science'; stuff with no practical application."

It becomes more and more doubtful if there really is such a thing as "pure science," with no practical application. It was an astronomer, closeted with his prisms and his Fraunhofer's lines, who first discovered helium ninety-three million miles away, in the sun. But helium helped us win a war—as did O'Brien's "black light"—and it is now of great commercial importance.

Here is one mundane application of this matter: The man who refinishes his own plugs might do well to see to it that two batches of paint which he uses not only appear alike to him, but that the chemical analysis on the cans show them to be compounded of exactly the same ingredients—which would mean buying paint of the same brand each time, and making sure that its composition had not been changed. The same precautions should be taken by the dyer of feathers, if he expects consistent results from the flies made from them; and he should expect different results from dyed and natural feathers—though I see no reason why, in spite of the popular theory, the dyed should not in some cases prove the more effective.

In conclusion, crude sciolist though I recognize myself to be, I go so far as to suggest that when scientists next experiment with color vision of fishes, they pay no attention to the matter of how the colors appear to them, but find out what the spectroscope, color filters and ultra-violet and infrared photographic plates have to say about the tints they use. Who knows but that they *might* find out something that would surprise them?

CHAPTER XI

To Return to a Spot on Water

I HAVE several times mentioned how necessary it is to be able
to return to an exact fishing spot again, even when it is far
out in a lake. Indeed, no matter how much angling skill a man
may have in other ways, he can call himself no better than a
third-rate lake fisherman until he is able, unerringly, to drop
his anchor in almost the identical place where he had it once
before, perhaps half a mile from land or from the nearest
visible weeds. If he is unable to do that, he can never keep a
list of those productive and little-fished deep holes found well
out—and such a list is usually the secret of some "miraculous"
angler's consistent success.

There is another useful application of the method which
I shall describe: finding sunken equipment—an outboard
motor, a rod, a tackle box dropped overboard. To show how
infallibly it works, I shall give here a letter which I received
after I had published a magazine article explaining how it is
done:

> I was much interested, and thoroughly agree with you,
> in your statement concerning triangulation methods of lo-
> cating oneself.
>
> Experience in the method you mentioned enabled me

to recover a rod and reel lost three hundred yards off shore in open water in Lake Geneva, Florida, two years ago. A bad cast shook the rod from my hand and it disappeared in ten feet of water. The lake was too rough for several days, to drag the bottom with a grapple. Then a fellow officer at Camp Blanding heard of my plight. "I'll dive for that rod," he told me. "I have seen you work in the field and when you say you know where the spot is, I'm willing to go down."

The first day the lake was calm, we rowed to the spot I had marked. He dove over the side and came up a few seconds later with my rod. The spot had been marked by resection of four points on the shore line which were at almost right angles to each other.—M. R., Waco, Texas.

Note ". . . a few seconds later . . ." A single quick dive, and he laid his hand on the rod, and brought it up. What better proof of the method's accuracy could one want? But do not be frightened off by the word "resection." No engineering experience is necessary, and it can be done well the first time one tries—though practice makes one a little better at it, or at least faster. And no optical instruments are required beyond a man's own eyes.

How does the average fisherman go about returning to his good spot, where he got all those big bass? To find out how vague his notions are, just ask him where he got the fish. He'll look a shade puzzled. "Why—why, about opposite that white house across the lake. And out about—about—uh— two hundred yards. Or maybe three hundred."

Next day he goes back and anchors "in the same place." No fish; not even a strike. The fact is that he may be a long way from the good spot. I believe this inability to return to a place on the water is the main reason why the grouping habit of large bass at certain spots in deep water has not been recognized—they rarely group thus in shallow water near shore, where the place would be easy to find again by anybody.

"Opposite that white house" means exactly nothing. And an even reasonably accurate judgment of distance across bare water is impossible for most of us; it is easy to be out one hundred per cent or more in our judgment.

A quite useless version of the method seems to have become current; no less than three different men have solemnly described it to me in the last year or so. Get your boat, they will say, directly between two marks—houses, for instance—on opposite shores, and also directly between two marks about at right angles to these but on other shores—and there you are!

That would be grand if only a man had an extra eye in the back of his head, and a set of surveyor's instruments between it and the others, to line him up, but I've never seen a man so equipped by Mother Nature. Obviously, those who recommend that method so gravely have never tried it; it's more armchair fishing advice. As well say that a man could find the center of a mile-square pasture by getting himself exactly in line with each pair of opposite cornerposts.

There is, so far as I can figure out, but one method of locating a spot out in a lake, and this is it:

Pick some object; for instance, the chimney of a house on the shore. Get the right side of the chimney exactly in line with, say, the left side of a conspicuous big tree farther back. Remember that I said *exactly*, not roughly. Imagine that you are firing a rifle so that the bullet will just graze the right side of the chimney, and then the left side of that tree.

Now turn and find similar marks in line as nearly at right angles to the first ones as you can. And—that is all.

Like anything else worth while, it may seem a trifle

difficult at first, but with a little practice it takes hardly more than a couple of casual glances while you fish. If you want to check on how surprisingly accurate the method is, notice that as your boat swings a little on a short anchor rope, each pair of marks swing noticeably out of line.

The whole trouble is remembering the marks. At first, this may be difficult, where they are not conspicuous objects —and they can't always be that. My own method is to glance and pick two marks, then turn and keep on fishing, trying to see them in my mind. Presently I get a strike, and forget them. But I bring my mind back to them again—without looking. Next, I do the same with the other pair of marks; then, with them alternately. In this, as in everything else, habits can be formed, and it becomes easier and easier to pick marks, and to remember them, the more one does it.

Still, it is difficult for one to remember them from fishing trip to fishing trip, and practically impossible to remember the location of more than one or two spots from year to year. And these good deep spots may stand up for years. So it is imperative that one keep a record of some sort. A pair of rough sketches would probably be best—if one has considerably more drawing skill than I have.

One man wrote to me of taking two snapshots at right angles. That sounds ideal for a small lake, or for near shore; but it seems to me that a telephoto lens would be necessary to make the marks show large enough on a wide lake. I'll admit that I haven't yet tried it—the reader may wish to.

My own method is to keep a notebook in my tackle box, and a stub of pencil. My notation will be something like this:

Tip of last big tree on Rocky Point, in line with peak of red barn, on ridge.
Right side of big clump of willows appearing barely to touch

*right pier of bridge. (Willows beyond bridge, seen under it.)
Cast about 60 ft. toward mouth of Jones' Creek.*

And if it should be fifteen years before I got back there,
I could still, first cast, lay my lure into that good hole which
is only a very few feet in diameter. And if the level of the
lake was still about the same, and it was the right time of
year, I'd probably start pulling out the big bass immediately.
If, of course, I hadn't lost the book. And if that big tree on
Rocky Point hadn't blown down years before.

From this last point, it will be realized that permanent
marks, such as big boulders or contours of the land itself, are
by far the best things to take, where they can be found. For
instance:

On one northern lake that I had fished off and on for
eighteen years, I had a hole that was remarkably good for very
big bass, and it had stood up season after season during all
that time. It was half a mile from shore, off the tip of a reef
that nowhere was nearer than eight feet or so to the surface.
Two years ago, during the middle of summer, a man who
lived a mile off cut down a big maple in his field.

If he'd only known the trouble he was to cause me, he
might have been kind hearted enough to spare that tree! That
was one of my four marks for the good spot. It might be
thought that, having one definite line, and a rough idea of the
other, it would be easy to find that little hole again. It wasn't;
it took me many evenings of pottering, off and on. Even then,
I wasn't sure that I had it exactly; I didn't seem to get quite
as many lunkers as I thought I should. But who does?

Invariably, one should write down an accurate description of the two lines marking a good hole which one had
found. Never should one trust to memory to be able to recognize those lines next day, or even an hour later.

Do I always do that? I don't. But I lose some fine spots for just that reason. Anyway, I've told you how it's done, so if you lose your good deep hole you have nobody but yourself to blame.

And now for another and slightly more involved application of what I have just described. Let's call this our Dirty-Trick Department. Concerning the instructions I'm going to give here, let us say: if the other fellow doesn't pull it on you, it's only because he doesn't know how. I got the trick out of my own diabolical imagination, and perhaps nobody else was ever quite fiendish enough to think of it. Now I'm divulging it for the first time.

Have you ever watched a dog go to bury a bone? He looks absent-minded, and pretends that he isn't going there at all—indeed, no; he's going to three or four other places. A similar game is played by the fellow-that-always-catches-them sort of bass fisherman in approaching one of his good deep holes, which nobody else knows. He'll spend a lot of time pottering in different places where he realizes it's no good; then he'll slip in there, catch four or five lunkers in a hurry, and row off in apparent disgust at having got nothing there, to do some more pottering around. If another angler tries to steal up on him while he's in his good spot, he quietly lifts his anchor a little, drifts somewhere else, and lets it down again—where he knows there are no fish. Oh, very clever! Have I done this foxy trick? Yes, many a time; I have that pup-and-bone technique down pat.

It's fair enough. One doesn't want everybody fishing one's pet spot, to ruin it by overfishing. Every good angler has such secret holes. But if he's that good a fisherman, isn't he, perhaps, trying to discover the other fellow's good spots too? Indeed, keeping his own places secret, and finding the other man's, is almost a mania with the really clever grade of angler, and as legitimate as bluffing in poker—though he may feel bitter when the other fellow beats him at it. Still, if your conscience is tender, don't read the rest of this chapter, which for the first time reduces finding the other man's good spots, in spite of all that he can possibly do, to an exact and infallible science.

A little instance of my working it:

Several years ago, I moved, in the middle of summer, to a lake up north. Being busy with some writing I had to get out, I didn't fish for the first week or so there—which was a great strain on me.

There were two brothers there, bachelors, middle-aged, who always brought in bass, and very big ones. That would have been all right if they hadn't been so cocky about it, hadn't bragged so loudly, hadn't been so ready to sniff and sneer at those who couldn't get as many; they were of that variety of mankind scientifically classed as *homo ornerycuss*. Somehow, a reputation for knowing something about fishing had preceded me, so they worked up a few particularly nasty sniffs and sneers for me, before I'd even fished at all; they bragged that they were going to show me up properly.

I got mad. And I said to myself, "*Bueno, señores! Vamos a ver!*"

Really, I could have gone fishing sooner, but I was up to those dirty tricks I've mentioned: I did not even go out on the lake in that preparatory period. When the time was ripe I went. And returned about sunrise with my limit of real lunkers. I hung the live net from my dock and, by pure coincidence, happened to be there when Jim and Jake came in later. I showed them my bass. They'd been skunked.

That happened several mornings in a row. They weren't always skunked; they got about half a dozen very small ones in all that time. And their tempers were not exactly nice to observe when I would meet them at my dock. If the penalty for murder hadn't been so strictly meted out in that state . . . Then they moved their docking place far out of sight of mine. But at any rate they kept still about their fishing, from then on, and either of them would walk a mile out of his way to avoid meeting me on the road. And all the rest of the neighbors got a good deal of satisfaction out of it.

How did I find their good spots, to fish them out before they got there, without even going on the lake? Simple enough: I'd just drive around the road nearest to the shore, watch them through glasses, and when I saw that they were on a really good hole and getting fish, I'd find my usual double marks for one line—and I'd find them right over the middle of their boat. Then I'd drive about quarter way around the lake and get another line in the same way. They'd been many years discovering these few best spots but, before I'd fished there once, I could just about have dropped my anchor into a sunken wash tub at any one of them.

Of course it's easier to do by swinging around a man, perhaps half a mile away, with an outboard motor.

Do I like showing fellows up that way? I certainly do not, unless they make me mad, as those did. Many and many a time I've had some fisherman, whom I'd be passing on my way home, joyfully hold up for my inspection a beautiful string of crappies averaging fully six inches long. I'd exclaim in envy—how ever did he get 'em, when I didn't have a single crappie? If he rowed close so that I could get a better view of those beauties, I might have to kick a couple of yard-long pike and a lunker bass or two under the stern seat out of sight. There's one thing I honestly enjoy more than my own fishing, and that's seeing the other fellow get enjoyment out of his; and if he gets it from a few small crappies—more power to him! But, of course, when somebody makes me mad . . .

And now, having told my method here, how about my own good secret spots? That's what worries me; there's always the chance that somebody will buy and read a copy of this book. At any rate, I hereby beg the reader never to pull this trick on a man who'd be too good a sportsman to pull it on him. But it will come in handy sometimes.

CHAPTER XII

Deliberately Seeking Lunkers

I F THIS chapter should seem vague in spots, it is because it deals with the most advanced stage of bass fishing—deliberately setting out to catch lunkers, not bass of ordinary size. It is, in fact, what one might call a post-graduate course in bass fishing. When I ran a version of this in *Sports Afield*, I humorously referred to myself as holding the chair of Applied Fishiology, and the editors carried out the spirit of the thing by calling me their "distinguished old angling professor." Imagine my amazement when one of the largest universities immediately began wiring me, and telephoning me long-distance, inviting me to give a series of lectures on advanced stages of the art and science of fishing. I had to decline the honor, owing to press of other duties—and, to be honest about it, the thought of it scared me stiff.

Fishing and poker are analogous: one has to become quite good at either to realize that, comparing one man's "take" with another's, the element of luck is almost nonexistent; the expert nearly always gets more. There are times when even the best bass angler cannot discover many bass that are feeding; and times when even the slickest professional gambler cannot find his suckers. But there is hardly a day when the real adept at either cannot at least do well enough for eating purposes.

True, the novice at poker has as good a chance as the expert of drawing the rare and unbeatable royal flush; but in his excitement he's almost sure to "tip his hand" and make nothing from it. And the greenest beginner may hook the record fish of the year, but in his excitement he's practically sure to lose him. I think it certain that far larger fish are lost each year than are recorded; the big one does get away, all too often—quite naturally; anybody can land a small one.

But the part of the analogy that interests us right now is this: the expert at either game goes deliberately after the larger fish, not bothering with small fry except when he can find no better. In short, the tyro at angling may chance to get an occasional big bass; but the man who has really studied how to get lunkers can bring them in with surprising regularity.

There are two odd things about the largest bass which help one get a good many of them. Strangely, I never have found these things commented upon either orally or in the books. Surely some others must have discovered them, but if so they have kept them to themselves.

The first is that the largest bass are far more gregarious than those of ordinary size. So where a person finds one there is nearly sure to be at least another, and often a dozen or more. This, though all bass beyond the fry stage are supposed to be mainly solitary in their habits.

The other is that these great ones always have small, scattered, and very definite spots in the water which they prefer; these are almost invariably in deeper water. Catch some lunkers in a place one day, and the chances are much better than even that you can go back there next day and get more like them—and often do it for days in a row. More keep moving in as the first are caught out and leave room for them. There was something there to attract large bass in the first place, and the same thing attracts more. As with so many matters pertaining to fishing, I do not know why either of those two things I've mentioned are so; I learned them not from thinking about it, but from long experience.

The average fisherman blunders when he hooks a big one, not knowing that the same spot probably holds more. In the first place, he almost invariably kicks up quite a rumpus in playing him. He splashes around, and knocks his shoes and oars and everything else against the boat—he may not even realize how sensitive fish are to such vibrations in the water. If he's drifting, casting ahead, he'll do all this while letting his boat drift over the spot where he hooked him, making sure of stopping the rest from feeding for a long time, and perhaps scaring them out of there.

If he succeeds in landing him, he'll keep right on going, fishing and rejoicing. Or he'll go in happy, the proud possessor of one big bass—and he'll think he's a wonderful angler. He'll never know that, in a thrill-packed half-hour, he might have picked up his limit right there, all perhaps averaging as large, with likely at least one considerably heavier. I know this can be done, for I've often got them that rapidly myself.

Therefore, when you hook a big bass, carefully avoid all disturbances. A commotion doesn't help one land a fish, and may lose him. In my experience, no amount of running and leaping by the hooked fish himself will put the rest there off their feed; indeed, it usually seems to make them strike better, by exciting them. And generally, in playing a fish, a man doesn't have to move anything but his hands.

Sometimes the bass runs under the boat, and it is necessary to pass the line around one end of it. If this happens, sneak along, and crouch as low as possible. That not only avoids your falling out and drowning, but it keeps the rest of the bass there from seeing an alarming bulk moving against the sky. Whether one nets the fish or lifts him in by hand, it can be done quietly, for a big fish should never be brought up to the boat until he's tired out—as mentioned elsewhere, hauling them close too soon is the principal cause of losing fish, as well as of broken tackle.

When he's hooked near the boat, try to dip the oars, alternately, very gently and back away. For a man who is alone, this isn't easy while playing a large bass, but I manage to do it as a rule. If he was hooked on a fairly long cast, and there is little breeze, you may have him in before getting too close to where he struck. But if at all near, the thing to do is to sit low on the seat and drift well past the place before moving, when you can cast back—I usually anchor very quietly before doing this.

It might be well to say here that the bass fisherman on a lake should invariably have some good rig which will enable him to slip his anchor up and down quietly without moving from his seat. Most bass fishermen do not use the anchor nearly enough; it is one of the most useful accessories of the game. That is, if it is operated properly, without jumping all over the boat.

If you have drifted quite a way past the spot, which means that there is more wind, you must note exactly where that spot is. Then circle it widely—do *not* row over it—and get back to what one might call comfortably long casting distance; then anchor. This avoids casting into the wind, which is especially difficult with light but bulky plugs.

Naturally, keep on using the same lure and retrieve that took the first. And if you had been retrieving slowly and absently, don't unconsciously speed up now; the slow retrieve nearly always takes the most bass, as long as you get some action into the lure. But occasionally that will have been the only fish in the group that happened to feel interested in that particular lure, depth and retrieve. So if you get no strike in a dozen casts—no more—try some others, fished in different manners.

Don't get the common notion that big bass always like big plugs. Sometimes they do; but sometimes they much prefer the most diminutive ones. Never forget that the smaller the lure, the more certain it is of hooking those that strike, for the fish will take the whole thing into his mouth, and that even the biggest bass rarely does with a large plug.

There's no use wasting too much time with one lure. Four or five casts with each should be enough to show if they are there and going to strike it. And end up with whatever you got the first one on. Maybe they were slightly disturbed, and will hit after the short rest—though I can't say that I've often found this to be the case; usually it's a long rest or nothing, and you had much better get away from there for the time being.

It's poor policy to stay long in one place, getting no strikes. If you do get fish after an hour or so in one spot, it means that you have been waiting for the fish to come accidentally to you or, if they're there, to start feeding. Go find where they're feeding now.

Even if you do catch several there on your first lure, it's a good trick to try some other lures before leaving. I sometimes have thought I'd fished a spot completely out with one plug—and then found two or three bass that wouldn't touch that, but wanted something else. These last, however, have almost invariably been smaller than the average I'd taken there, but often good ones at that.

If you got only one, by all means try it there again later on, preferably between sunset and dark; possibly more were there but it wasn't their feeding time. And if you're out at dawn next morning, see what a few casts there will do; that's a propitious time for big fellows.

One of the great secrets of getting big bass consistently lies in being able to find your *exact spots* again, even if they're half a mile or more out in the lake, with no visible weeds near by. For one who hasn't learned the proper method of locating a spot, a poor second-best way is to mark the place with a tight can anchored with a piece of old line and a heavy sinker. The trouble here is that some other angler may disturb this, or start fishing there, suspecting that it means something. A large, weathered cork, or a piece of stick, is less conspicuous— but you probably can't find it yourself if it's far out and you don't know how to take lines from shore. Much better to do it the right way.

And remember, well out from shore is where one does run across most spots that are regular producers of lunkers. That is particularly true on hard-fished lakes, where the inshore water is continuously disturbed by anglers.

Sometimes, even in deep water, that big one might have been only a stray; near the shoreline, he's almost sure to have been that. But as the water goes over six feet or so in depth, the chances are increasing rapidly that you've found a spot which draws the big fellows regularly. At twenty feet, it's practically a certainty. Also, at that depth, you may pretty well count on having the place to yourself, for few use heavy lures and let them sink deep before retrieving, and generally the bass won't come up after more shallow-running ones.

How big are these extra good spots for lunkers? It's risking a lot to make any flat statement about fishing, but I will say that a fair caster can easily reach all over one of them from an anchored boat. Often they seem hardly more than ten or fifteen feet across, with water all around them barren of fish.

Why do the big bass pick these spots? That, to me, is a mystery. They will often not look half so good as some other places close by. And I know long stretches of shoreline that

seem ideal for bass, where I can get them when about everywhere else fails me—but where, out of hundreds caught, I've
never got one of more than small average size. And then, in
the middle of a poor stretch, there will be a spot that appears
only fair; but it will be a regular gathering place for lunkers. Of
course there is some reason for all this—but what it is I can't
say.

How long will such a place hold good? I've seen some
produce well for only two or three days; others, rare ones—and
always the deeper ones—for perhaps a couple of months at a
time. Then the fish are gone, and one must find their new locations. Usually, then, the old place holds nothing whatever;
it will be good for big ones or nothing at all. But next year,
when the weeds down there are in just the same stage of
growth, they'll be back there again; I've never seen this to fail.

One's first guess would be that these changes of location
would be governed mainly by water temperatures at different
levels. I cannot find that this has nearly as much to do with it
as one might expect.

And now for the second secret of getting big ones, the
thing which has been responsible for my bringing in nearly all
the biggest bass of my life. It is this: When you find a big one,
catch him!

This sounds like a gag. It isn't; I'm deadly serious. Here is
what I mean:

When the average angler loses a very big bass, he goes on,
bemoaning his hard luck, and that's that. And it seems that
most of these really big ones do strike and get away after a run
or two, generally by leaping and throwing the plug—as if to
taunt one with their great size before escaping.

But what else is there to do besides going home dispirited,
and trying hard to refrain from telling anybody about "the big
one that got away," knowing you won't be believed?

Parenthetically, I must say that I always believe that story, unless I know the teller to be a habitual liar in other matters. True, the inexperienced angler will invariably imagine the fish bigger than he really was—but that isn't lying; it's an honest mistake caused by excitement. But in spite of all the moldy jokes, I can't see that fishermen are any worse liars than golfers or duck hunters or tiddleywinks players, and I've certainly been around fishermen enough to know something about them. Indeed, things have reached such a pass that it has to be a very big one that gets away before the loser, fearing ridicule, will mention it.

But—this is the point—he hasn't got away! The chances are at least even of bringing him in yet. That is, unless the water is very shallow, or you've made a disturbance around there.

Keep after him! Keep resting him at least an hour or two at a time, and going back. If he's a real whopper, spend several days after him if necessary, hardly thinking of the others that you may get while giving him time to start feeding again.

Yes, he'll stay there; he'll return to the exact spot in which he was lying when he darted out at your lure. I believe that playing and losing a bass almost never makes him change his location, if the angler hasn't frightened him otherwise. Of course there is the long chance that it may happen to be his moving day, to go to another spot; barring that, or a rumpus on your part, he's pretty certain to remain there. Remember, I'm speaking here only of very large bass; smaller ones change locations much more often and more readily.

All that I said before about not disturbing a good spot holds here with double force, for you know that there's a big one here. Slip quietly up to your longest comfortable casting distance when you return; ease your anchor down carefully, without the least splash, by means of that lift controlled from your seat. Imagine it's a whitetail deer that you're slipping up on—don't do as most do, and act as if you're picking mushrooms, which won't scare off.

Place the lure where you did before, and retrieve it over exactly the same spot—that's pretty sure to be where he'll strike, and not six feet away. There lies the one catch to going back and finding your big bass that got away; being able to cast into the same place, exactly. Of course, if you don't know it that well, you can cast in a segment of a circle until you're sure that you must have brought the lure past him—but there's always the chance that the lure splashing around him will have alarmed him enough to keep him from striking.

He'll generally take the same plug as before. It sometimes happens that he'll strike at it more than once, and so lightly that you will not hook him. But he may be in a mood to hit another one much more savagely; bass are queer that way.

Do not keep whipping the place very long at one time; that may run him out, and will practically never catch him. Leave, and fish elsewhere. But keep coming back so long as he even bunts the plug lightly once on most of your return tries— as I say, these bunts mean, almost always, that you should change plugs, to find one which he either likes or dislikes enough so that he will hit it harder.

He'll rarely strike more than once on a visit, and it's best not to try to make him; he may get mad and decide to go where he'll be bothered less. Of course, you're not certain of him until you have him in the boat, but the chances are fine that you'll eventually land him—if you make no blunder.

Why do I sound so sure of all this? Simply because I've proved it to myself over and over, by going back and getting those that had escaped from me once—or twice, or three times or more.

I've given an outline of how all this is done but, naturally, variations will be necessary according to conditions. A man must figure these out for himself; he will not have a more experienced angler there to do his thinking for him. But this chapter wasn't written for the kindergarten class in angling. One should be at least a B.F.—Bachelor of Fishiology—to get the most out of it.

CHAPTER XIII

"Fished-out" Lakes—Aren't

IF WHAT I shall say here makes sufficient impression on the reader, it should prove the most useful chapter in the book to him. It is meant to show what fine fishing there can be in a "fished-out" lake near home—if one learns to fish it properly. And in this chapter lies the main secret of why most men who fish it get practically nothing.

One day in fall I woke up and looked out the window at the first peep of dawn, to find it a heavy, lowering morning with the clouds almost down to the ground; it seemed ready to rain any moment, but somehow I had the feeling that it wouldn't. In other words, it was the most ideal bass morning imaginable.

Now, dawn fishing, practically always the best bass fishing of the day, was then a pleasure almost unknown to me, for, like most other men, I have to earn a living, though I'd much prefer to fish all the time. If I went fishing early instead of sitting down to write, I either couldn't force myself home until dark, or I'd come in too hot, or too cold, or too tired, or too mosquito-bitten—or with my mind too much on how I'd fish that place next time—to get any work done that day.

Being a writer, I lived where I pleased, which, all the year round, was within a few feet of good fishing. But having to write mornings sadly cramped my piscatorial activities; it was only by starting to work always at about five A.M. that I could manage to get in a bare eight hours a day or so, average, of fishing for the year through. That isn't enough. My notion is that to be perfectly healthy, contented, and able to get along without vitamin pills, a man should fish an average of at least twelve hours a day, every day in the year.

That, of course, was before I became an angling editor, when fishing was purely an expense to me, and spending so much time at it, when I might have been working, kept my conscience in a perpetual squirm. Also, it caused my best friends to smile tolerantly when they met me; they thought I was slightly touched in the head, to fish so much.

Now, it is otherwise. To get out and fish mornings regularly is a plain obligation to my readers, my bounden duty to the magazine that trusts me—generally over two thousand miles from the office—to earn my salary. Otherwise, how could I honestly advise readers about early-morning fishing? So out I get, come rain, snow or sleet, a conscientious martyr to job and duty. . . .

On that perfect bass morning in question, the temptation was too great for my conscience. I slipped out of bed and got a hasty breakfast. ·

A little while later found me a mile or so off, my boat drifting along the shoreline before a gentle breeze. I was being extremely careful to keep my casts at least six feet out from the edge of the bushes, or I should certainly have connected with a large bass, which might have ruined my temper and my day's fishing.

·That may sound pretty silly, but if the experienced and foxy angler will think a moment he'll probably chuckle; he'll have done the same thing himself. I was being watched, and I was afraid that if my observer knew I was catching fish he'd immediately start tossing a many-hooked plug uncomfortably close to my ears, while at the best he'd put the bass down so that they wouldn't strike again for a long time.

Presently the young man in the other boat called to ask how they were hitting. I pulled a long face and shook my head. "Why-y—so-so." Which can mean anything. Still, being by nature a friendly sort of chap, I wanted to help him to some sport if I could do it without having him ruin mine, so I asked him if he knew the lake hereabouts.

"Sure! I live in that house down there a hundred yards. But I haven't fished here in a couple of years; I've been away, where there was no fishing."

No fishing! And the man was polite, even pleasant, after two years of stark tragedy. He had fished a lot too, and he was a real sportsman; he was keeping far enough off not to scare any fish that might be near me.

"I got these," I said, and I pulled up my stringer. Generally, I liberate about all the fish I get, but we were having friends out for dinner and I wanted some for them.

His mouth flew open, and got stuck that way. At last he managed to gasp, "Wh-where did you get 'em?"

"Right along here."

"And they're running that big!"

"Oh, no—I've kept only the biggest."

He seemed dazed. That string of huge bass was, obviously, a damn lie—the kind of lie we fishermen are accused of telling. But there it was! He was silent a moment; maybe he was trying to decide whether he was still back in bed, and dreaming.

"But, listen! I looked out the window only half an hour ago, and you weren't here."

"No—got 'em since."

He shook his head, looking at me in awe. "Do you always get 'em that way?"

That I certainly didn't, as I assured him. This was the finest morning for big bass I'd seen in at least a year; they seemed to have gone crazy, to be attempting mass suicide. But he—as I had noticed—hadn't been getting a single strike. He asked me deferentially if I'd show him how I did it. I told him to watch.

There were two trees growing out from the shore, about fifty feet from my boat. Since the lake was unusually high, their lower branches were in the water. They made a pocket about eight feet in diameter, with a sort of little gateway two feet or so across facing me. I sent my plug through that opening, let it rest several seconds, and then started it toward me just fast enough to keep it barely under water.

It had not gone a foot when it stopped gently, as though it had hung on an underwater twig. That was how the bass were taking that morning; they seemed torpid, lazy—until they found they were hooked, when they went wild. They acted as if they had been overeating and it took a good jar to wake them up.

A peculiar thing about a bass hooked far from a boat, on a slow-moving lure, is that one can invariably rush him some distance, even on very light tackle, before he gets his wits and begins to scrap. That let me get this one safely out of the bushes before he went into action, but when he did, it began by his breaking water with a splash that would have done credit to a muskellunge. I glanced at the young man in the other boat, and I probably chuckled at the astonishment on his face.

The fish landed and released, I looked around. Almost a hundred feet down the shore was another particularly promising pocket. Normally I'd have made perhaps a dozen casts before reaching it, but now I tossed my plug that way, watching to stop it in the air if I missed the opening—which at that distance was more likely than not. It chanced to go straight, and within five seconds I was battling another bass, a particularly rambunctious four-pounder.

I made two more casts, one a dud, the other picking up a very nice one. Three good bass in four casts—not bad, considering that this lake was within ten miles of downtown in one of our largest cities, and supposedly fished out two generations ago.

The last one released, I rowed over to the other man's boat to see how he was equipped. He had quite a good outfit, and there was a pike-scale plug on his leader—that usually worked well around here, as he probably had found out from former experience. But this particular morning they wanted no dealings with pike-scale plugs, for some reasons known only to themselves. They wanted a red-head, and as he had one along I advised him to put it on. I asked if he could cast into the pockets without tangling up.

"Lord, no! I'd be hooked in the branches every time."

I might have known that without asking him. I'd seen him casting sidewise—sideswiping—and, doing that, one needs a crystal ball along to foretell where one's plug may go. The only accurate cast is the overhead, and the more accurate one wants it to be, the more pains are necessary to keep it perfectly vertical. It is much as though one had a very long knife and were trying to chop straight down through the spot aimed at.

So he shouldn't try the pockets; it would mean rowing in every other cast to get the plug loose, thereby putting the fish down for a considerable distance along.

"Then," I said, "cast as close to the bushes as you can; watch your plug and stop it in the air if it's going too far. But remember: this morning they just won't come out more than three feet after it; and if it's moving much faster than mine was, they won't bother with it at all. You won't get as many as in the pockets, but you'll get plenty of good ones within half an hour."

I advised him to begin at a big tree down the shore, where I'd started, and fish the other way. He headed back there, while I kept on. Since I had my limit, I became interested in experimenting with various lures and retrieves, to see if I could learn something new. Even at that, I was regularly picking up nice ones.

Presently I glanced around to see how he was doing. I got an object lesson in the sheer, utter perversity of human nature.

He was staying well out from the shore, as he'd been doing before, and not putting his casts within fifteen feet of the bushes. And as soon as his plug struck the water, he'd start reeling back about as fast as he could. He'd begun at the big tree, all right—but he was following me along where I'd probably caught every fish, where those I'd released certainly wouldn't strike again so soon.

A suspicion came to me. I casually dropped back close enough to see what plug he was using. Yes—blamed if he didn't have his old-reliable pike scale back on again! It was a good plug, and he knew it, and he wasn't going back on it. Like all too many anglers, he had his favorite plug, type of water and retrieve, and he was sticking loyally to them, come hell or high water—or an empty stringer.

He could have lashed the lake that morning until his arm gave out, and never got even a strike. Which, the last I saw of him, he was well on his way to doing. He'd probably go home and tell of the fine bass "that other fellow" got, and moan about their having stopped striking just as he got there.

I have told this because it brings out all the points I want to make: A so-called fished-out lake can furnish superb sport, really much more true sport than a wilderness lake, because it calls for real skill to fish it; there's the satisfaction of knowing that one is using skill, not doing what any novice can do. But the average angler stubbornly persists in fishing the wrong spots, and in using the wrong plug for the time, and the wrong retrieve.

Why does he? Probably because that method calls for no thinking whatever. It would seem sometimes as though a man, intelligent in most things, likes to check his brains at the boat house when he goes fishing.

That just won't work, with bass! I know of no other type of fishing which calls for so much ingenuity, and thought, and study, as bass fishing—and that, together with the bass's astonishing gameness, is what makes bass fishing the great sport it is. It is not for the man who likes to do only easy things. Neither is it for one so vain that he can't bear having fish make a monkey of him—bass are very, very good at that. In short, if a man isn't willing to use more intelligence than a fish, he had better leave bass alone.

I'm not trying to insult anyone by insinuating that he has less intelligence than a fish; I'm merely suggesting that he use the brains that came with him as standard equipment. A bass's brain is bean-sized, while a man has a noble dome filled with pounds of cerebrating cells.

There are actually more large bass in some of these "fished-out" lakes—which in many cases one can reach any evening after work, and in which most of our fishing is done— than in some of the famous angling lakes of the north. In these home lakes, bass are kept thinned out by anglers until those left find much more food than they can eat. So, they grow into big, sassy brutes with a strong propensity for smashing tackle and escaping when they do get hooked.

There's a catch to it! The more innocent ones die young,

and those which attain the lunker stage know all about wooden nutmegs and wooden plugs—plastic ones and other kinds too. And moribund minnows impaled on hooks have long ago ceased even to amuse them. They are never hungry, and so they can afford to cast a bored eye at anything which doesn't appear just right to them. To complicate matters still further, it is safe to say that every last one of those whoppers has felt a hook at least once in his life, and probably several times, which doesn't tend to make him overly gullible. But they're there.

"Sure!" I'm told. "Everybody knows they're there. But they can't be caught except by a miracle."

To reply to that—and to encourage the man who fishes such a lake, which is what I'm trying to do—I must point out that for six weeks before the incident I related, fishing daily, I had not once failed to get my limit of big ones in that lake; I dare not test the reader's credulity by telling how many I released on the best days. And houses around the shores of that lake were closely packed; they were in regular blocks, with numbers on them. Over a million people could have reached that lake by a few minutes' drive any evening. Sometimes, from the congestion of boats, it would seem that the whole million were fishing on it at once.

I've said things like this to men who couldn't call me a liar, because they and their friends, living right on the shore, had seen over and over again what I was getting—they could see from their front windows a few yards off. Here would be the answer, given in a bored tone:

"Oh, sure! That's all right for you, Jason. Fishing as much as you do, you can learn all the tricks. But I haven't time for that, and can't expect to get any."

Of course he hasn't time to learn—from his own experience, which after all is the hardest and slowest way to learn anything. Or he isn't as big a fool as I, to spend all his days fishing, and his nights meditating about it. Or . . . maybe it *is* better than inventing atom bombs to blow everything to pieces, or piling up money to leave to nephew Cyril, who would go to pieces blowing it.

Anyway, there's no reason why the ordinary fisherman should have to learn everything from his own experience. Every time he buys a copy of this book, or of a magazine with an article of mine in it, he's helping pay me to get out and do the experimenting for him, and let him know what I discover, so that he can use it. And I can assure him that I don't want to hold back anything that I may learn—just consider the last part to Chapter XI.

Tackle
Selecting—Correct Use—Repairing

CHAPTER XIV

What Casting Rod?

This is a case of one man's meat being another man's poison. Few seem to realize that the casting tackle which will prove ideal for one man may prove all wrong, even completely useless, in the hands of another. And here I am not even considering the matter of individual tastes, which may be changed.

I am taking into account the fact that tackle will be used under widely varying conditions, by men totally unlike in the amount of skill which they have developed—and I might add that this has little to do with how long a man has fished, for some become really good casters in less than one season, others, never. For these last, I have no sympathy; either they keep plugging along clumsily and stubbornly refuse to learn, or they won't get good outfits and keep them in proper shape —most often the latter, for the man who gets a correct outfit generally learns to use it right.

Still more important perhaps, on the whole, but a thing rarely mentioned, is the matter of personal fishing habits. Two men about alike in skill may be fishing so near each other that they can talk across the water. Still, they may need entirely different casting tackle, and what just suits one of them might be sheer misery to the other. This is not exaggerating, for on more than one occasion I have been one of those two men.

141

From this it will be seen that I cannot set down specifications for "the best" casting outfit, any more than I could tell a man by mail what size shoes and hat he should wear. Of course if he sent me his measurements in inches, I could pick up a mail-order catalogue and translate them into sizes, and send him what he wanted. And if he gave me full data on his fishing experience, conditions and habits—which wouldn't be likely; he'd be sure to leave out some of the most important things—I could tell him exactly what tackle would be best for him.

What I am going to do here is to give some information on the things that should govern choice of casting tackle, so that a man may pick his own and be pretty sure that it will suit him. Mainly to show what great differences do exist in requirements, I shall begin with an extreme case.

A man in the East wrote to ask my advice about a casting outfit. Here is the data he sent me:

He was only five feet tall. That had nothing to do with it; his wrist might have been stronger than mine, and I'm well over a foot taller—and any man's wrist is strong enough to cast with any well-made rod. He fished entirely on a long, narrow lake formed by damming a river. There were cliffs on both sides, and the water, practically always crystal clear, dropped suddenly past rock ledges, with scarcely any vegetation and no snags. The bass ran large, and were so extremely shy as to stop feeding before a boat could come within ordinary casting range; this was the whole matter that had him baffled.

There could be but one answer to his peculiar problem: He needed what was almost a tournament-distance rod of six feet—not quite so stiff as that, of course, but on the same order. And he should have a delicate, open, free-spool tournament reel, and a line of not over four or five pounds' test—I also advised him to try long, light nylon leaders. I specified three-eighths-ounce lures, to avoid the bigger splash that heavier ones would make.

Such a very light line would be satisfactory for him because he was an experienced angler, and had used a fly rod a great deal; therefore he would not be likely to lose his head and unnecessarily break the line in playing a fish—an easy thing to do. Also, he would not have to contend with any weeds or snags whatever, and could play a large bass as long and as lightly as he wished. All he'd have to consider would be whether his line could cast a plug without whipping in two.

This, with a lighter and more flexible rod, makes a beautiful outfit, of the kind which I love to use. And I hereby warn the reader to avoid it as he would the plague, for using it could only mean one break after another in the line, until soon the rod would go smash. Besides which, very few men would fish enough to learn to cast with it.

Why do I give such a blanket warning, admitting that I like it myself? Simply because the few for whom it is suitable are skilled anglers of long experience; they do not need my advice, and would not take it—I know many who use such outfits, and would have nothing else.

As further discouragement, I will add that such a rod, of six feet, can be had only made to order, as a rule. And tournament reels are sometimes hard to get hold of.

Now we'll jump to the other extreme—the man who does a lot of fishing among lily pads on thick snags, and a good deal of it from shore. Advising him is equally simple: Get the outfit plenty strong. There can be no playing a fish; he has to be "horsed" in as fast as possible. Nor can there be real casting; it's a case of chunking the plug out there any way you can, without hope of any distance or much accuracy. It is crude fishing, which the expert angler avoids if he can possibly find any other.

These are two extremes, but such cases are far from equal in quantity, so to speak. At the summit of the pyramid stand the very-light-tackle men, in lonely dignity. The whole big base of the pyramid is a mass of very-heavy-tackle men jammed together like sardines. And the sad fact is that most of these could immediately climb up at least a grade or two higher, and then keep on going up. Indeed, many of them would now be climbing but for one thing—they don't know that the things they use are not casting tackle.

True, a few are so unfortunately situated that they must employ the snake-'em-out methods in snags or weeds, or not fish at all. But even one of these should, as a matter of pride, have a lighter outfit to show his friends, as what he fishes with where it can be used.

This heavy outfit is nearly always recommended for the beginner. I am in a quandary here, not quite sure what to say. If I recommend a light outfit, and it is broken, I should be blamed; if I recommend the heavy rig, the user can never learn to cast properly—and I'd be blamed for that. What shall I say, with a horn of the dilemma threatening from either side?

Perhaps if the man doesn't expect to fish much, the heavy things would be best—but then he might as well stop reading this right now and go his crude way. If he does intend to take fishing seriously, I recommend something considerably lighter from the beginning, even if it would mean some broken lines and fish lost at first. There may be, here and there, a rare man who could start right in with the expert's very light outfit, and have no particular trouble—but he'd have to be unusually cool-headed and dexterous. The whole trouble is that one who starts with a heavy outfit will get the habit of whale-lining bass in, and that habit is very hard to break.

There is one sort of beginner whom I should have no

trouble in advising: the man who is not a beginner at fishing, but only with the casting outfit, being already experienced with a fly rod. I would tell this man unreservedly to get about the lightest casting outfit, and the longest rod, that he could find. If he should start with the heavy stuff, he'd be almost certain to quit casting in disgust, and to spend the rest of his life damning casting as a crude method of fishing, and no sport whatever, never realizing that it can be refined to the point where it is actually more sporting than fly fishing.

There is one piece of advice that I can give unreservedly to the novice: If there is any chance whatever that he may fish much, or grow to like it, he should by all means avoid the cheap outfit usually thought good enough for the beginner. He cannot learn to cast properly with the thing, and he will probably soon become so discouraged that he'll give up all fishing. I've seen it happen. And I've more than once wheedled a man into trying it again, by much Dutch-uncle talking, some coaching, and lending him a good outfit—to see him, within a month, a fanatical angler.

Now for the man who is somewhere between the two extremes, or who wants to climb, but not too rapidly, from the bottom of the pyramid. It is men like him who each year waste thousands of dollars on wrong equipment, though all too often they never find out that it is wrong, and keep on using it. I am going to discuss casting rods for his benefit, rather than blindly recommend a rod for him.

We'll begin with the old-fashioned tubular steel rod, consisting of sections of level, seamed tubing which one fits together. It has no action, and it isn't strong—it is hardly a casting rod at all, though one can manage to heave a plug out with it if one swings and grunts hard enough. So we'll end with it right here; I advise it for nobody.

Then comes the solid steel, either round or square—the

latter often called "rapier" steel; the first of these square ones, sixty or eighty years ago, were actually made from rapiers. The solid steel rod is very strong, and so it is best for the man who likes to step on his rods, and slam car doors on them, and do things like that—some men do.

Many experts will say that there is no such thing as a good solid steel rod. I beg to differ with them; some have recently been developed which have nice feel, action and balance, and I know some experienced anglers who think there is nothing else quite as good; they are real fishing rods. Do I use them myself? No, I do not, except for my heaviest fishing, muskellunge and such. But I do not damn a thing just because it doesn't happen to be my own personal choice.

Owing to its construction, the solid steel rod necessarily has slow action for its length and weight; therefore a man should proceed with caution in getting one of over four and a half feet, or he may find it either too slow in action or with too top-heavy a feel to suit him—steel enough to stiffen a long one makes it top-heavy.

In fact, I personally consider four and a half feet as just the right length for a solid steel rod. And I want my casting rods of other materials to have somewhat the same action as a good solid steel, for about four feet at their tips, with the lower part quite stiff, acting mostly as a sort of throwing-stick to give more swing to the top part. But this extra length in the butt cannot, as I have said, be added to a solid steel rod without making it either too slow or too top-heavy for most of us.

It is perhaps worth mentioning that in my own experience a solid steel rod is not more durable than one of the lighter type, which I shall come to next. That is because of "fatigue," or "crystallization"—molecular changes caused in all steel by constant flexing. I have had two solid steel rods break unexpectedly in my hand when I was making casts of hardly more than moderate length; and it is almost always a long cast, not playing a fish, that will break an experienced angler's rod. On each occasion, it was on a frosty day in late fall; cold seems to have something to do with crystallization of steel, but I am not metallurgist enough to know why. However, this matter of crystallization is of little interest to the average angler, who will never use his rod enough to cause breakage from that.

Now, for the latest development in steel rods—those of drawn, seamless steel tubing. These are made not jointed, but with a detachable butt—though I have been discussing with some tackle companies the advisability of making the longer ones in two sections, for convenience in carrying. They are made in two types: in one, the tube is brought to a taper by steps; in the other, smoothly. One seems to have no particular advantage over the other; of course, it would be possible to make a poor rod either way, so it becomes a matter of relying on the reputation of the manufacturer.

Owing to quantity methods of production impossible with bamboo rods of good grade, the best of these drawn steel rods can be had for far less than the best bamboo. The experts have stopped sniffing at such rods as these, and have come to recognize them as really fine fishing rods in all respects; many veterans have switched over to their use, both for fishing and in tournament casting, although the top-notcher, unless he is connected with a steel-rod company, will still usually be found using a bamboo—and an expensive one.

There is a thing about a rod of this type to which some object: it has very fast action, much faster than a light bamboo. But others like this. Personally, I could wish that the action were slowed down considerably, but in spite of that I use rods of this sort a lot, and like them. Also, it is difficult to procure them in the six-foot length that some of us like—I have been pestering the makers assiduously about this, and they promise to have some out soon. Then I must try to coax them to make one in six foot six, for use with the very lightest lures; it should be a dandy—with sufficiently slow action because of its length —but I'm afraid I cannot promise them very great commercial possibilities for it, since its use would be restricted to a very few.

One great advantage of a rod of this construction, for the average man, is that it does not call for nearly the care and "babying" that a bamboo does. Still, one must remember that it is not a pole; it is a really good rod, fitted for artistic fishing, and must be given the respect that all good fishing tackle requires. It is very far from unbreakable, just as are all real fishing rods.

In the bamboos, one finds the very worst rods; stiff, lifeless things with the action of broomsticks. These are the cheap ones. And about all the short ones; if there ever was a short bamboo rod with anything resembling real action, I never happened to get hold of it. In this class, too, we find what many will call the very best rods—and at least I'm not going to get into an argument about that. There is something individual about a really fine bamboo rod that appeals to the veteran angler, so that he actually likes tinkering with it, rewinding it, varnishing it, trying to take out sets. If a man doesn't want to do these little things for his rod, he might be as well off to avoid the bamboo. Of course he could take it to a rod repairman.

Some of the worst bamboo rods appear at a single glance, to the man who knows rods, as fakes. But others may fool an expert; just looking at them, he cannot see their internal flaws. In fact, there are some sneaky tricks used to make a bad rod look good on the outside. About the only thing the average buyer can look for is two nodes of the bamboo—darker, crooked-grained little stretches—lying alongside or too near each other; that is almost sure to mean the rod's breaking there before very long. And, of course, little open, glue-filled cracks between the strips show the very worst and shoddiest kind of construction. This last is rarely seen; it is simple to make the inner angles of the bamboo strips too blunt and fill the spaces inside with glue. Then the outside edges meet neatly, and look well—but you have a very poor rod.

A bamboo rod can be built with about any action one wants, since the higher-priced ones are made largely by hand. Any individual action could probably be built into the drawn steel too, but this would be a matter of changing heavy machinery, which, of course, is impractical.

A first-class bamboo casting rod costs much less than the best bamboo fly rod, simply because it is shorter, not because it is inferior in workmanship in any way; it just takes less hand work.*

Now for the proper length—and it is here that most men go entirely wrong, by not getting their casting rods long enough to cast well or to play a fish properly. While I think four and a half feet just right for a solid steel, I consider that far too short in drawn, tubular steel or in bamboo, and especially in the latter.

For fishing in thick snags or weeds, one must necessarily use a heavy line, and a heavy line simply won't cast lighter plugs well; for it, they must be at least five-eighths ounce, and often heavier. The rule is, the lighter the plug, the longer the rod, to give best results. But even for this heavy-line fishing I do not recommend a rod under five feet, except in solid steel.

I might mention here another letter I received. The

* See Chapter XXXIII, Glass-Plastic Rods.

writer said that he used plugs of all weights, from the lightest to the heaviest, and that he insisted on having a rod that would handle all of them well. Would I kindly tell him what that would be? I told him what the drunken cowboy said when he saw the giraffe—there ain't no sech animal!

As I see it, one can diverge only one-eighth ounce up or down from the plug weight for which a rod is best fitted. With the lighter, it will be a trifle stiff in action but good for long range; with the heavier, it will be flexible and accurate for close work, such as fishing pockets. Another eighth ounce below, and you have a hopelessly stiff pole. Another eighth higher, and the thing "goes dead"; it is too limber by far— and probably breaks on the first very long cast attempted.

The reader may think it impossible that an eighth of an ounce could make so much difference. Remember that the speed of the rod tip in casting—the momentum of the swinging plug—multiplies that eighth ounce many times over; remember that an eighth-ounce bullet, at high speed, acquires a force of over a ton. That explains why the slightly heavier plug, in casting, feels like a flatiron on a light rod. One actually has added the weight of a flatiron.

More and more. I see half-ounce plugs coming into use; they've about become standard in some parts of the country. For these, I recommend a rod of five and a half feet. And when one gets down to the three-eighths-ounce lures—which cast so beautifully on the right outfit that one will never go back up again—it is well for some to push the length to six feet. And I personally like one of six feet six for lures around a quarter ounce, and not over three-eighths—but a rod of that length must be made to order.

Still, I do not advise anybody to get a rod of six feet or over. This, again, because the man who has to ask my advice— or anybody else's—about a rod has no business with such a long one. Not to feel clumsy, it must be light and pretty fragile; it's a rod for an experienced angler and for nobody else.

Rods of all these lengths can be obtained in different weights, which means different strengths. One might think that all one should consider in choosing a certain weight is whether it is strong enough to handle a fish without breaking. This certainly has something to do with it for most anglers, but not for the veteran, who can play a large fish on a very light rod, with no danger whatever of breaking it.

But there is another angle to it: different actions go with different weights. With a given plug, a very light rod will have the slowest action, call for the slowest wrist movement in casting. A heavier one is naturally stiffer, and it takes a faster snap of the wrist to bring out the action. Some like fast action, some slow; it's purely a matter of taste.

Or not quite purely; there's still another point that has to be taken into consideration. Sometimes a man, picking up my rod, will remark that it is somewhat stiffer and heavier than he'd expect me to use, with my experience. That is partly because I make considerably longer casts, on the average, than most bass fishermen, and the more forceful snap of my wrist necessary for that brings out all the action in this stiffer rod. The man who fishes closer would prefer a more whippy rod; it would be pleasanter for him to use, and perhaps more accurate at close range.

I should say here, to prevent misunderstandings, that I do not hold these long casts to be often necessary, or even the least bit better than shorter ones. I know some extremely expert anglers who, for all I know, cannot send a plug more than seventy-five feet, and rarely cast more than fifty or sixty. But they are sharpshooters when it comes to accuracy. And they get as many bass as if they were casting twice as far. One reason why my own casts average longer is that I fish deeper water much more than the average bass angler, and my retrieves out there are good right up to the boat. In fishing the edge of weeds, or a brushy shoreline, if one doesn't get a strike in the first few feet of the retrieve it is usually as well to rush the plug back and try again; therefore, in such places, very long casts are largely a waste of time and effort.

My Eastern correspondent, with whom I began this chapter, was the man in a thousand who really must make long casts. They are also often useful to a man wading, who has to reach far out into a lake, or to some hard-to-get-at spot in a river. But I really believe that the average man would get as many bass if he did not, or could not, cast over sixty feet or so. Therefore his rod should be quite whippy—unless he just prefers fast action in casting. And if I think most drawn-steel rods to have perhaps somewhat too fast action for a good many men, I believe that the action of most longer bamboo rods could be speeded up a little to advantage. But this speeding-up should *not* be done by stiffening the whole rod, which would make a mere pole of it; I think the butt part should be quite stiff, with action mostly toward the tip—much like the action of a good dry-fly rod. I know a great many expert anglers who prefer a rod of this type.

Should the casting rod be of one- or two-piece construction? Those of solid steel will probably always be one-piece. At present we are given no choice in the drawn, tubular steel, which are all one-piece, with separable handles, though we may see some in two sections before long. So the following will apply to bamboo rods only.

I recommend the two-piece, with the butt considerably shorter than the tip. In these, the butt section is generally quite stiff, so it really is little more than the throwing-stick I mentioned a while back, to give full swing to the more flexible tip with a very slight movement of the wrist—the action which I prefer.

We have heard a great deal of the far superior action of a one-piece bamboo. Frankly, I cannot see any great superiority; just a mere trifle, hardly worth mentioning. That is, in rods of five and a half feet and over; in the shorter, the difference is much more noticeable, the stiff ferrule taking up a greater percentage of the length. There is a slight difference; and for the best action of all I favor a rod without detachable handle —one piece of bamboo from tip to butt.

The whole trouble is that a one-piece rod, especially if it is of the latter construction, is just a nuisance when traveling. And even around the house, the tip has an uncanny knack of butting into tops of doorways and such things, to be broken or damaged. And if there's a slamming car door anywhere around, it just loves to get into it.

The main advantage of a one-piece rod, as I see it, is strength, durability. It cannot break at the ferrule, not having one. Almost any two-piece will eventually break there, after a great deal of hard use. But the remainder can be fitted back into the ferrule, leaving a slightly shorter, stiffer rod, good for many years more. However, long before the two-piece gave way, a one-piece would probably have deliberately butted its tip into something and been smashed. So I'll take a two-piece, and let somebody else bother with the one-piece, and its slight superiority of action.

What guides should one specify? One need give oneself no concern over this; they will come of a grade to match the rod one is paying for. However, we may discuss them briefly.

I have no equipment for testing various guide materials for hardness, and the information I've been able to get is somewhat conflicting. However, it seems that the real agate guide is the hardest of all, by a trifle. And it takes a very high polish, so it should cause little wear on a line. But many of them are not highly polished inside; they are fairly rough. Therefore they would act as sort of mild emery wheels to wear a line; and, since they are so hard, the line itself will not polish them. From this it would seem that a real agate guide might be the best, if it is highly finished inside.

Lately, when even good manufacturers speak of "agate" guides, they do not always mean real agate; often, when the rod comes, I find that they are imitation agate—this because real agate guides have been so scarce that the manufacturer takes it for granted that I do not expect them. But I do! Any imitation agate which I have seen was very poor stuff indeed. It breaks more easily than the real thing. And it is usually so soft that with steady fishing the line soon cuts a deep groove into it. I thoroughly dislike imitation agate guides.

The best steel guides are now made of a hardness but slightly inferior to that of real agate. And they are always perfectly polished inside. They are not brittle, and they are light. Thus, it should be evident that first-class steel guides are the most practical in nearly all cases.

Of late years, about all casting rods except bamboos are made with sunken reel seats; most fishermen have come to regard these as standard. However, a great many expert anglers and tournament casters prefer the straight reel seat and handle, believing that better casting can be done with them. I admit that I am among these, but I suspect that it is only because I learned casting with the high reel seat and am more accustomed to it. I believe that I should like the sunken reel seat better but that all reels are now made with a very low rear pillar; when my thumb is braced upon this, its tip jabs somewhat into the rear of the spool, instead of rocking down more gently on the top, to permit more delicate thumbing.

How, somebody may ask, about a trolling rod for bass? I shall not devote much space to that, for I consider trolling an ineffective method of getting bass, owing to their habits. However, the man—if there is such a one—who always trolls and never casts, should use a longer rod, with a longer butt, for convenience and for more spring in playing a fish. Since no casting will be done with it, there is no question of action, so it could be anything that suits his fancy.

All of us troll occasionally, though the more experienced bass angler rarely does. There is no need whatever for a special heavy rod for this. Just point the tip of the regular casting rod back along the line, and of course it cannot possibly take a set or be otherwise damaged. There is another advantage to this method; the long line which is used—or should be used—in trolling has quite a bit of stretch to it. Add the spring of a rod stuck out sidewise, and far too many strikes will be missed.

From all the foregoing it will be seen why it is impossible to specify "the right casting rod," without knowing the inquirer very well, and having often watched him fish. But if a man whom I knew to fish a reasonable amount should pin me down and make me give some definite specifications, I should say: Get a solid-steel rod of four and a half feet, or a drawn-steel or bamboo rod of five and a half feet, either with medium action, and avoid lures that weigh over a true five-eighths ounce.

CHAPTER XV

The Casting Reel—Selecting—Overhauling

I HOPE that the reader has realized by now that I have a sincere desire to help him to better and more sportsmanlike fishing. For that reason I wish that I knew of some way to impress on him the extreme importance of a good casting reel, in perfect condition, and well oiled. Unless he can cast correctly, his fishing can never be either pleasant or as successful as it should be. And he simply cannot cast properly without the right tackle.

In casting, *the reel plays the most important part*, though, of course, a suitable rod and line are also necessary. This is the exact opposite of what holds true in fly fishing, where the reel is of little importance, hardly more than something to store spare line on, and to balance the rod for comfort. Indeed, one can fly-cast without any reel, and tournament-distance casting is always done without one.

But there can be no long and useful discussion of reels, as of rods; there is little more to say than, "Get a good one, and keep it in proper condition." But I shall make a few remarks on the subject which should be helpful.

The most necessary thing is to be sure that the reel was turned out by a good maker, one with a good reputation, and that it is at least of his medium-priced grade. Even the best companies manufacture cheap casting reels which are almost useless. For the man who does not fish a great deal, this medium-priced one will perhaps serve his purpose just as well as the most expensive; it will cast smoothly, which is the main thing. The man who fishes a lot should certainly get the best obtainable, and he will never regret it. Not only will it cast a shade more smoothly than the lower-priced one, but it will wear much longer, with far fewer trips back to the factory for overhauls.

And now here is something which the manufacturers will not like my saying: The higher-priced bass reels sold at present are not bass reels at all; they are muskellunge reels. They are much larger and heavier than is necessary; they go back to designs of the days when casting was crude, and extremely heavy lines were used. They seem to be geared as a rule to spool a line of about twenty pounds' test, which certainly is muskellunge line, not bass line; and they hold more line than is necessary even in musky fishing. They do not work so badly until one gets below twelve pounds' test, but when one comes down to the expert's light line, it is laid on the spool in coils so far apart that the next line coming in squeezes down between those widely spaced ones under it and is pinched, especially if it is brought in under tension, as in playing a fish. Result: on the next cast, that pinched line is whipped down under, to cause a jerk and a backlash, unless one thumbs far harder than should be necessary. But in spite of all that, these are very fine reels indeed for the average angler.

For smoother casting, the man who uses light lines will generally be found with a reel of the skish type, geared to lay a nine-pound line smoothly, and working well with much lighter. But the trouble is that these, which so far have not been in really great demand—though I predict far more for them—are made only in quite inexpensive grades. They are small and light, and cast beautifully—but we hear complaints of their not standing up to hard and steady fishing. However, a trip back to the factory for an overhaul will always make one like new. Some of us have been trying for a long time to get makers to turn out for us a higher-priced reel made for the light-line angler—and of course many of the skish fans would buy it too. But our pleas seem only to bore them; they'd rather sell the heavy-line reels they make now.

Any casting reel should have some sort of anti-backlash device. Even the expert may wish to use it occasionally—for, say, fishing on a dark night, when a chance backlash could possibly stop his fishing. And when the device is completely released, it generally has no effect on the casting of the reel. A few reels are made so that they will not operate at their best with the anti-backlash device completely off; but since a majority of anglers will never learn to thumb a free-running reel, that is nothing against them—and some of these reels do have unusually smooth anti-backlash devices, which of course is in their favor.

A very few men use tournament reels for fishing; these have no level-wind nor anti-backlash devices. There is no question that a tournament reel does the finest, smoothest, and longest-distance casting of all; moreover, it causes less wear on a line than any other. But it is, to put it bluntly, a nuisance for most fishermen; it takes a lot of practice to learn to spool the line evenly enough with the fingers without watching it, which would keep one's mind off the proper working of one's lure— and that, after all, is *the* important thing in fishing; it's what gets the fish. And it is all too easy, in playing a large bass, to let the line pile up and jam against the pillars, probably meaning a lost fish.

For years, I used tournament reels almost exclusively in my fishing. Then I lost them in a fire. and could not replace them, so I had to use level-winds. At the time of writing this, I have not yet got another tournament reel; I hope to soon. But the question I cannot answer now is whether I shall ever go back to it for my fishing; the level-wind does simplify things a lot and it casts well enough for all practical purposes.

The only man to whom I would recommend a reel of this type for fishing is the man who uses it a lot in tournament casting, and so is accustomed to it. And it might just possibly be a good thing for the user of quarter-ounce lures, if he fishes so much that he will learn to spool his line by hand almost automatically. But a good level-wind reel will handle three-eighths-ounce lures very nicely, and most quarter-ounce ones quite well.

There are some free-spool level-winds made for fishing. But these are not really completely free-spool; they could more accurately be called free-handle reels, since the gears do not—and cannot, on a level-wind—come out of mesh, so we still have the drag of the gears, and of any heavy grease that may be on them. But some of these are excellent and smooth-casting reels.

If you already have a good reel, check it closely, to see that it is in the first-class condition which is so necessary. Here's how to go about it, and how to remedy what's wrong:

First, take hold of the spool and jiggle it sidewise, not endwise. On most reels, the oil cups on the ends can be removed, which permits inspection. If the end bearings are badly worn, they won't hold oil, and they may even permit the spool flanges to touch the end plates, which absolutely precludes good casting. So if they show noticeable wear, send the reel to the maker for an overhaul; it will come back just like new except perhaps in outside appearance, which has nothing to do with its casting.

Has your reel a light aluminum or plastic spool? None

of the older reels have, and too many newer ones are made without that. Good casting cannot be done with a heavy spool, because it acts as a flywheel, hard to start and stop, and under the thumb it is inclined to jerk and cause backlashes; there are many things against it, and nothing in its favor except perhaps strength—a strength totally unnecessary if one fishes right.

So, if your reel hasn't a light spool, order one, if it can be obtained. If the end bearings are in good shape you yourself can slip it in. This, of course, does not apply to hand-made reels, which must be sent to the makers for fitting.

There are some quite antiquated reels in use. Some of these have what is called a "balanced handle"—a single handle, with a small weight on the other end of the crank, which is supposed to balance it. But this handle is balanced statically, not moving, instead of dynamically, whirling. And the air resistance against the handle and the small weight vary in relation to each other according to speed. With all this, the "balanced handle" cannot possibly balance in actual use, and it sets up a jiggle to the hand that makes for poor casting. The handle of this type is years out of date.

If yours has this, a different one should be put on. If you can order one to fit—fine. If not, any good repairman can make one fit for you. A man of some mechanical skill can do it for himself; I've often done it. If the hole in the crank is too small, simply enlarge it carefully with a little file. If too large, drill the place out round and solder in—preferably hard-solder —a piece of suitable material. (I have even used a filed-down penny, which is an alloy of copper, and rustless.) Then drill a small hole in the middle of this and file to shape. I am not going into further details, for if a man cannot quickly figure out for himself how it's done, he is not mechanical enough to do the job.

Of course, all this doesn't apply to reels that are completely or partly free-spool, those on which the handles do not revolve in casting. I slightly prefer a single handle for these, but it is of no consequence which is used, merely a matter of taste.

One of these old reels is sure to have an extremely heavy spool which must be replaced. But by fitting one with a light spool, and double handles, you may find yourself with a very fine reel indeed; some of these old-timers were beautifully and accurately made by hand, on watchmakers' lathes, and cost a small fortune, as reel prices go. Their faults came from the fact that for a long time the whole matter was not properly understood, and only very recently has sound casting technique been developed.

If this first casual inspection shows that you don't need a lighter spool, and don't have to send the reel in for new bearings, take it apart and see what it looks like internally. This is so simple that even the least mechanical-minded man should not hesitate to attempt it. Just remember never to force anything, either in taking it apart or in putting it back together again, or you will do serious damage—if something seems to require force, you're doing it wrong, which calls for a little thinking on your part. And if, when putting it back together, parts don't just drop into place, or screw in very easily, try fitting them another way.

To avoid scarring things, be sure to use a screwdriver that just fits the slots in the screws; if it doesn't, file or grind it until it does—and always leave the end of a screwdriver flat, with parallel sides; a cold-chisel point shows the rank novice at mechanics. The smaller the screwdriver, the better; it's too easy to force things with a larger one, and those screws are of very soft metal and will easily twist in two. Putting them back in, turn them just comfortably snug, no more.

When the reel is apart, clean it thoroughly. The handiest thing is a bowl of gasoline and an old toothbrush—but this should always be used outdoors. Do *not* use it indoors, assur-

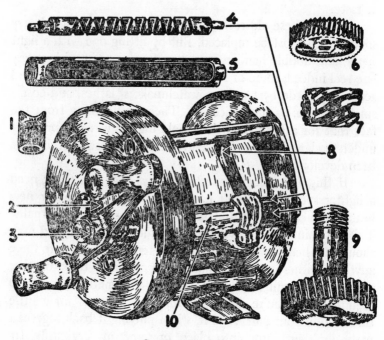

Casting Reel Parts

1—pawl; 2—oil cap; 3—crank nut; 4—double-thread shaft; 5—carriage tube (on some reels); 6—shaft pinion; 7—spool pinion; 8—line guide; 9—gear; 10—shaft cover (on some reels).

ing yourself that you'll be careful. Gasoline fumes in a confined space are always dangerous; and an open flame even in another room may easily cause them to explode.

Soap and water will clean the reel too. In fact, if there is old slime from weeds clinging to it, soap and water are much better, for gasoline is effective only in cutting grease. After you are through with the soap, rinse the parts well in very hot water and they will dry quickly and thoroughly.

When inspecting the parts, a small magnifier is useful if you have one handy, but it is not necessary. The pawl—the little gadget that runs back and forth in the grooves of the double-thread shaft—is by far the most likely to be worn. It is hard to judge its condition from its looks, so if it was working perfectly last time you used the reel, retain it; a broken-in pawl works a trifle more smoothly than one just inserted.

This pawl might be compared to the distributor points of a car—they're tiny things, but if they are wrong the whole two tons or so of fine car limps along or won't run at all. Few realize the importance of the pawl, so it might be well if we consider it pretty thoroughly.

Nearly always, when I find a man cursing his reel for being worn out, and for being a pure gyp in the first place, or when I see him casting with a wild effort and backlashing almost every time, there is nothing wrong but a worn pawl. The pawl, from its very nature, cannot wear long; it is not meant to wear long, and it takes only five or ten cents and a few seconds' work to put in a new one. So next time you start backlashing too often—and your reel is well oiled—notice if the backlashes begin when the line guide is at one end of its journey across the double-thread shaft, and ready to reverse. If so, the pawl should immediately go to the bottom of the water and a new one be fitted right then.

Sometimes the pawl quits suddenly, allowing the line to pile up in one spot, but it is rarely so considerate as to give this plain warning of what's wrong. If your reel does do this, or sticks for any reason, above all things don't force the handles, or you are almost certain to do damage that will necessitate sending the reel back to the factory.

Neither science nor metaphysics has been able to explain it, but it is a well-known fact that a pawl almost never goes bad except when you are miles from camp, and the fish are striking madly. There is but one way to fool it—*always* carry a spare pawl, and when you insert this one, get another immediately. Not to do this is sheer carelessness. (Which just reminds me—I forgot to put a new spare one in that little place on my reel for it, when I took the other out, weeks ago; I hope I remember to do it when I finish writing this chapter.)

Some reels have a receptacle for a spare pawl—a very useful feature. If yours hasn't, don't carry the spare loose in your tackle box, to rust or to be lost. When there is no special place for it on the reel, here's a way of carrying one which I devised long ago:

On most reels there is waste space under the head. If yours is like that, remove all trace of oil or grease from some angle, using gasoline (otherwise cement won't stick permanently). Smear a little quick-drying cement—sometimes called airplane glue, because used in making model airplanes—on the spot. Grease the pawl with petroleum jelly, so the cement won't stick to it, and wrap it in a tiny piece of paper. Then lay it on the cemented place and run more cement over it, letting one layer after another partly dry before adding more. When the whole thing dries, you have a fresh pawl completely sealed up from air and water, in a cocoon of lacquer, ready to be dug out and peeled off with the point of your knife when you need it. Of course, you should always have a little reel screwdriver along to take the head off, but most anglers carry that anyway, and all should. In a pinch, your knife will remove and replace those screws, but probably leaving them looking somewhat the worse for wear and tear.

The pawl matter settled, see to it that the line-guide block doesn't wabble too much on the double-thread shaft— or on the carriage tube outside it, if that is what it travels on. If it does, get a new block. And if the double-thread shaft or carriage tube shows the least signs of wear, get a new one too.

Now you are ready to reassemble the reel. Before putting the head back on, grease the gears lightly; too much grease makes them drag, makes the reel feel dead in casting, and in cold weather may cut the length of one's maximum cast down to one-third what it might be. Some makers put out special graphite grease for their reel gears; some advise against using anything containing graphite on theirs. Since each knows his product better than you or I, it is well to follow his advice.

Many use petroleum jelly on the gears. I do not like this at all, for in cold weather it gets almost solid, and in the hot sun it becomes so thin that it is practically a light oil, and runs off quickly. A little piece of mutton tallow rendered out, without burning, in a frying pan, and poured into a small jar, makes an excellent gear grease. This tallow, I believe, works well on all reels, and it never becomes sticky, and never thins out noticeably.

Before putting on the head, it is well to apply some oil to the gear shaft, for the oil is a little while working down there well when placed under the crank nut.

With the reel assembled, oil the end bearings and the level-wind mechanism. Some use petroleum jelly on the double-thread shaft, but that makes for dead casting, and oil is much better. Put some oil where it will work up around the pawl; hardly anybody thinks of doing that, but it gives a little more smoothness in casting.

In fact, oil everything that moves against anything else— with one exception! Never oil the reel handles, especially if you are dude enough to fish in a light-colored shirt. Those reel handles whirl rapidly, and there's such a thing as centrifugal force, and little dots of blackened oil on a shirt leave small stains that just won't wash out.

A few words about reel oils:

The oil should be of the correct density for the temperature if you want to do the best casting—though I'll admit that that is getting down to too fine points for most fishermen. Still, any angler should know about it, and have reel oils of two densities. I long ago remarked about that in magazine articles, but I never saw it mentioned elsewhere in print until recently, when Earl Osten, executive secretary of the National Association of Angling and Casting Clubs—the tournament sharks—himself a champion caster with all sorts of medals, came out with his book on tournament casting: it is now the standard authority on the game. Many years ago, when I myself did tournament casting, it was customary to use watch oil, almost as thin as gasoline, on a reel for the distance-plug events. Now, according to Mr. Osten, a distance caster may have so many little bottles of oil—thirty or more!—that he might be mistaken for a Standard Oil research man; and which one to use, or what two to blend for the temperature at the moment, is a matter for serious thought.

All that would, of course, be nothing short of ridiculous in fishing. But it does show that the matter of oil viscosity should   at least be considered. And I must say that some of the companies making our very best reels are sadly careless about the oils they sell and recommend for them; in hot weather, they are extremely thin, and on a frosty morning they become stiff.

As an example of what may happen: One cold evening last fall I, who certainly should know better, since I believe I was the first to call attention to the whole matter, oiled my reel carefully with an oil that I had used with perfect success just the day before, which was much warmer. The reel spun freely in the house, testing it, but by the time I had run across the bay, a distance of a mile, it had cooled down to outside temperature.

I began to fish. To my disgust, I found that I could not cast much more than a third of my usual distance, and that my casting was heavy, soggy, inaccurate. My oil was too thick for that cold evening—and maybe I had too much grease on the gears, to make things worse. It was too late to go home and clean and reoil the reel. By the time I got through fishing, enough oil had worn off to let me cast perhaps half as far as I sometimes wanted to. Because of inaccuracy, and feeling disgusted by the need for extra effort in casting—the clumsiness of it—I am sure that I did not get nearly as many fish as I'd have got if things had been going more smoothly.

Again, a fairly heavy oil for the temperature, especially if applied liberally and often to the level-wind, will act to some extent as the smoothest possible anti-backlash device. And that is the chief reason why the tournament-distance man goes to such pains in selecting his oil for the time; he does not thumb his spool at all, and cannot, with the extremely fine silk thread which he uses instead of fishing line—the thread would break if he did.

The point is that you should experiment a little, and find out what grade of oil suits you—and the temperature, and the amount the reel bearings are worn. An old reel, like an old car, needs heavier oil than a new one. And I've used ordinary automobile oil on my reel; I believe that any good lubricating oil will not do a reel damage.

Perhaps some reel makers will not thank me for things I've said here, since they all sell special oils for their reels—though sometimes, as I remarked, these oils are not what they crack them up to be. On the other hand, they should thank me for trying to make men keep their good reels lubricated, with any oil, so that they'll wear well and there will be fewer complaints.

When one is fishing, the end bearings should certainly be oiled at least once a day—find out how often your own reel bearings need it; that varies with make and age of reel. And, every day, place a little oil where it will work in to the gear shaft; it goes in somewhere at the crank nut, the exact way of oiling here varying with different reels.

The level-wind should be oiled every hour or two when fishing—a few bad casts, or a backlash or two, is often the sign that the time has come for oiling it, though few men recognize the signals. In short, oil often, and lightly, if you wish to do good casting. And take your reel completely apart and clean it several times during the season, if you fish much. A gradual falling off in ease of casting may remind you that this is advisable.

There should be a wire applicator on the stopper of your oil container, so that you can place a drop or two exactly where it will do the most good. The method sometimes seen, of squirting oil on from a can, is—well, just awful!

Now, with your reel back together, in perfect condition, with a light spool and all properly oiled, are you ready to do the smoothest casting possible? Sorry, brother; you're still far from it. You must have the correct arbor (reel filler). So, with a sigh at all the complications this pestiferous writer is bringing up, turn to the next chapter.

CHAPTER XVI

The Reel Arbor, and Making One

I HAVE just pointed out that a heavy spool in a reel will act as a flywheel and make good casting impossible. But one may have the lightest spool possible and still have a flywheel—one worse than the heavy spool, because of being off-center.

This is because for anything resembling casting—I do not even say "good casting" here—the spool must be filled with line until that line, when wet, just comfortably misses brushing the pillars or line-guide block as it goes around. If you have the spool only half full of line, it is whirling just twice as fast as it should be for the amount of line passing out, and the level-wind is doing double the necessary work. Also, a partly filled spool is much more difficult to thumb correctly than a full one. For this reason, I cannot understand why some advise thumbing against the spool flange, rather than on the line. How does one's thumb reach that flange on a full spool?

The usual thing among careless or less experienced anglers is to use a filler of old line. This soon soaks full of water in casting—and there's your heavy flywheel again. Not only that, but all this wet line is sure to squash flat on one side, throwing the spool badly off balance, and making it jiggle under one's thumb, which, of course, precludes smooth thumbing. This is perhaps particularly true with nylon line, which is not removed daily for drying, as silk is, and wound back on. The jiggle is caused by the circumference bobbing up and down under one's thumb. In short, a big filler of old line just won't permit really good casting.

The answer is an arbor of cork, balsa or plastic, and it should be large enough so that little or no line is needed to fill the spool beyond the amount actually necessary for fishing. One can go to the nearest sporting-goods store and buy an arbor of the right size, and just slip it in—if one uses a line of very heavy weight, a line of muskellunge size.

If you are not too particular about doing fine casting, you can can get the largest arbor obtainable, and then fill the rest with old line under the new. The way to get the right amount of old line is to wind the new on first, the old outside; you can cut the old line at the right place and not damage the new—then, of course, reverse it. Or you can manage to build up the arbor some more by cementing on layers of cork gasket material; but these really should be turned as in making the new arbor which I am about to describe, if you want the best results. However, the man who is really particular, and likes his casting to be as good as possible, will make his own arbor. Here is a method I've often used; the advantage of it is that it calls for no special tools.

First, let us consider how long a line is necessary; that will decide how large the arbor has to be made.

A twelve-pound line is about the heaviest that will cast properly with modern bass lures, and certainly no stronger is necessary in bass fishing, except possibly in bad snags or weeds. A single fifty-yard spool of this is enough for the average man, fishing the average amount in a season, for with his longest cast he will have plenty left to play his fish, and he can keep cutting off the worn end for some time and still have enough.

I personally fish mostly with lines of five pounds test for bass—I often use a leader of two and a half pounds test on that; and I lose very few fish because of its being too light. I mention this because I am trying to get the reader away from the usual heavy stuff; I am trying to show him that a light line will get them in, if it's handled right. But I do not recommend a line so light as five pounds' test unless a man has had a good deal of experience in playing fish.

Those using lines of such light test usually put on a hundred yards at once. That is partly because far longer casts are possible with it than with heavy stuff, and also because the worn end must be broken off much more frequently. But a hundred yards of this takes up surprisingly little space on a spool; it will look almost full of arbor before the line is put on.

One must allow for swelling of the line when wet, or it will strike the line-guide block in going around, causing a jerk and a backlash. With soft silk, this swelling is fairly large; with hard, waterproofed silk, much smaller. With nylon, either hard or soft, it is hardly noticeable, since nylon absorbs practically no water.

Now for the construction of the arbor:

First, remove the spool from the reel. Obtain a piece of cork at least as big as the spool, measured to the outside of the flanges. (I say "cork" to simplify things, but exactly the same procedure is used for balsa.) It must be good, smooth-grained cork, or otherwise it will be hard to work, and it will probably soon get out of round in use. You may have to do a little searching in hardware stores to find some really good pieces.

If it is tapered at one end, as a cork usually is, trim it to a fairly accurate cylinder, making sure that you do not get it noticeably smaller than the flange diameters. Cut the ends off, as squarely as possible, until it is of the same length as the spool to outside of flanges. (See Fig. 1.) A sharp knife can be used for all this, or a fine rasp. Any attempt at perfection of the cylinder is unnecessary, for you are later to turn it on a lathe.

You say you haven't got a lathe? Oh, yes, you have! I'll tell you where it is pretty soon.

Wrap a square-cornered piece of paper around the cork, having one edge even with the end. Cut the paper off until two edges just meet along the cork. Draw a pencil mark down the cork along one edge of the paper, making sure the edge at right angles is still even with the top while you do it.

Fold your paper carefully in the middle, and use it to measure halfway around, where you will draw another line. Measure both ways a time or two as a check, to get the thing as nearly centered as possible. Connect these lines by one across each end. You now have your marks to split it down the middle. (A, Fig. 1)

With a very sharp knife, split it in two lengthwise, as accurately as you can follow the lines. Keep the cut clean, not jagged. Make a pencil mark (X, Figs. 2 and 3) on one edge of each half, and be sure that these come together in all operations.

Next, you shape the four ends of the cork to fit down inside the ball-shaped flanges of the spool. The simplest way, I found, was to use a piece of coarse emery cloth over the end of my forefinger. It eats into the soft cork very rapidly, so you must watch out not to remove too much. Remember that none should be removed from the corners (marked C, Fig. 2), nor from the edges (D).

Keep placing the cork down often inside the flanges, and examining the fit closely. It sounds difficult to get a good fit, but it isn't, by exercising a little care. And it should be a good fit—it won't be perfect, but that doesn't matter; leave it a bit tight, so that it will squeeze into place.

When you get down to where the flat side of each piece of cork touches the spindle, with a small rat-tail file (some

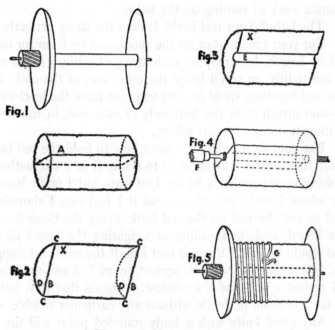

How to Make a Reel Arbor

medium emery paper wrapped around a small stick, and glued, would do in a pinch) start a groove along the middle of each flat side (E, Fig. 3). You can get them centered accurately enough by eye, if you're careful. When you have them started well enough, place the flats of the cork exactly together and push the file (F, Fig. 4) through the hole. File the hole round

while held thus, and to a good fit on the spindle of the reel
—test often as you go along.

You must alternate the filing with more work at the
ends, using the emery paper on your finger. Soon the pieces
of cork fit down snugly; their edges should just stay together
without being squeezed. Now you are ready for the fine and
accurate work of turning on the lathe.

The lathe? Your reel itself! It does the thing perfectly.

Put your rough arbor on the spool, and tie it on for only
half its length, by wrapping with string (G, Fig. 5). Do not
tie too tightly, or you'll bulge the other end of the cork. Fit
your reel together, spool in—but you may leave the level-wind
off—and attach it to the butt only of your rod, in the same
position it occupies when fishing.

Use your own judgment about how to hold the rod butt
steady for turning. Making a jig to clamp it in a vise without
crushing would probably be the best way—but I rarely have a
vise where I make my arbors, and if I had one I shouldn't
need to put the reel on the rod butt. Tying the thing firmly
to a board, and then nailing or weighting the board down
solid would be fine. I'll admit that I do it the hard and sloppy
way, by pressing the rod butt against my midriff and the other
end against a wall under a window. It jiggles that way, but I
get the job done perfectly without any particular trouble.

Any good knife with a fairly rounded point will do, if
you make it very sharp, and keep it that way. That's what I
use, but if you have a small, sharp wood chisel it should be
better. Lay the blade of the knife flat on the rear pillar of the
reel, pointing about toward the middle of the spindle. Hold
it firmly against the pillar with the left thumb (see Fig. 6),
and turn the reel handle with your right hand.

If you have never used a lathe, the main thing to remember is that the blade must *barely tick* the cork lightly at first;

otherwise the thing won't work at all. You'll seem to be getting nowhere at first, but before you realize it you'll have a neat groove all the way around. Do not go any deeper yet than just enough to make your cut meet at the ends.

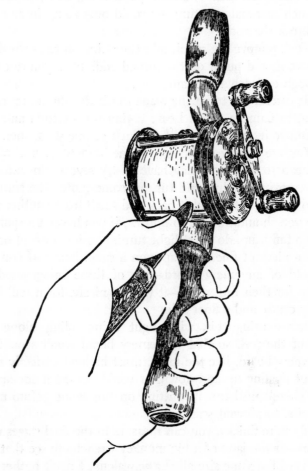

Reel Arbor Lathe in Operation (Fig. 6)

Now work along slowly and gradually. And back and forth until you have the cork perfectly round at all points, and as nearly of the same diameter all the way as you can get it by eye. You'll discover how it should be done, better than I can describe it. The main point is not to try to remove too much material at a time, or you'd only gouge in and perhaps break the cork.

Next, remove the spool, take the string off the end where you have it, and put it on the turned end. Then you can turn the rough end down the same way.

Be careful not to let the blade touch the aluminum spool flanges, to damage them. Leave a tiny rim of cork, and you can remove it, last thing, with a touch of fine sandpaper.

You are now ready to try on the amount of line which you mean to use. You may have to try several times to get a fit, removing the line and turning some more. The simplest way to do this is to wind it back and forth from another reel, which you should be able to borrow, if you haven't a spare.

To finish up, do a last light turning, using, instead of the blade, a piece of fine sandpaper on a small board. If you can get hold of an emery board—one of those things used by women for their fingernails—it will do nicely, for it will have a fairly coarse and a finer side.

Before using this, wind light twine solidly along the pillar of the reel, so that the emery board won't scratch it. The emery board, like the knife, must be held perfectly solid without jiggling up and down, or you'd get the arbor out of true. There's no harm in putting on this twine before using the knife, to prevent scarring.

If you're finicky, you can measure in the final stages with calipers—or the jaws of a big monkey wrench—to see that the arbor is of the same size all the way along. I don't bother, for it works just as well without that, being in perfect balance.

If you are no better mechanic than I, the first arbor will come out fitting badly at the ends; and the second will, before you know it, be too small for the line. But the third should be perfect; you'll have, for keeps, the knack of how to do it. So now, if you use lines of different weights, you can make an arbor that will just allow each to go on without hitting the guide block when wet. To keep from getting them mixed up, you should mark both sides of each.

Cork gradually rots and gets out of shape if left damp. Especially if you use nylon line, which is never taken from the reel for drying, it is well to give your arbor a coat of something suitable. Shellac will do; varnish, for some reason, I haven't found so good. Or get a ten-cent bottle of nail polish, clear or otherwise; it will have a little brush in it, and it will leave the arbor with a light coat of pure lacquer.

Never cement such an arbor on; you'd have to tear it up later if you should want to get it off. Just slip it in, and the line wound over it keeps it perfectly in place.

So there's your arbor. You'll be astonished at how neat and professional it looks, coming from that crude, whittled piece of cork you started out with. And of course, being turned on the reel itself, it will have to be in perfect balance. But your biggest surprise will come when you find how it smooths out your casting.

CHAPTER XVII

Casting Lines

ONE day not long ago I was in a tackle store talking with my friend Jerry when a man came bustling in. I guessed he was a professional man; he was well-dressed, and keen-looking. From his hurry, he evidently was darting in there during his lunch hour.

"Give me a casting line. . . . What kind? Oh, something about eighteen pounds test, a good one."

In a matter of seconds he had it in his pocket and was hurrying out again; he had hardly glanced at it. Jerry looked at me, shook his head, and grinned. I shook my head too, but I didn't grin; I take all things pertaining to fishing far too seriously. To me, the transaction was painful; I wanted to follow the man down the street and shake him—and tell him something about casting lines.

Of course Jerry couldn't take the matter seriously as I did. He frankly admits that most of the tackle which he sells is totally unsuitable for its purchasers, and that some of it is hardly better than junk. But neither that tackle store nor any other is a philanthropic institution; it's in business to make money; it must make a living for Jerry and the rest there, or go broke. Jerry would rather sell good tackle, even if he made less money on it. But what can he do? He must give customers what they ask for.

The sad part of it all is that Jerry is one of the finest and most enthusiastic anglers I know, an expert with either fly or casting rod. Also, he's been in the tackle game almost all his life. He knows tackle—which few tackle clerks do; most of them only know what sells best, which is all too often the wrong thing.

Now, if that man had come in when he was in less hurry; if he had talked to Jerry as one angler to another, not in the impersonal way so many talk to clerks in stores; if he had asked Jerry's advice—all that would have taken four or five minutes of his time and a friendly smile, and it would have repaid him a hundredfold in pleasure during his season's fishing.

When a man goes to buy a rod or a reel, he will sometimes pore over tackle catalogues evening after evening—which is a grand indoor sport. Then when he goes to the store he will inspect a number of different things, taking as much pains as if he were picking a wife. A lot more, judging by the many men divorced from their wives, and the few divorced from their fishing rods. And then, almost as an afterthought —"Gimme a line."

The finest exhibition caster in the world would look like a beginner if he had to use the line we find the average man fishing with. Hardly anybody seems to realize the great casting difference in lines of different types and weights.

We'll begin with silk lines:

I believe there is no question that the best casting can be done with a soft, square-braid, non-waterproof silk line— it will give the greatest distance with maximum ease, and the most freedom from backlashes. The fact that, so far as I know, it is almost universally used for tournament and exhibition casting is proof of this.

However, many would call it somewhat impractical for

fishing, especially in the lighter weights. The trouble is that it just won't wear at all. A single hard day of fishing and it is assuming the flat shape of a ribbon; it is already becoming decrepit. One must be eternally watching the front end and breaking some off, or it soon is so weak that it will flip plugs off in casting; either that, or it will part unexpectedly and let your big fish escape, even when you are playing him properly and not trying to clothes-line him in.

Still, I know a few men who do use the tournament silk line, of four and a half pounds' test, for all their bass fishing; it does let them cast beautifully and pleasantly, and it does bring out their skill to land heavier fish on it, especially when it is partly worn—as it always is. But I long ago gave up using it; it is just too much bother.

At the other extreme, we have what is by far the most popular line, the biggest seller. This is a silk line of very hard, round braid, waterproofed, and generally black in color. Many men even seem to think that a black line is best, for some reason. Theoretically, it should be worst, showing up most against the sky, but I have never been able to find that the color of a line makes a noticeable difference in one's catch—still, I prefer one of a neutral color, if I can get one without too much trouble. If this hard, waterproofed line is of good grade, it wears a long time—and that is the sole reason for its popularity. It has comparatively poor casting qualities, because it is somewhat wiry, and so it is inclined to spring up in coils on the spool and cause backlashes.

This does not mean that it isn't a good line, nor that quite good casting can't be done with it; I am merely saying that it cannot be expected to cast as well as softer lines do. It certainly will save one money to get a line of this type, if a few cents' saving during a season is a matter of importance. And it can be depended upon, more than any other silk line, to be strong after a good deal of use, and so perhaps keep one from losing a lunker bass.

This is the difference between a square-braid—also called soft-braid and solid-braid—and the round-braid line: The square-braid is made up of a number of strands plaited pretty loosely, almost as one might do it by hand; that is why it is soft. The outside of a round-braid is woven firmly over a round core.

There is quite a difference in these round-braids. Some are woven much harder than others—though all are called hard-braids. The softer one is, the better it will cast. And the less it will wear. But the softest of these should wear long enough to suit anybody but the most penny-pinching.

Almost all these round-braid lines are waterproofed at the factories by a special process. This helps them to wear longer, and avoids dragging in so much water. As they are used, they lose some of their waterproofing—but gain in casting qualities, become "broken in." Some men try to re-waterproof them with oil, or with fly-line dressing; others have queer formulae of their own for the purpose. I have yet to see any such home refinishing that did any noticeable good, and most of it does harm.

From all this, it will be seen that, for the average man, I am inclined to recommend about the softest round-braid that he can find. And by all means, if he fishes much, he should get the best obtainable; it will cost but a little more than a poor one and will wear many times as long—and possibly save that Big One. When you look them over in a store, it is generally impossible to tell a good line from a poor one, or even to tell just how hard one is braided. And, as with everything else, some companies make much better lines than others. So it is a matter of getting a line made by a company with a good reputation, and of reading its catalogue to find out how it describes its lines.

Why it never occurs to most anglers to send for catalogues of lines and other tackle is a mystery to me. They contain a wealth of valuable information. At least half a dozen tackle catalogues studied in conjunction with this book would permit one to get far more benefit from it than one could otherwise—and going over tackle catalogues, I'll repeat, is a grand indoor sport for the angler. I believe I know much more about rods, reels, lines and such things than most readers of this book will; but I would not even think of buying any of these things without first carefully reading what the maker has to say about it in his catalogue. The average man depends on what some tackle salesman tells him. It's probable that that salesman knows no more about the article than the purchaser does, or very little more.

Naturally, one cannot always accept at face value what a maker says about his own stuff. Some things are every bit as good as the catalogues say. On the other hand, a maker of shoddy stuff can hire some good advertising man to "prove definitely"—in print—that what he makes is unquestionably the best in the world; some of their arguments are specious indeed, and should be taken with a great deal of salt. And even the best makers are lax in pointing out how very much inferior their cheaper stuff is to their higher-priced. This is particularly true of rods and reels. In casting lines of a good manufacturer, there will not be nearly so much difference between the best and the worst; but there will be enough to make it well worth while to buy the best, if one fishes much—it will prove the cheapest in the end, as well as give far more satisfaction in use. One must take care of a silk casting line. The most imperative thing is to see that the guides on one's rod are perfect. The least crack, and the line is ruined in a few casts.

A silk line, to wear long, must be dried each evening after use. There are many line dryers on the market—big reel things onto which the line can be wound quickly. But with a little ingenuity a man can make his own. An effective and convenient way of drying a line is to drive two nails into the wall of a room, one at each end, near the ceiling, and walk back and forth, hanging the line onto them with the rod tip; then, the rod can be stood in a corner under one. These nails should invariably be covered with scotch tape or something of the sort; otherwise they will cause rust spots on the line, which are certain to cause it to break soon. The trouble with this method is that the nails should be in a living room, where the line will dry quickly and thoroughly, and some women object to having nails hammered into the walls, and lines being strung all over the place; so the advisability of this method depends chiefly on one's wife's disposition, and on the amount of resignation she has developed toward fishing matters.

Now for nylon casting lines:

Occasionally I hear somebody maintain that a nylon line is no good—but I hear it less and less frequently. When I pin one of these men down, I can get but one definite complaint; that nylon has too much stretch to it. Because nylon has considerably more elasticity than silk, some think that it is hard to hook a fish with it. I can only say that it has never given me the least trouble in this respect, and I fish with a longer line than most men, and so have more stretch to contend with. But I keep my hooks needle-sharp, which few men do—many needlessly lose over half their strikes because of dull hooks. I hook bass just as well on nylon lines as on silk.

On the other hand, this very elasticity has a great advantage in that it will often save the line from being broken, when a big fish whips around suddenly before the angler gets his wits. In short, it helps play the fish. Even if it did cause missing a few strikes—and it doesn't, for me—that would compensate for it.

Nylon lines are made in both round and square braid, the same as silk. But the round-braid nylon generally seems slightly harder than the hardest silk, and therefore it is somewhat more wiry and a trifle more difficult to cast. And it doesn't break in; it doesn't wear out; it just stays as it was, almost indefinitely. The wearing qualities of a first-class nylon line, even a very light one, are astonishing. And in a line of the round-braid type, the difference in casting qualities between the silk and the nylon is not really so great after all.

When one comes to the square-braid, the difference is slightly more noticeable, the superior casting qualities of the silk more evident. But the square-braid silk just won't wear at all, and the square-braid nylon will—very well indeed if one has good guides.

This is especially noticeable in the lightest weights, which, of course, cast the best in either silk or nylon. I have said that most men would regard a silk line of five pounds test or so as impractical, because of its short life. A man could put one hundred yards connected of five-pound, soft-braid nylon of good make on his reel and, if he fished no more than the average, it would wear until he was tired of seeing it. Also, nylon does not, like silk, deteriorate with age, so it is good year after year.

Another thing in favor of nylon: it does not have to be taken off the spool and dried daily—or ever. Few indeed are the men who, getting home tired from a day's fishing, never forget to dry their silk lines. But drying a nylon line is pointless; it does no good whatever.

As mentioned in the chapter on reels, a nylon absorbs practically no water, and hence swells little on the spool. Therefore there is little danger of its striking the line-guide block and causing backlashes, if the spool is a trifle full. And a nylon line does not carry in as much water to the spool as does a silk.

So, on the whole, I prefer a nylon line for fishing, even though I believe the silk to have somewhat superior casting qualities. But nylon is still being improved, and we may soon find it casting fully as well as silk.

Lines of material other than silk or nylon are no good in casting for bass and such fresh-water fish, so there is no need to do more than warn the reader not to try to use them.

Of what strength—test—should the bass-casting line be? I have referred to that matter several times elsewhere, but I shall go into it a little more here and summarize it.

One of twelve pounds is about the heaviest a man should use if he wants to cast well, and it is certainly strong enough to land any bass that ever swam. The exception is the man who must snake his bass from among snags or dense weeds; such a man may use a line up to eighteen pounds test, or even heavier—but he cannot expect to do good casting with it.

As a man becomes more expert at playing a fish, and especially if his fishing is done in fairly open water, it would be well worth his while to try a nine-pound line; this casts beautifully, especially with plugs of a half-ounce or under. Perhaps hard-braid at first, and then soft-braid.

Then when he feels that he's getting up into the expert class, and especially if his fishing is done in weed-free water as a rule, he can come down even to a five-pound test—indeed, in a few small sections of the country that size is becoming almost standard. But this is no line for the beginner, or for the man who does not fish a good deal, to keep in practice. It must be used only with very light lures, or it will not wear long. And if it is used on a stiff rod, it will be flipped in two sometimes on the cast, allowing the plug to go flying off and be lost. I am not recommending such a light line to anybody—if a man thinks he's experienced enough to use it, and that his fishing conditions will permit it, let him try it and see how the experiment works out.

A very few fishermen use still lighter lines, which, of course, have wonderful casting qualities. But the man fitted to use them certainly does not need my advice.

It is useful for a man to be able to determine the actual test of his last year's line which he is considering using again, or of a line which seems partly worn out. This is very simple: Put the ring of a spring balance over a nail, or have somebody hold it; then slip the snap of your leader over the hook of the balance. Pull on the line, watching, or having your assistant watch, the pointer of the balance as it creeps up the scale—and suddenly flies back, as the line breaks. The highest point is the test of the line. That may not be the test as it might be determined at the factory, but it is its actual breaking strain in fishing, and it includes a test of the knots you use; that is all that you are interested in. If the line is wet when you test it, it shows still better what you can expect from it, for there will be some difference between wet and dry breaking strains.

But all too many test their lines by jerking them as hard as they can between both hands—if one holds, it's a fine line. To a real angler, that is almost pathetic. Many crack bass anglers have the following method of determining the strength of casting line to use: if one will lift the dead weight of the largest fish likely to be caught, it's too heavy for sport. Roughly speaking, it might be as well for the less experienced angler to use a line of twice that strength, for he will have to allow for his own excited jerking and pulling, as well as for the fish's.

For maximum sport, and maximum ease in casting, there is just one rule: use the lightest line with which you can trust yourself.

CHAPTER XVIII

Correct Casting *

THERE are many ways of heaving a plug out sloppily, with nothing resembling accuracy or ease. There is but one way to cast correctly.

Instructions in proper casting can be found in almost any tackle catalogue, but somehow they seem to make little or no impression, possibly because the space allotted to them is necessarily brief, and the thing is often presented in a pretty sketchy manner. Psychologists insist that if one wants a child to obey one should not only tell him to do something, but should always explain just why he should do it. I believe this holds even more true for adults, or at least for those who have the habit of using their heads, instead of docilely accepting whatever they are told. So after giving actual casting instructions briefly, I shall discuss fully exactly why each thing should be done in one certain way, and in that way only. A careful reading of this discussion will, of course, make it easier to follow the instructions—easier, in other words, to learn, and learn very quickly, how to cast right.

Fairly wide disagreement will be found among experts regarding the best method of using a fly rod. On the use of the casting rod, there is no disagreement worth noting. The

* For demonstration photos see Plates 3, 4, 5, Photo Section.

method I describe here is the only correct one, and no other can achieve anything at all resembling satisfactory results.

Hardly one angler in fifty whom one sees fishing really casts a plug; the rest heave it out by some awkward method more or less resembling shot-putting or shadow boxing. This is, of course, partly due to pure ignorance; they have no idea how clumsy and bungling they look, or how dangerous they are to any person within range. Moreover, nobody could guess where the plug is going—it's pure chance. Proper casting is smooth, effortless, and can hardly help being quite accurate.

Not always, by any means, is the man himself to blame; more often than not real casting is practically impossible with the tackle he uses, though a correct outfit would usually not cost a cent more. I have discussed tackle elsewhere; now I will only repeat that the rod must be long enough, and flexible enough, for the weight of lure used; the reel must be of at least medium grade, in good repair and well oiled; and the line not over twelve pounds test for bass, and not too heavy for larger fish.

The beginner will be greatly impressed upon seeing an exhibition caster do tricks of all sorts; the veteran fisherman will smile tolerantly. Some of these fancy casts are utterly useless in fishing, and it would be nothing short of ridiculous to employ them for that. Even the "underhand" cast, so commonly used by demonstration casters—often for safety, when there are many persons standing close by—has practically no place in fishing. One cannot use it when sitting in a boat, or even, because of the gunwale, when standing in one; wading, it cannot be used; and it would be awkward and difficult under any circumstances with a long rod. Furthermore, only an exhibition caster, after much practice, can attain any degree of accuracy with it—and then never nearly as much as by more orthodox methods.

For practical purposes, there is but one cast to learn—the overhead, overhand, or vertical. It is incomparably the most accurate; a tournament caster would not even think of employing any other in the accuracy event. When one has learned that, one can easily, without special instructions or practice, make any other casts—with one possible exception—that overhanging branches or other conditions may call for.

The necessary instructions for a correct overhead cast are so simple that I can give them here in three sentences:

Always swing the rod in a vertical plane, from straight toward the mark up to your hat brim, and back.

Always keep the reel handles on top (backward, of course, when the rod comes up), and never let them tip to right or left.

Always keep your elbow hanging loose and practically still by your side.*

The man who obeys these three simple rules cannot help casting properly; the other things will come to him with a very little practice. Now for explanations, to show why he should follow these rules. And some tips to hurry his learning.

Don't grasp the rod too tightly; don't "strangle" it.

The plug usually hangs six inches or so from the rod tip; the exact distance isn't important, but there should not be too much line dangling. A plug that is really too light for the action of the rod will cast better with more line out; a heavy one, when drawn up pretty well.

The cast must be begun with the rod tip straight toward the object aimed at. Sight over the tip guide very much as if it were the front sight of a shotgun or rifle. Some say to sight over the guide next the hand, but in fishing, as distinct from tournament casting, it may be found more comfortable to use the tip guide, with the hand not so much in front of the body.

* See Plates 3, 4, 5, Photo Section.

This leaves the whole rod pointing well to the left, but so long as the elbow is held near the body—to avoid a large arc—and the tip swung in a vertical plane, this doesn't matter.

Here, the tournament-accuracy man generally lowers his rod tip several inches, after which his upswing comes directly through his point of aim; this to get a good bend in his rod tip without going far back with it. But he is standing on a clear platform over the water, and this method is not always practical for fishing; so the man fishing takes the tip right up from his aiming point, and a little farther back. Correct "form," if one wants that, calls for the lower part of the rod going up to no more than the vertical, but in actual fishing few adhere to such form.

While mentioning form, it might be said here that in fishing, especially in deeper lake fishing when no particular accuracy is required, even an expert caster will often permit his rod tip to drop a good deal to the side. There is nothing wrong with this, and he will always use the same wrist movement, not "sideswipe" with his whole arm. But watch him when it suddenly becomes necessary to place his plug exactly where he wants it—up comes his rod tip to the vertical.

From this it will be seen that I am not trying to teach exhibition casting; I am not an exhibition caster myself, nor do I want to be one. For a tackle company's demonstrator, strict adherence to form is business, and necessary; for me, it would be little more than showing off.

The upswing should be sharp and fast, and it should stop suddenly; that is what lets the flying plug pull a good backward bend into the rod, and the bend shoots the plug forward, much as a bow shoots an arrow. The rod tip should not go too much beyond straight up, except on an extremely long cast. The elbow staying low helps keep the rod tip well up, and also keeps one from trying to throw the plug with one's whole arm, "by main strength and awkwardness," instead of allowing the spring of the rod to flip it out.

This is where the vertical plane needs close attention. It is as though a string were stretched from the mark directly back over one's sighting eye, and the rod tip were pointing to it all the way up and forward again. Of course, this cannot be done just right every time—if that were possible, tournament casters would make perfect scores so regularly that the game would lose interest—for reasons which will presently be seen, a good tournament caster rarely undershoots or overshoots the ring. But with very little practice it can be done perfectly enough each time to lay the plug well within the feeding circle of a bass whose hiding place is known or suspected.

Here is a method, one which I have never seen described before, of keeping to this vertical plane; it will help greatly in keeping one to it. When the rod comes forward, sight instantly past the tip again, and see that it has stopped upon or directly over the mark aimed at. If it has, you certainly cannot miss the mark much, for even if the tip swung in a slight curve it would make the same curve going forward as going back.

There should be no pause at the top of the upswing, as in fly casting, or the rod would lose the bend pulled in it by the plug. The whole thing is a snap up and immediately forward, the speed of which depends on the speed of the rod you are using; also, with the same rod, a heavy plug will call for a much slower snap than a light one. And the wrist helps the bend of the rod shoot the plug forward. Remember—the wrist only!

The distance the rod is brought forward depends on how far one is casting; it stops quite high on a long cast. The line should shoot straight out from the tip guide, not sidewise from it.

The thumb is, of course, held pressed against the spool,

to keep it from revolving, on the upswing and part of the forward swing. It is impossible to describe just when it is released, but a very little practice gives one the knack. The beginner invariably releases the spool too late, and shoots his plug down into the water a short distance off.

With a good anti-backlash device, properly set for the weight of the plug in use, the thumb may now be completely removed from the spool. Indeed, it need not be placed back on as the plug strikes the water and stops, but that is a very poor method of casting, since correct aim for distance is almost impossible. It is much better to aim higher and somewhat farther than the mark, watch the lure in the air, and stop it with a thumb pressure so that it settles down on the right spot. Thus, too, it *settles* down, instead of plunging in with a big splash.

Always aim above and beyond the mark, and stop the plug in the air thus. But do not aim too far beyond, or it will be traveling too fast to be set down accurately. In casting toward a brushy shore, this method avoids hanging the lure in branches and having to approach it to get it loose, thus ruining the fishing around there for a long time; it also avoids losing it if one is wading and casting across a deep river. And if your aim is short—well, you can't very well leap out there and kick the plug up a few feet before it stops.

Now for using the free-running reel, which certainly does *not* mean a free-spool reel; it merely means that the anti-backlash device is not employed. And remember that anything which helps thumbing is an anti-backlash device, no matter what it's called.

The thumb must at least feel the line on the spool all the way out; releasing pressure too much, or jerkily, is the cause of backlashes in casting—the sole cause. There are exceptional conditions in which the spool may be allowed to run without thumbing, but they are not worth going into here. A good deal more pressure all the way out is necessary with a light, bulky plug than with a small, heavy one.

This thumbing cannot be done evenly unless the thumb is braced firmly against some part of the reel frame to steady it. The conventional method is to brace it against the tail plate. A strict stickler for form may look askance at anybody who does otherwise, but that is just nonsense. When the pillar of the reel is in a suitable position, the ball of the thumb may be rested on it, with the under part of the tip against the line; many, especially those with rather small hands, will find this the most convenient way. However, some of the newer reels are made with such a low rear pillar—to leave a wide opening for working on backlashes—that this method cannot be used comfortably on a rod with a low reel seat. I think reel makers would be doing much better to leave that pillar in its old position, for the benefit of the many who thumb thus. The tackle buyer, like every other consumer, has two types of producers to contend with: those who refuse to advance, and those who make too many "improvements."

Learning proper, delicate thumbing of a free-running reel is pretty difficult for most men; that is why I recommend the use of the anti-backlash device for those who don't fish a good deal—casting with it can never be so smooth and effortless, but it does save wear and tear on a man's disposition.

The principal reason for not letting the reel handles tilt sidewise has nothing to do with the reel itself; it is that the wrist has a far freer action that way, bending backward, not sidewise. In my own case I have found that, with my knuckles held horizontal, by actual measurement I have over fifty per cent more swing to my wrist up and down than from side to side; and the up-and-down movement is easier for me to do and under far better control. Bending the wrist sidewise in casting, there is always a tendency to throw the plug with the whole arm—the beginner's way. Correct wrist action is very important, indispensable if one wishes to cast at all well; that is why I am emphasizing it so much here. And it is just as easy to learn as the wrong way, perhaps easier.

There seems to be a fairly prevalent notion that at the end of the cast the reel should be turned until the pillars are horizontal; many have written to ask me about that. This just isn't so. A spool spins considerably more freely on end than horizontal; also, the wet line whipping through the guides is not slapping and dragging against the rod, so it has friction only against the narrow, polished guides. All this naturally makes for smoother and better casting, greater distance when it is needed, and fewer backlashes.

Whether one is using an anti-backlash or a free-running reel, remember that the whole cast is made entirely *with a snap of the wrist*, timed to speed of rod and weight of plug. The forearm moves quite loosely, following the wrist, but not really helping with the cast, and the elbow is hanging straight down by the side and practically motionless, but not stiff.

If one has difficulty in keeping the elbow still, it is a good idea to do quite a bit of casting with something such as a handkerchief or a stick held between the body and the arm, just above the elbow. This may bring about a temporary stiffness in one's casting, but one should soon lose that, and elbow-swinging *must* be eliminated.

As soon as one has stopped the spool, the rod is switched to the left hand. A friend of mine told me recently of having read somewhere that this switch should be made *before* stopping the spool—a feat I want to see! Very soon, this switch will be made unconsciously, with immediate control of the lure when it is set down, so that one can hook the occasional bass that seems to strike the plug almost before it has touched the water. Now, of course, one reel handle is taken in the fingers of the right hand.

How one holds the rod in the left hand is purely a matter of convenience. Personally, I pass my little finger and the two next it under the forward grip, my index finger above it. Since I learned to cast with reels having no level-wind, and used that sort for years, I still have the habit of taking the line between my thumb and forefinger, or at least holding one on each side of it. Some pass the line between thumb and forefinger thus to press most of the water out before it reaches the spool, to go flying on the next cast. Though I use mostly soft, absorbent lines, I am never even conscious of this water; possibly that is because I use such light lines that they do not carry in much water.

Many "palm" the reel—cup the tail plate in the left hand. And our stickler friend might possibly insist that that is the "right" way. If this is so, then I have caught a good many thousand fish using the "wrong" way, for I could not do this at all well or comfortably on the few occasions when I tried it; perhaps my hands are not large enough. As I see it, this method is all right if it feels comfortable, and all wrong if it doesn't.

In retrieving, the butt of the rod is usually held against the pit of the stomach.

Now for casts other than the overhead which one may need on occasion, as under branches. It is as well, if fishing conditions will allow it, to avoid these entirely until one has grown so thoroughly accustomed to the vertical cast that it can be done automatically, without thought.

The horizontal cast to the left is exactly like the overhead, but done in a horizontal plane. It calls for little or no practice when one has mastered the overhead, but one should see to it that the arm is not employed, which would make it degenerate into a sideswipe.

The "backhand" cast—a horizontal cast to the right—is a trifle more difficult to learn, but a lot of instructions would do no good, and might possibly confuse the reader; it is a matter of a little practice. This is almost never used except when one is standing immediately in front of brush and wants to cast to the right; even then, one can generally turn and use the overhead, sometimes tilting the rod well to the left above the head.

One cast that is very useful in cramped quarters is a short, quick flip of the rod, the plug drawn up close, the rod tip not moving far. But this is merely a slight variation of the plain horizontal cast, and presents no difficulty.

Any other casts I might list would be nothing but variations of the overhead or the backhand casts which would suggest themselves instantly to a man when they were needed, and which he could do quite well the first time he tried. Indeed, many good anglers manage to go through life and catch thousands of fish without bothering to learn the backhand.

Which brings us right back to where we started: Practically speaking, there is but one cast to learn—the overhead. When a man masters that, he is fully equipped to place his plug just where he wants it on almost all occasions, and to catch any bass that may be around.

CHAPTER XIX

The Fine-Line Caster

THE beginner at bass fishing, and the man who gets to fish only occasionally, might as well skip this chapter, for it will not concern him: it is addressed only to those who fish a good deal all through the season, and so can hope to refine their tackle and methods to the utmost possible.

How much must a man fish before he can think of getting down to the lightest tackle? That I cannot say; too much depends on the man in question. Some few are naturally so quick-witted, cool-headed and dexterous that they can use extremely light tackle almost from the beginning of their fishing. Many never can learn to use it.

Just how light tackle can be successfully used? Recently I had an article on light lines in a magazine, and right in the middle of it the editors ran a cartoon, and under it the caption: "Just practice! I kept using a lighter and a lighter line; finally I was able to dispense with one altogether." The picture showed a man with a wildly quivering rod, a bass trying to throw a plug—but no line between. Well, I'm not *that* good! I'm not sure but that those editors were poking a little good-natured fun at me because of my many efforts to coax them to use very light lines, lighter than they would trust themselves with. Still, I do use them pretty flimsy sometimes. Here's an example of how it may work out:

In one of his wittiest essays, Addison (or maybe it was Steele) holds that Truth and Good Sense are the ancestors of humor, while Falsehood and Nonsense are forbears of a foolish young jackanapes who tries to pose as the real thing.

By that standard, "The Fisherman's Prayer" would assay as true humor, for probably every angler, deep in his subconscious, has the hope that some day, somewhere, he'll catch a fish bigger for its species and locality than anybody ever got before. My own great ambition is to catch a fifty-pound muskellunge. This, analyzed, isn't very likely; still, if I spend enough time trying—well, who knows? There are fifty-pound muskellunge, and a very few have been caught over sixty.

For a long time my seemingly unattainable goal was a six-pound northern smallmouth. Finally, one memorable day, I hooked one! I'll tell about it briefly, just to prove what usually happens when one gets a real whopper on a line which he knows is very weak, about worn out, a line that should have been discarded long before.

It was many years ago, up close to the Canadian border, where even largemouths rarely grow to six pounds. It was in a clear, rocky lake—and how the bass in that cold water could fight!

I was using, as I still so often do, a very light bamboo casting rod of six foot six—so long that a green angler often mistakes it for a fly rod; the chief difference between them is the position of the reel seat. This will flip a quarter-ounce plug 'way out with little more than a slight twitch of my fingers, and it places a half-ounce with extreme accuracy and delicacy at close range. I had a line that was nominally eight-pound test. Nominally, because I always forgot to cut off the worn end until I noticed it completely fuzzy. Or until, attempting a long cast, I popped off one of my pet lures, which always managed to be of the sinking kind and go right to the bottom in deep water.

I was in a boat with a friend, Jim McChesney. We weren't doing so well. In fact I remembered afterward that I'd about lost interest in fishing and had been singing—a bad habit which I picked up as a child, and of which I have never quite broken myself. At least I generally refer to it as singing.

I was fishing deep with a sinking plug, and I was retrieving slowly and absently when it stopped. Just stopped, with no jerk. In a case like that, I use the old Western adage and "shoot first and ask questions afterwards," so I gave a couple of jiggles to the rod to work the barb into whatever it was. If it turned out to be a snag, I could get loose at my leisure, but one can't set hooks in a bass at leisure. And, my fingers being wet, I automatically threw on the click of my reel.

The reel gave a sudden screech that made me leap in my seat, and something was heading for somewhere else. Let's admit the truth here: my reason for throwing on the click when playing a fish isn't solely to prevent a tangle in case my fingers slip from the handle; I like that screech of the reel when a fish runs—whatever may be said about my singing, I still know good music when I hear it.

Jim yelled "Musky!" and started whipping in his line to get it out of my way. Muskies, the most pernickety and maddening fish in the world, simply hadn't been hitting for nearly a month, though there were lots of them in that lake.

A big splash out there, and we saw the fish. A bass! Wow!

I heard a sound from Jim that might be set down as "Glug-ug-ug!" He sat a moment with his mouth hanging open, and then he got his voice. He let out an incredulous yell of, "It's a smallmouth!"

No bass had any business to be doing all the things that one was doing, or doing them so fast. We were watching closely next time he came up, and he seemed to run ten feet on the very tip of his tail, shaking himself in a way that should have thrown any plug. Jim made another glugging sound, and managed to get out, "Holy Jupiter!"—that isn't quoting him verbatim—"He's well over six pounds!"

He was. But I said nothing. I couldn't say anything. I had an awful, sinking feeling. It had suddenly come to that I'd been fishing with that old eight-pound line for days and days without cutting off the worn end. I knew that a good yank on a bluegill would break it.

I used to hold—following, without thinking too much, what I'd heard others say—that an old, overgrown fish is easier to handle than one half his size, that it would take longer to land him, but that it would be a slow, logy fight. This certainly is true for muskies, pike and most other fish. But what mental aberrations ever made me say that of northern bass, I don't know. The bigger and older one is, the swifter, the more acrobatic, the more everything else that breaks tackle. Maybe one does finally reach an age where he becomes logy, but I've never caught one that old; perhaps, like the one-hoss shay, he gives out all at once if he's not caught before that age—just suddenly rolls over on his back and dies. And this one certainly showed no symptoms of wanting to die, even with assistance—he was a natural-born tackle wrecker.

He proved it by heading back straight for me; he seemed to know that it's the close-up stuff that smashes things. I kicked hard against the bottom of the boat; I've found that that will sometimes turn one and make him keep his distance —it's the vibrations in the water. He paid no attention, but tore right under, so fast that I couldn't hurry to the end of the boat and pass the line around. All I could do was plunge the rod upside down in the water, almost to the reel—well down, so some splinter on the bottom of the boat couldn't catch the line.

Then I did manage to reach the stern and I got the rod around safely. By then, he was heading for the surface again. This thing of breaking water is all very fine, and thrilling—but there is hardly any other fish that can throw a hook as easily as a leaping bass, and I'd probably have fallen into a decline if this one had shaken loose at that stage of the game. I'd seen him often enough by now to know that *this was my six-pound northern smallmouth,* and no question about it.

There is but one thing to do when a bass starts to break water: keep tension enough to hurry him along the surface with only his head out, and not let him get all the way up to leap or "dance." It doesn't take much pull—but it would take a lot more than my old line could stand; I hardly dared bend the rod tip more than six inches.

For some reason, a bass leaps far more on very light tackle than on heavier—and much higher too. So I gulped and watched him do flip-flops and fin-springs, my heart doing two to his one. Yes, I do take my fishing too seriously, and, in spite of all the fish I've got in my life, I still almost have a nervous breakdown when a lunker like that starts doing the gymnastics he was doing. I hope I never get over feeling that way.

He went down deep, and apparently made an attempt to cross the lake so fast that he might have shot clean up on the other shore. And into the air again, 'way out.

I can't remember half of what he did. But it couldn't go on forever, and finally I felt him weakening. Now was the time to be very cautious—only a beginner loses a fish after he has him played out. At last I judged it safe to lead him close. He tried the last resort of a tired fish: sounding, heading straight for the bottom under the boat. He did it three or four times, each dive a little shorter than the last. I had to lead him by several times before I dared try to slip my thumb into his mouth, my finger under his lower jaw; it had to be done with extreme care, in slow motion, for even then a quick jerk would have lost him from that old line, with so little of it out now that there was no stretch to it to take up a slight shock. But finally I did manage to get my thumb into his mouth.

And there he was!—flopping in the bottom of the boat. If I let out a whoop like a drunken Apache, what of it? Maybe I did it because of how Jim was thumping my back; Jim's a big fellow and pounds hard.

I noticed Jim looking at him queerly. He stooped, took the hook between a thumb and forefinger, and lifted. Before he could nearly raise the bass, the bend of the hook tore through a little thread of skin on his lip, and he flopped back to the boards.

I dug out my spring balance and weighed him. Six pounds, three ounces. No world's record, even for the border country—but that's plenty of northern smallmouth in any language, including the Chippewa.

Jim reached for my balance and hooked it into the snap of my leader. Watching the scale, he pulled slowly until the line broke.

"I'll be cow-kicked by a mule!" he said. (Again, this is not verbatim.) "Pound-and-a-half test! How you ever got him in on *that* thing, I don't know. And if you were half as scared of losing him as you looked, maybe that'll teach you to keep a stronger line on your reel in future."

I didn't want to argue then, but that evening, over Scotch and soda, I made him see the truth of the matter:

I'd inevitably have lost that bass, probably in setting the hook, so that I'd never have suspected how big he was, if I hadn't had on such a weak line, and known it was weak. For, as Jim readily admitted, that piece of skin holding him could hardly have tested two pounds. With stronger line, I just couldn't have made myself play him lightly enough to land him.

Jim and I and a couple of other anglers staying at the resort had what one might call a well-flavored argument long into the night. Strangely, Jim, despite all the fishing he had done, didn't know exactly a bass's manner of taking a lure; but I hauled out a scientific book and made him read passages from it. I was trying to convince them of what I've always maintained:

In reasonably open water, a skillful angler can land many more bass on a very light line than on a heavy one.

When I first said that to those three men, they remarked that it would take "some proving." I have little doubt that the reader feels the same way about it, so I shall explain.

As I previously pointed out, a bass seldom follows up his prey; he dashes at it like a cat, from below or from the side. So, he has no opportunity to catch any odor it may have left in the water through which it passed. And since all fishes are nearsighted, he's had only a rather blurred view of something which from its size, color and movement suggests that it might be desirable food.

I do not subscribe to the theory that a bass strikes from belligerence, except when guarding his nest, when he does not eat at all—and that really isn't belligerence; it's self-preservation, an instinct that keeps the eggs from being eaten by small fish. I have never found any reason to think that a bass is the only living creature that goes hunting trouble just for the sake of getting into it. Certainly I have caught bass—other fish too —when they were full of food up to the neck and even beyond it. I have also seen men, hogs and hounds that didn't have sense enough to stop eating when they were full. When a man stuffed full of turkey reaches for a second piece of pumpkin pie, it is not usually taken as a sign of pugnacity on his part; nobody thinks of putting him up for the world's heavyweight championship.

Granting that the bass darts at that moving thing only because he regards it as probable food, what would he do—since he hasn't had time, before approaching, to smell it, or to examine it well? He'd be a foolish fish indeed, fitted out with some very poor instincts, if he just gulped it down immediately. Many small fish, both in salt water and fresh, are equipped with poisonous spines; if he gulped down one of these, he'd be lucky to get off with no more than a bad case of laryngitis.

He does what one would naturally expect him to do; he seizes the thing lightly in his lips, to test it, to find out what it is before proceeding further. If it tastes and feels right, and seems to be an edible fish, he carries it off some distance, and mouths it a while to investigate the matter further. Then he always turns it in his mouth so that he can swallow it head first. Such a thing as a hard lure is, of course, immediately ejected.

And that method of feeding explains perfectly why so many bass are badly hooked, by a lip only, and often by a mere thread of skin.

That is just why so many strikes are missed in bass fishing, and why a bass can throw a plug so easily when he leaps and shakes himself. As for the latter, I am convinced that many more plugs are pulled from their light hold on a bass by the angler than are actually thrown—somehow, the sight of a leaping bass seems to make the average man want to heave back on his rod.

Here I must, with apologies, go even further against the experts. They say the bass is a hard-mouthed fish, so one should give a good yank and set the hooks hard. I believe that if the point of the hook comes against skin and flesh, and if it is sharp, some little jiggles will make it penetrate; but if it comes against the bony plate, it can't be set at all. The result would be that when a bass is being hooked by only a thin piece of his lip, a hard "setting of the hook" merely tears the hook through instantly. When this happens, it's called a missed strike, and little is thought of it. I'd call it a completely wrong strike, losing a fish that should be landed. Maybe I'm in error, and all the others right—but I do bring in a surprising number of bass hooked only by a thread of skin, so that a hard jerk to set the hook would have pulled it loose.

Possibly somebody else can play a fish very lightly when he knows that his line is strong, but I can't—it appears senseless to me (though perhaps it really isn't) to use only a small percentage of the strength of one's line; it seems like playing with a fish, rather than playing him.

With a very light line, one must play the fish lightly. And set the hooks lightly, by a series of jiggles rather than with one wild heave. Result, with those very lightly hooked bass? It's obvious enough; if the water is reasonably free from weeds and snags, they're finally led in—as that smallmouth of mine was.

Just how light a line is practical? I'll tell of another experience of mine—a good joke on me:

During the war, I bought some five-pound nylon leader material in a store, to use with my casting rod; I had a five-pound line. The stuff did look pretty thin, and it obviously wasn't any too strong. "More wartime junk!" I said to myself. Still, it was marked five-pound strength, and I didn't bother to test it.

For a couple of weeks, fishing every day for long hours, and getting plenty of fish—not only bass but some fairly good-sized pike and walleyes, and a bowfin or two—I had a pretty hectic time. But I wouldn't go above five-pound test. Happening to be in town again, I bought some more marked five-pound test. It was much heavier! So I sent a piece of each to Du Ponts—I didn't have a micrometer with me where I was.

Back came a letter. The first package had been mislabeled by whatever jobber put it up. It was .009 inch, or 2X, with a test of 2.25 pounds—two and a quarter pounds new, less when worn! Mr. W. F. Jensen of Du Ponts wrote that if I'd been getting the fish I said I had on that stuff, with a casting rod, I could call myself a fisherman and not get into an argument with anybody.

I sat staring at that letter a while, and then sat down and had a good laugh—the best joke in years. I'd been a lot better fisherman than I'd had any intention of being; if anybody had suggested my using 2.25-pound leaders for fish of the size that were around there, I'd have snorted at him. With a casting rod, I mean; the long spring of a fly rod makes a much lighter leader safe.

But the more I thought of it, the more one thing became obvious: never in my life had I landed so many bass in proportion to the number of strikes. And never in my life had I seen such a large percentage of those I got in hooked by a mere filament of skin on the edge of one lip. And the latter explained the former. Plainly, I wouldn't have got nearly so many bass if I'd been using a heavier leader; I'd have torn the hook loose on a good number—and called it "missed strikes."

Just to see what would happen, I decided to stick to 2.25-pound leaders for three months, for all my fishing. I tried to get a line of about that test—its casting qualities would have been superlative—but I was unable to at the time. Now that I knew definitely how weak my leader was, I was more careful than ever in playing fish. And I was, too, becoming used to handling them on such frail stuff; that makes a lot of difference.

In that three months, I caught 865 fish, counting all sizes. They were mainly bass, for that was chiefly a bass lake. I got a few northern pike, but none very large. Still, one of those which went ten pounds wasn't exactly a minnow, for such tackle. He fought hard a very long time, through tall, spindly weeds, but did not tangle in them and gave me no particular trouble; just enough to make it real sport.

I lost five plugs because of that light leader's breaking, either when they'd tangle in weeds, or when I tried to head them from the weeds. And I kept on landing a great number of bass hooked only by a small filament of skin, bass that I'd never have got in with heavier tackle.

Still, I'll admit that it was a relief when the three months which I'd set for myself were over. As might be expected— it's how such a thing always goes—those plugs I lost were very good ones, and of types that I couldn't replace at the time. And, with the shortage of plugs then, the strain of playing a large fish was pretty hard on my nerves. But I had at least proved definitely to myself that I could land a lot more bass on frail tackle than on strong. Remember, I am speaking of bass only; most other fish take a lure in a different manner, and far more deeply into the mouth. So I went back up to five-pound leaders, though at first I felt a little ashamed of myself for using such heavy stuff.

Am I recommending five-pound lines for every bass fisherman? I certainly am not; I should say that there is hardly an angler in five hundred whose experience and fishing conditions will make it practical.

In fact, no matter how skillful or experienced a man may be, the lightness of line practical for him depends on where he fishes. For instance, in one of those cold, clear, rocky, weed-free northern lakes I should not have the slightest hesitation in tackling any bass that ever lived with a line of one-pound test, or even half that, if it would cast a plug without whipping in two, for there I could play him as long and as lightly as I wished. Trying to use such a light line among even moderately bad weeds or snags would be utterly ridiculous.

The lake where I made the test had the usual assortment of weed beds, the weeds varying from scattered and spindly to very dense. I found a five-pound line quite satisfactory there; but I had to stay clear of the denser weeds with it. Sometimes I didn't. I recall one calm morning when for almost an hour I sat in my boat looking down at a lovely bass six feet below, one of my best lures in his mouth, and the leader tangled in weeds. I tried pulling gently on the line with my fingers; I tried poking down with an oar. It ended with my losing bass and plug. I really should have carried along some sort of small grapple on a few feet of strong line, for such occasions.

One may see what I'm getting at: Almost every bass fisherman I ever met uses lines of one strength for all his fishing. For the beginner, that is undoubtedly the best way, the simplest. But I think the experienced angler should make a practice of having lines of several weights, down to some extremely light ones, to use as water conditions—freedom from or plenitude of weeds and snags—will permit. The ideal thing, if one can afford it, would be to have two or three reels along, each with a line of different test on it, to be changed quickly on the rod. Or one can switch lines on one reel, according to where one is going to fish that day. This would not only allow one to do the best casting possible under the conditions, but would bring one in the maximum number of bass, letting one land those lightly hooked ones where there are not too many weeds; where there are very many, they just cannot be landed.

Few will want to use lines of less than five-pound test, because of their poor wearing qualities. But a nylon leader just as light as one wishes may be used with this. There's another advantage to this very fine leader: the lake free from weeds is generally crystal clear—I am speaking here mainly of natural lakes, not artificial, which are sometimes muddy—so if the bass are at all wary one can get many more strikes with a practically invisible leader. This is recognized as a cardinal principle of trout fishing, but it often applies to bass too, and in some districts a fine leader is almost imperative if one wants to hook many of them.

How long should such a leader be? Nearly always, it is of such length that it comes almost to the reel when one is ready to cast. A single water knot, simple as it is, seems about the best and safest to fasten it to the line; it casts perfectly through the guides, but it is well to test it with a pull of the hands occasionally to be sure that it is not weakening. From scattered spots here and there in the country, men have written to tell me that they could do much better by using a light nylon leader of up to twenty feet. I have never found occasion to use such long ones for bass, but I am certainly not controverting the words of my correspondents; I have never happened to fish where they do.

After all, why, barring dense weeds, should a man use something resembling tuna line for bass? It isn't sport—or at least it is a crude and almost childish form of sport. Look at the "3-6" fisherman of salt water—his six-foot rod of six ounces, and six-thread linen line, which originally meant twelve-pound test, though improvement in line manufacture makes it stronger now. With that rig—which our average fresh-water angler would think too light for bass!—he consistently lands great sea fish.

What's the point of this chapter? It is simply that the bass fisherman should steadily develop his skill until he finds himself able to use extremely light tackle when conditions permit, instead of getting stuck at his first crude, heavy-handed methods. The player of every other game tries to develop his skill, to refine his technique, not only from year to year but from day to day. Why shouldn't the bass angler?

CHAPTER XX

How to Play a Fish*

THIS is going to be a pretty short chapter, but it might easily prove the most important in the book, especially to a reader who wants to get out of the novice class and to use lighter lines. We'll begin with an axiom:

It is utterly impossible to break a rod or line, no matter how light, while a fish is being played properly.

And now we'll start with the strike, and battle that fish until he's in the boat, to show the right way to do it.

I have just discussed a bass's delicate way of taking a lure in his lips, to test it, and how that so often leads to his being hooked lightly, by a thread of skin on his lip. And I advised working the sharp hook in by a series of jiggles, rather than trying to set it with one strenuous jerk which would tear it through its hold.

Still, the ideal way would be for those first quick pulls to be the hardest to which he would be subjected throughout the fight. The point being that if he is hooked very lightly, but the hook held while being set, it would not be pulled through later on. This ideal can be lived up to only where there are no weeds or snags from which one may have to attempt

* For demonstration photos, see Plates 6 and 13, Photo Section.

211

to head him. And it might be remarked that if the point of the hook is only slightly embedded in the bony plate in his mouth —it can't be embedded far in it—he is soon going to get loose in spite of anything that one can do.

When a fish is hooked, the first thing I should advise anybody to do is to throw on the click of the reel; the left thumb can do it quickly. A large fish whirling away from you may cause wet fingers to slip from the reel handle, resulting, if the click isn't on, in a snarled backlash at the very time when it is most undesirable; if you are using a reasonably light line, it means that line broken and the fish lost.

Of course, such a mixup *shouldn't* happen; one should invariably be cool-headed and do everything just so. There-fore the man who never gets excited, no matter how big the fish, who always does everything perfectly, may disregard this advice—but I'm not certain that this book will be read in the celestial realm where he is.

Immediately on hooking the fish, another switch of the left hand is made; it is brought down to the lower grip of the rod, with the thumb braced against the reel frame and its tip touching the line on the spool. In fact, it takes about the same position that the right had in casting. Then a braking action can be maintained with the thumb when the fish runs.

A warning here, especially for the man changing from heavy lines to light ones: In the excitement of playing a large fish—the only one likely to smash something—that braking action will always be at least three times as heavy as you think it is. But this warning will do no good whatever; it will take about a dozen parted lines to teach the lesson. And don't say the line was rotten; it was your own flustered judgment that was that way.

Of course, you use one crank handle to reel the fish toward you. But do not attempt to let him run by allowing your fingers to go backward with the handle, whether exerting pressure on it or not. Above all, try to break yourself as soon as possible of the beginner's invariable trick of "freezing" to the handle, holding it still; with reasonably light tackle and a large fish, it means a certainty either of the fish being lost or of broken tackle, and a high probability of both.

Hold the handle so that you can release it like a flash in case of a sudden whirl back; in learning to do that lies one of the great secrets of successfully playing a heavy fish. The muskellunge and his close relative, the true pike, are particularly likely to catch one off guard with an instantaneous, powerful and totally unexpected whirl; for that reason, they are notorious tackle-smashers. But a bass can do it too.*

The only safe way to play a fish is with the rod held well out from the body, the lower part at right angles to the direction of the fish. If you "give him the butt," which means pointing the tip toward him and giving him the butt to pull against, you are not taking advantage of the spring of the rod to fight him, and a quick jerk on his part will probably break the line. Giving him the butt is excusable—even necessary—in but one case: when a large fish is heading into bad snags or weeds where he is almost certain to be lost; then, it is as well to give him the butt and try to snub him, at the risk of breaking something. Far better break a line than the rod. This isn't playing a fish properly—but it's the best one can do in these circumstances.

A great many misconstrue this expression, "to give him the butt"; they take it to mean pointing the butt toward him. That is giving him the tip. And it is likely to give it to him literally, for, doubled back on itself, it will probably break off and go sliding down the line to him. This is the sole cause of practically all breakage of rods in playing fish, and it is

* See Plate 6, Photo Section.

inexcusable at any time. Be extremely careful when a large fish comes alongside a boat, for if you have your rod tip high in the air, and he lunges down or under—it's too bad; your rod is done for.

Another point in holding the casting rod well out is that, lacking the much longer spring of a fly rod, it can do with the assistance of wrist torsion in playing a fish. An unexpected run will force the wrist to lower the rod tip temporarily, if your thumb does not release the spool quite soon enough. This will break the first shock of the run.

I say that holding the rod out thus is the only safe way. But one's wrist may become too tired to continue it during a long fight with a big fish, so it may be necessary to put the butt back against the body. But always remember the danger to tackle in doing that, and be ready to thrust it out immediately in a pinch. Be sure, invariably, to keep it away from your body when a fish comes close, for that is the dangerous time, the time when almost all smashups happen. Never try to lead a fish near you until he is exhausted, or you may get what you are begging for.

In handling a large, hard-fighting fish, especially with a lighter line, all this is pretty difficult; it calls for experience, quick wits and a considerable amount of manual dexterity. So what is the man to do who doesn't fish enough to catch on to all of it? That's easy: get a drag handle for his casting reel.

This drag handle is purchased separately, for a dollar or so, to replace the regular one. It is not made to fit all reels, but a watchmaker or any skillful mechanic can adapt it readily to most of them, using the methods described in the chapter on reels. There is a friction clutch which can be adjusted to well below the breaking strain of even the lightest line—and remember to allow for a worn and weakened line in fishing. The best way to get it right is to tie one end of the line to the hook of a spring balance, and have somebody watch the pointer on the scale as you reel until the clutch slips. Setting this clutch right calls for a little time and care.

With this on your reel, it is not necessary to hold the rod out from the body in playing a fish, except when he comes close and could double a frail tip and break it. Nor is it necessary to switch the left hand down in playing him—in fact it may be better not to, to avoid the temptation to use the thumb on the spool too, and probably break the line. Just hang on to the handle while he runs—or, if you are excited enough, keep on "reeling in"; he'll still be going on his way, and your tackle safe. Now and then a fish will run into weeds or snags and be lost—but you would likely have lost him even sooner without the drag handle; and it will probably save you five big fish to replace him.

Some men are disdainful about the use of a drag handle—they feel that it is not quite ethical, since it makes playing a fish so much simpler. But such a thing is found on nearly all sea reels, and also on spinning reels using extremely light lines—"threadlines," as they are appropriately called in England. I think it far better for a man to use a drag handle and light line than the usual crude, heavy tackle. Indeed, the critic of it—Well, if it isn't our old friend, the stickler, back again! And holding a rod and line that would almost toss his fish over the moon. No need of a drag handle for him!

And the beauty of the drag handle is that it will permit a man with little or no experience in playing large fish to use a light line, and so find out how smooth and effortless casting can be.

The last thing, of course, is landing the fish. Most experienced bass anglers do this by hand. He should be completely tired out before it is attempted. When he is, lead him gently up to you, and slowly, carefully, slip a thumb into his mouth, the forefinger under his lower jaw. This gives a firm grip from which he cannot possibly escape, no matter how big he is.*

There is one trouble with this, especially when one is using multiple-hook plugs: the danger that the fisherman will, through some hurry or clumsiness on his part, find a set of hooks through his hand, with a heavy fish flopping in the air from another set. I know of one man who had his hand partially crippled for life by this; it might not have been so bad if he hadn't become excited from the pain and done things he shouldn't.

So, I recommend a net. In fact, in spite of all the bass that I have landed by hand, I like a net myself. If one fishes entirely from a boat, and lives near where it is docked, the usual long-handled boat net may be found most convenient. Even under these circumstances, I prefer a short-handled one of the trout type, but stronger and larger than is generally used for trout. There is a slight knack to using this. Jabbing at the fish, or striking his tail with it, will rarely net him, and is likely to permit him to escape. The net should be held under the surface, and the fish led quietly into it, when an easy sweep lifts him up. Indeed, the more quietly and gently this whole netting procedure is done, the better.

The shallow net one sometimes sees used is no good whatever; often a fish, especially a big one, will flop out of it as he is being lifted, and in using it there is always a tendency to hurry too much, to try to toss him into the boat or ashore. Use a deep net, and when he is in the bottom of that, he is safe.

Some object to the net because multiple hooks on plugs tangle badly in it, and it takes a little while to get them loose. But no angler is in such a great hurry that he should grumble

* See Plate 7, Photo Section.

about this, if it saves him a good fish now and then—and averts all danger of hooks in his hand.

There are other advantages to using a net. Especially when one fishes with small lures, one will very often catch crappies when fishing for bass, where they are present. The crappie is notoriously soft-mouthed, and cannot be landed by hand like a bass, so a net is really the only way to land one. Where there are pike or pickerel, they are, of course, often caught, since they strike freely on any bass lure. These can be landed by hand, but there is a trick to it that few learn; a net is much the best thing for them. And if there is a good way to land a walleye by hand, I have never discovered it.

There is one sort of fisherman to whom not one word of what I've said about playing a bass will apply, especially if he casts from shore: he who gets his fish in thick, tough weeds or among snags. All he can do is use a sort of slightly modified crowbar, with what one might call moderately light sash cord for line, and snake his fish in tail-over-fins as fast as he can. And he must, with that rig, use the shot-putting, or biceps-building, technique in casting. If he really prefers that sort of thing—why, there's no accounting for tastes. If he doesn't, but can find no other fishing—well, that's tough luck.

CHAPTER XXI

The Tackle Box

THE man who fishes wading usually wears a wading vest. In this matter, it is impossible to advise one, for it's so largely a matter of taste. But the more pockets, the better; somehow, there are never quite enough. And anybody who fishes a lot should really have two vests—one warm, with long sleeves, for cool weather; and one of the skeleton type for hot days. If I were getting only one, it would be of the skeleton type, for it is always possible to put on something warm under it.

Small trout may be carried in a rubber-lined pocket in the back of the vest, but that doesn't work out very well for bass. So a creel is desirable. And, for bass, it should be of eighteen-inch length.

In boat fishing, of course a tackle box is needed, so we'll consider what sort is best.

I am repeating that I think consistent success the only true measure of an angler's skill. The comparatively inexperienced fisherman will have his good days—days, even, when he'll be lucky and beat the expert. Provided, of course, that he isn't too green. The trouble is that he'll find so many times when the bass "just aren't striking." He'll get back to the dock to find other anglers dolefully standing around, and agreeing that they're not hitting at all today.

Then another boat comes in; the man in it is probably old enough to have some deep sun wrinkles on the back of his neck. And usually he'll be alone. At other times he may be the most friendly man you could find, but he takes his fishing far too seriously to want it interrupted by conversation, or even by a slight sneeze from anybody else. Almost all the most successful anglers I've met have been lone wolves at the game, concentrating so hard on their fishing that they'd hardly be aware of another man if he were along. Maybe the man who always has a pal with him, for a little kidding, gets more fun out of it. But men are built differently, with different preferences.

Anyway, the doleful group around the dock eyes the arrival gloomily. Just to be sociable, one of them asks, "Any luck?"

The veteran shakes his head. "They're just not striking today." Then, after a pause, he pulls up his stringer. "I had to work like blazes to catch these little things."

He's got his limit of bass! And the "little things" are so big that any of the others there would be pretty happy to get them any day.

The rest look over his equipment, trying to find out "what he's got that they haven't." There will likely be but one noticeable difference; his tackle box is much bigger and heavier than anybody else's.

A man usually begins his angling career by using a light, cheap tin box, with a few very new-looking plugs which appear, somehow, sort of lonesome in it. One could well imagine the box and its contents standing on the counter of a hardware store, marked "Clearance—$1.98." They're the sort of plugs that would be sold at clearance rates, to get rid of them.

The box becomes more cluttered as time passes—and, since it's badly finished, pretty rusty. So he gets a larger, better one, of which he's very proud. Only to find in a year or two that this also is too small. And so the succession of tackle boxes begins. It ends, not when he at last finds one big enough to satisfy him permanently, but when he's got the largest to be purchased, or the heaviest—counting its contents—that he can carry. He's reached the stage where there isn't any tackle box big enough, and if there were it would have to be mounted on a barge and called a houseboat.

One can make a rough guess at how consistently successful a bass fisherman is by glancing at his tackle box closed. It may be pretty new—it probably will be, for the finicky angler likes to have his stuff look as well as possible; if he's of the careless type, he wouldn't have become a good fisherman. But we must see the box open to confirm our first guess.

If all the plugs and things in it are nice and new and shiny—well, we got fooled; and the bad selection of plugs, too, shows that. Certainly the veteran will have some new, shiny plugs, but they'll range from that to disreputable-looking relics that one would think should have been thrown away years ago. As if any angler ever threw away a plug—except possibly some patent weedless affair designed by a mouse-trap inventor; any experienced angler would feel ashamed to be caught with one of these.

Just why can one guess a man to be a consistently successful angler from the fact that he carries a big, full tackle box? Simply because he's prepared for anything that may turn up, for those occasional days when bass will touch nothing but some plug which ordinarily doesn't interest them in the least.

You will notice that I say "bass." Pike, muskellunge, walleyes and other fish ordinarily caught on casting lures are not nearly so temperamental and choosy; two or three good lures will do quite well for them. But no fish that ever flopped is so fond of laughing at an angler as is a bass; he likes to reverse evolution, and make a monkey out of a man. And is he good at it! That is one reason, besides his gameness, why bass fishing turns into a mania for so many of us; we want to see if we can't outsmart him—and he takes some outsmarting.

Therefore our consistently successful bass angler must have a box that will hold plenty of plugs. Since there is no greater nuisance than a cluster of plugs with their hooks tangled together, that means plenty of little compartments for lures. And this in turn means at least two trays, both so divided. A few of us reach the stage where we have to have ten-tray boxes, big things looking like a plug salesman's sample case—and then we end up with two large or three small lures to a division. And wishing we had that Wiggly Whatsit we left at home in the main collection; probably that's just what they want right now!

These trays should invariably be of the cantilever type, swinging out and sidewise when the box is opened. Loose trays, to be lifted up every time one wants to change lures, are pestiferous things. Also, one will often want to reach in a hurry for something in the bottom of the box; so that should always be exposed, with everything available instantly, while one is fishing. When changing plugs, the one taken off should always go back into its compartment. Leaving it lying on the boat seat means that sooner or later it will somehow be caught in the line, jerked overboard, and lost. Or it will get stuck in one's clothes, and perhaps in what's inside them.

There is but one length of tackle box for the man who takes his angling seriously, and that is the 21-inch. It is the longest standard size; any longer would be too unwieldy. The trays will, of course, have more plug divisions than shorter ones, but one of the principal reasons for this size is that the bottom, below the trays, is long enough for certain things which most good anglers like to have with them regularly.

Another thing: the box should be large enough to hold all that one takes fishing, except the rod. Then one hasn't a lot of loose objects to carry, or to forget and leave at home.

So here we have a tackle box of twenty-one inches, with two cantilever trays for most men, and more for the veteran—the man who, on the rare day when he gets no fish, will wait till well after dark and sneak home through the brush, risking poison ivy rather than have anybody witness his disgrace.

It goes without saying that it should be a good box, well made, though there's no need for its being fancy or too expensive. Cheap boxes rust and dent too easily, as well as having other faults.

The first thing to see to is that when it is closed little or no rain gets in, even in a downpour. That is another reason for a box of the cantilever type; during even a light drizzle, the careful angler will keep it closed, but it can be swung open instantly, something taken out, and the box closed again. This avoids rusting and messing up everything in the box, and will make a better-grade box a paying investment, in preserving tackle.

If there are seams on or near the bottom of the box, see to it that they are tight, for a rented boat, or almost any boat which has been out of the water a few days, will sometimes leak. Even with a dry boat, a downpour will often leave some water sloshing around in the bottom, where the tackle box generally rests. It would be a good plan with a new box to pour it half full of water and see that it all stays in. If there is a leak, it can be fixed by soldering or with cement of some sort.

Should the plug compartments be cork lined? There is some controversy about this. Some do not like the cork, holding that it will rot fairly rapidly when exposed to the weather, and will then soak up water like blotting paper, to rust things.

But it is a simple matter to remove the old lining and cement in new, cut from light cork gasket material such as can be bought for very little at any auto supply house. Cork lining does help prevent dull hooks. However, the plain, painted metal will not dull them if one is careful in putting plugs in and, especially, in removing them.

Unlined trays often have thin paint, so hooks on plugs jiggling around will soon scratch through it—and some rust will eventually be found even on sound paint, from wet hooks. This will stain the sides of plugs, giving them a poor appearance, and rendering them less effective, since they don't show the finish which they are supposed to have. One should watch for this rust stain on the bottom of trays, and at the first sign of it, repaint.

Undoubtedly the best thing for this purpose is a good aluminum paint; nothing else seems to stick so well on a surface not fully prepared, to get quite so hard, or to be so resistant to weather. Many object to the glitter it has in the sun, saying that one gets enough of that from the water without having it in the boat too. Some don't mind it; it's a matter of preference.

Green is most restful to the eyes, and also it looks well in trays. Therefore a dark green enamel would perhaps suit most men best. If it isn't of a very good grade, let it dry thoroughly and give it two or three light coats of high-grade spar varnish—indeed, that will make a more durable finish for even the best enamel. Remember to use light coats of varnish, and to let each dry thoroughly before applying the next; twenty-four hours should be the minimum.

All working parts—the hinges, the lid catches, the rivets on which the trays swing—will rust, because they must have bare metal. So oil them occasionally. Use your reel oil, placing a drop at each spot with the applicator on the stopper. Don't squirt oil on; that's messy.

Here's a tip. It's something that will do more than any other one thing to keep your plugs and stuff in good shape. It's almost a matter of religion with me but, oddly, I've never seen anybody else practice it:

Invariably, just as soon as you get in from fishing, bring your tackle box into a dry room in the house, open it, and leave it open until everything in it is thoroughly dry. If through mischance or carelessness you have allowed a noticeable amount of water to get into the bottom or into the trays, wipe it out.

In connection with this, there's one point that it is advisable for the married man to remember, or he will run the danger of his tackle box not being allowed in the house. If the box contains a collapsible landing net, a live net, a cotton stringer, or anything else of a porous nature, remove it immediately and leave it outdoors to dry. There will be wet fish slime, either new or old, on it, and it will—well, stink's the word.

Of course, no true angler dislikes the odor of rotten fish slime; it's reminiscent of happy catches. But remember, it's only the fisherman who looks at it that way; take my advice, and don't expose slimy nets and such things in the living room. Leave 'em outside—but bring the box in and dry it.

What goes into the box besides plugs?

I'd begin by advising the last thing anybody thinks of putting into it—an inflatable boat cushion. It's a fine life preserver in case of accident; for that reason there should be tape or heavy cord around it to hang onto. It is much more comfortable to sit on than a hard boat seat, and if one fishes nearly as much as I do, it will save many times its cost in a year—twisting around on a hard, rough board to cast is tough on trousers. Some may prefer a kapok cushion; it's all right if one always takes it along, but who does? Since thin rubber deteriorates fairly rapidly when exposed to the weather, a cushion of plastic may be found more durable, and less likely to spring an air leak in time.

A long-nosed pliers is needed, for removing hooks from fish, and for other things. Some recommend that if a hook becomes embedded in one's flesh, the barb be pushed all the way through and cut off. Unless it is deep indeed, I think it better to back it out with a jerk. Best of all, let a doctor do it.

In the last chapter the use of a landing net was recommended. A folding metal one can be found that will go nicely into the box, handle and all.

Of course, one needs a stringer of some sort. I prefer the wire, safety-pin type. But there would be no harm in having a strong cord one along too, which can be tied solidly to the lip of one's largest fish, the real prize.

We always read that a bass should be strung through both lips. Why? He can't breathe very well that way, and when his upper lip is torn he looks pretty messy. I string mine by the lower lip only, and avoid dragging them through the water, which forces their mouths open so that they can't breathe.

Some, after getting their limit, keep on fishing, liberating the small ones from the stringer and putting the large ones on. I can't express my opinion of that in print. An injured fish should never be released, except when keeping him would be illegal.

I recommend a large, strong live net to hang over the side of the boat. This keeps bass looking at their best, not all red and damaged-looking around their mouths where a stringer has been. And one can be released from it entirely uninjured. The usual hoop-type mouth on the net won't do; it won't go into an ordinary tackle box. One can be made up by just buying a strong net and running a heavy stringer around the mouth so that it will draw shut. It's much better to tie on a lot of little brass or plastic rings—get the kind used on potholders, and tie them on with strong fishing line.

One should always have a hook hone; I've pointed out several times how lax most men are in keeping their hooks sharp, in spite of all the strikes that makes them miss. A small file might be more convenient, but it will rust badly in a tackle box.

A pocket knife will rust too if left lying around in a boat —and it might be dropped overboard. I keep a little cheap kitchen knife, always sharp, and always right there in the box, ready when I reach for it in a hurry.

Reel oil is imperative, and there's no harm in having some gear grease along. And if the spare pawl isn't in the reel itself where it should be, it can be kept in the box, in a tiny vial of grease; this pawl, being so important, shouldn't be permitted to rust.

Most experienced anglers always carry a spring balance to weigh their fish. It's provoking how much smaller it makes them—but think of the reputation for almost superhuman veracity it gives a man to be able to say definitely, "This bass weighs five pounds, two and a half ounces, exactly." A clever little spring balance has come out lately which also includes a ribbon-type steel rule to measure the fish. And one needs that balance, too, for determining the test of the worn end of one's line.

Where large fish such as pike are hooked, it certainly is very advisable to have a priest along. I do not refer to a Roman Catholic or an Episcopal clergyman, but to a thing which may be only a small piece of light iron pipe, to tap a fish on the head—I've always wondered if it is called a priest because it administers the last rites. There's a slight knack to using this: never **swing** hard; just give a light blow behind the eyes as the exhausted fish is led past. And be ready to lower your rod tip instantly if a last convulsive movement of his body sends him driving five or six feet in a circle. Then he'll come up limp, and can be lifted aboard at leisure.

Few carry goggles, but they are restful to the eyes on a bright day; the sun reflected from the water can be quite disagreeable at times. But never wear cheap goggles; they can even do permanent damage to the eyes.

If one is going into the wilds, it is a good idea to have a spare rod, in short joints, in the box. This will not have good action—but it might avert an abrupt end to one's fishing if one breaks the other.

A small magnifier is something else that nobody thinks of carrying, but it is useful in helping one pick out a tight backlash, especially on a light, soft line. It's good, too, to inspect hook points when honing them. An expensive one is not necessary; a few cents will buy one that will serve the purpose.

If there is any chance of being out after dark, a flashlight is handy. It will be more than that, to use for signaling, on a lake where there might be some danger of being run down by a larger craft at night.

And mosquito dope! Nothing can ruin a man's fishing more than these pestiferous insects; never go out without some dope for them.

Then there will be a reel wrench, and some spare hooks, and snaps, and leaders, and perhaps a waterproof matchbox, and various other odds and ends. It all adds up to a pretty heavy tackle box to lug around, but I think it's well worth the effort, since it makes one's fishing go so much more smoothly and pleasantly.

And it does look impressive, very different from the rank amateur's little cheap tin box.

CHAPTER XXII

Fly Tackle for Bass—Selecting

THERE is a prevalent belief that fly fishing for bass is more sportsmanlike, or more sport, than plug casting for them. To me this seems sheer nonsense. In fact, I am inclined to hold the opposite to be the truth. I believe these notions come from the fact that the fly rod is far older than the casting rod, which is a quite recent American invention; the fly rod has long tradition and an extensive and well-written literature behind it, to dignify it. Let's analyze the matter a little.

It is true that we cannot say much for the sporting qualities of the usual crude casting rod and heavy line. But what of the fly outfit we so often see a man using for bass, with a gut leader of perhaps twenty pounds' test? And he has a very long rod to do most of his battling for him, to take up sudden shocks; the rod, to a great extent, plays the fish for him, instead of his doing it himself. I think it unquestionable that a man has to be more dexterous, quick-witted and cool-headed to play a large fish successfully on a casting rod.

As far as the pleasure, the sport, of the thing goes, a fly rod certainly does not give one the feel of the fish that a casting rod does; the long, pliant spring takes up nearly all the vibrations. With a casting rod, you can almost feel every quiver of a fin on the fish one is playing. And you are doing things

228

swiftly with both hands, to meet every swerve on the fish's part—there isn't that long rod to do it for you.

Sometimes I find a man going around with his nose in the air, boasting that *he* always uses a fly rod for bass; he wouldn't *think* of using a casting rod—heavens, no! But when I see him on the river, he's bass-bugging with his fly rod. As a matter of plain fact, bass-bugging is an extremely crude form of fly fishing, if fly fishing it can be called. It is hardly different from "skittering"—flipping a bass bug around on the end of a line tied solidly to a long cane pole. A child of average mentality should learn bass-bugging in a few minutes.

This is not condemning bass-bugging; I practice it a good deal myself, and have lots of fun with it. But it is ridiculous for a man employing bugs on a heavy leader to feel superior to the user of light casting tackle, who must have much more skill than he, both in casting and in playing a fish.

There is fly casting and fly casting—and plug casting and plug casting. It does take long practice and study to lay a dry fly skillfully. Nice casting with very light tackle takes time to learn too—but not as much as good dry-fly fishing. On the other hand, the light-line plug caster, as already noted, needs more coolness and dexterity in playing his fish, which tends to make the total skill required for each somewhere about even. I am so fond of both methods that I would not admit either to be superior.

Because I have often come out so strongly as champion of the casting rod, some people have got the notion that I have a grudge against the fly rod, or that I don't like it. Nothing could be further from the truth. My feeling is only that it's high time plug casters stop taking that nonsense meekly—and maybe ask one of those fly-rod snobs to play a large fish on light casting tackle, to see how foolish he looks at it.

Really, I stick up for the casting rod only because it's been the under dog. But every dog will turn, and when the casting rod does, I hope it bites some of the smug fly-rod men where it would hurt most. And if one objects to jumbled metaphors, I'll settle for some triple hooks through seats of pants—well through. As the old saying goes, every rod has its day, and it's time for the casting rod's.

If somebody should ask me what is my own favorite type of bass fishing, I'd have to confess that it is—dry fly. There is perhaps no form of fishing that I enjoy more. But I must add that only on comparatively rare occasions have I found dry-fly fishing for bass effective enough to be interesting. I think the casting rod the more effective for bass a major part of the time, in most places; but when fishing from a boat I nearly always keep both fly and casting rod rigged up under my hand, to use alternately as conditions warrant, or as the mood strikes me. And I believe that anybody who aims to be an all-round bass fisherman should learn to use a fly rod.

But if that superior-acting, straight fly-rod man only knew it, common, ordinary fly casting, as distinct, for instance, from artistic dry-fly work, is far and away easier to learn than good plug casting with a free-running reel.

Here I see a caster shaking his head. "You're completely wrong there!" he says. "Why, I've tried over and over to use a fly rod—tried my hardest. And I had to give up. The fly-rod man has a right to feel superior to poor pluggers like me."

More mistaken notions! The whole trouble comes from two things which he doesn't understand: One can chunk a plug out somehow using a golf-club shaft fitted with guides, if one employs enough body-English. But one simply cannot cast a fly with the arm, or with a bad rod. Nor can one cast it at all unless one learns the right—and very easy—technique.

A great mistake that nearly everybody makes is buying a

cheap fly rod as "good enough to learn with." It isn't; the beginner must have a good fly rod, one with proper action. And must pay pretty well for it—thirty-five dollars or so will get a nice one, though not the best, but I don't advise going much under that. The rest of the outfit need cost but a negligible sum. And, unlike the plug-caster's tackle, there is little expense or replacement after the initial cost; a good fly line, for instance, may last a lifetime.

Perhaps the greatest misconception the casting-rod man has at the beginning is that he is casting the fly. He isn't; he is casting *the line*, and the fly just rides along as excess baggage; the lighter the fly, the better and farther he can cast. So it is always well to begin with very small flies, for ease in learning. I'd suggest a few days put in fly-fishing for sunfish as the ideal start; they can be found almost anywhere that bass are—they're called "bream" in the South, which, however, is a wrong name for them.

Let nobody turn up his nose at fly-fishing for sunfish. It's great sport; I've spent many a long day having a fine time at it, when I'd only have to put on larger lures to catch bass, or even muskellunge. And it's very useful to know how to do it, and to have the outfit along for it, on days when one has no luck with the bass; it may send one home grinning happily instead of scowling. Nor can using a heavy bass fly rod for sunfish be thought in the least unsportsmanlike, or poor fun; just put on a 5X leader, about six thousandths of an inch in diameter, of less than a pound test and—a big bass is almost sure to take the tiny fly, and then you'll find out how good an angler you are, and have a whale of a time, no matter whether you land him or not.

While, in casting rods, tubular steel and bamboo are coming down the stretch neck and neck, we must admit that in fly rods most fishermen prefer the action of bamboo. But steel fly rods are being improved rapidly, and more and more anglers are coming to like them; though I doubt if we shall see, for a long time at least, a steel fly rod with the "feel" of a really good bamboo.

There is but one kind of bamboo for fly rods—Tonkin. All others are out of date, and do not compare with it. There are many grades of Tonkin, and still more grades of fly rods after they have been made up by different companies, the price one pays not always, by any means, being a measure of their worth. The beginner, who knows nothing of what action should be, must rely on the reputation of the rod's maker. If he doesn't do this, he is practically sure to be stung, and badly, finding himself with a worthless rod, no matter what he pays.

Many seem to think that the main difference between a cheaper fly rod and an expensive one is in the mountings and finish. It would be hard to find anything much farther from the truth. It might be well for me to touch briefly on how a good bamboo rod is made, to show the reader why he has to pay so much for one.

The skill which some of the best craftsmen develop at this, through inborn knack and long years of practice, is almost incredible. One of them can quickly plane, by eye, a strip of bamboo with almost micrometer precision. And when he fails to do that, he breaks the strip and throws it away, disgusted at himself for being so unskillful.

He must also be a structural engineer of a sort to know where, for a given piece of bamboo, the rod should run nearly straight, where taper pretty sharply, to get the action desired. Naturally, you have to pay well for his skill, and for the years it took to develop it; if he's a top-notcher, he is more artist than craftsman. But the rod you get is worth all you pay, and more, though it may not look a whit better than another at less than half the price. Neither does a Stradivarius violin look better than one which can be bought for a tiny fraction of its price; and rod making and violin making are comparable.

Not only does the manufacturer have to pay the crafts-man a high salary, but he must keep the bamboo for seasoning at different stages of the game; even the final "glued stick," ready to mount, is seasoned for several months before finish-ing it. That is "overhead expense," or something of the sort, which the purchaser must pay if the manufacturer is to make money and stay in business.

Cheap bamboo rods are made almost entirely by swift-working machinery, of low-grade bamboo, with little seasoning at any time, and little inspection of the finished product. This inferior bamboo comes in at one end of the factory, and pretty soon shoots out the other as a fly rod—at least, it is called a fly rod by those who know no better. No matter how little one pays for it, it isn't worth it. It will do very well to catch panfish on worms, and that is all it's good for.

Now and then, by a near-miracle, a cheap rod does hap-pen to have good action, and a really expert fly-caster, looking through a great pile of those rods, might pick it out. But the average angler is not at all likely to run onto it; he'd buy at least fifty cheap rods before he found one with even passable action. And if he did happen to get the good one, it would be about sure to "go dead" and lose its action in a short time. I have known well-made fly rods to be used for more than fifty years, and still retain their original action.

There is something which I must say here, though with great reluctance. Much as I like to see a home craftsman work-ing in his own shop, I must admit that such a man is not likely to have access to the huge quantities of seasoned and first-class bamboo that the larger maker has, to select the finest for his best rods. Nor, generally, does he have the knack of working swiftly and surely. Therefore in buying from him one is likely to pay far more than a large company would ask for a similar rod.

Indeed, practically all these small makers do no more than buy glued sticks from the larger companies, and mount them—often rather messily, sometimes very well. But the larger maker will not usually sell him his best glued sticks; he keeps them for his own more expensive rods—he wants to build up his own reputation, not the smaller maker's. And the reader could very soon learn to mount glued sticks himself; there's no trick at all to that. But, having bought glued sticks and mountings at retail, he would not save a penny by doing so, and he really wouldn't have "made" a rod. It's the making of the glued stick that's the whole thing; it's the time and skill that goes into it that costs.

Yes, one has to pay for a good bamboo fly rod. And it has always been a mystery to me why a man will spend well over a hundred dollars for an outboard motor to take him across a lake, and then go fishing with, perhaps, a five-dollar rod, getting no pleasure from it. And he will lay out anywhere from sixty to a hundred dollars or more for a gun which he can use only a few days in the year, and then think he's "blowing himself" in paying fifteen dollars for a rod which he can use many, many times as often. It's particularly illogical when one remembers that the cheap and the higher-priced rods differ far more in performance than do cheap and higher-priced guns.

I have said a great deal here in an attempt to make a man avoid buying a cheap fly rod "just to learn with." You can't learn with one. And I wish that tackle makers would be much more explicit in their catalogues in pointing out the immense difference between their cheap and their better rods.

Having, I hope, convinced the reader that he should not

buy a cheap rod, let us consider what sort of better-class rod he needs for bass.

The thing one nearly always finds discussed first is the difference between "wet-fly" and "dry-fly" action. I become more and more convinced that there is no such thing as wet-fly action; to me, the "wet-fly" rod, bending limberly all over, is just a very poor fly rod, not nearly as well fitted for wet-fly fishing as is a rod with so-called dry-fly action. I have been saying this, with variations, for years. Indeed, when I find a man using a rod with wet-fly action, he is usually just letting his line wash down-stream with the current, hardly attempting real casting; he has found out that he can't do it with that rod.

So, I call dry-fly the only action for a fly rod, including a bass rod. With it, the lower part is quite stiff—but never poker-stiff—and one finds more and more action as one gets toward the tip. This rod has what is known as "power," or "backbone." But if it is well made, it will not feel harsh, nor too stiff, in the hand—and one that is too stiff is not only tiring but tricky in timing, hard to cast with.

There is the "sharp-taper" rod—one stiff nearly all the way up, with most of the action near the tip. This, too, is hard to cast with, and does not feel at all right in fishing. It will do wonderful things in the hands of an expert; but it is a rod for an exhibition caster, a trick caster, rather than for a fisherman.

At the other extreme, we have "parabolic action," when the bend comes mostly down near the hand, all the rest quite stiff. The advantage claimed for this is that it will lay a straighter line than any other fly rod, owing to lack of vibrations in the tip at the end of a cast. But the fact is that the practical angler finds its very slow action resembles too much that of the really obsolete wet-fly rod, and he will have nothing to do with it. The choice of a huge majority of experienced fly-rod men is regular six-strip construction, with regular dry-fly action.

Of what length should the bass rod be? Nine feet seems the leading choice, with some preferring one of eight and a half feet, and a very few—generally large, strong men—choosing one running up to nine and a half.

What weight? That, a matter about which much fuss is made, is the last thing one should think of; the actual weight of a rod on scales has little to do with how light it feels in one's hand, or how tiring it will prove. The matter is still further confused by the fact that various makers have various methods of arriving at the weights they list for their rods: some weigh the rod just as you buy it, with a substantial locking reel seat; some weigh only the *glued sticks*, with no reel seat, guides, varnish, or anything else; and there are other methods in between. So, when buying a fly rod for bass, specify "bass action," and don't bother about weight. It might be mentioned that the usual bass fly rod will weigh somewhere in the neighborhood of six and a half ounces in nine-foot length; if it is a quite expensive one it will weigh somewhat less, and still have sufficient power.

Incidentally, this is exactly the same rod, in all respects, that a great majority of men use for steelheads and other very large trout. Really, there is no such thing as a "bass fly rod"; it is merely a modern, standard fly rod powerful enough for bass fishing. There is no reason why one cannot use it, with a very fine leader, for much smaller fish, especially when it is desirable to make long casts—no reason except that a lighter rod is more pleasant to use, less tiring.

Recently there was devised a treatment for bamboo rods which is supposed to improve them greatly. In answering queries, I reserved judgment to see how these rods turned out in actual fishing. I am now receiving some complaints from readers that these, while excellent at first, become brittle and break after a few months of use; this brittleness seems to be the result of rapid deterioration due to aging rather than of constant flexing.

It is quite possible that this is due, not to the treatment, but to inferior bamboo used by some makers because of post-war conditions, to insufficient seasoning, or to faulty workmanship—no treatment can make good bamboo out of bad nor, for instance, change the position of two nodes which have been placed side by side, leaving a weak spot. I am always entirely frank with my readers, giving my personal opinion, right or wrong, for what it may be worth; so in this case I see nothing to do but continue reserving judgment until time tells us more about this treatment.

For this same reason I am not here discussing some recent and very promising developments in rods, fly and casting. I am waiting to see that they not only have action comparable to bamboo rods of similar price, but that they give promise of reasonably long life. I hope to be able to discuss them fully —and favorably—in future editions of this book, and in my writing in sportsmen's publications. To give an opinion at the present time, for or against them, would be considerably short of honest on my part.*

Having said so much about the rod, the rest of the fly outfit can be disposed of quite briefly.

Practically every novice with the fly rod gets far too light a line; this prevents anything remotely resembling real casting. The weight of line desirable has nothing whatever to do with the size fish to be caught; on a given rod, one would use the same line for sunfish as for muskellunge. Remember, you are casting the line, not the fly, and the line must have weight enough to carry itself out. This weight will vary with the power and

* See Chapter XXXIII, Glass-Plastic Rods.

action of the rod, but it *must match the rod*. Nowadays, most rods come with a tag bearing recommendations for the size line to be used on it. But often the line recommended is one size too small, for me at least; I will find a D recommended, but I can do much better with a C, and consider that necessary to bring out the action of the rod. This is particularly true of nylon lines, which are lighter for their diameters than silk.

That is for level lines. And most bass fishermen do use only the level line, which works well, and costs much less than those of other types. A double-taper is meant chiefly for dry-fly work. And I should recommend that the bass fisherman very soon get a "bug-taper" line, if he does not do so at the beginning; it permits much more distance than the level line, with no more effort. In these, the belly—the heaviest part—will always be heavier than the level line that fits the rod; since they vary in construction, it would be well to consult the maker's catalogue to find what is advisable.

About all that the foregoing can do is to keep one from the usual blunder of getting too light a line; one almost never sees a man go to the other extreme, and use one so heavy as to "kill the action" of his rod. But for the best results, the best and pleasantest casting, there is but one thing to do: find out from experience what line best suits your own rod—and your individual method of casting; yes, that counts too. The beginner, of course, cannot do this, but he will soon learn to.

The plug caster taking up the fly rod will always give himself a great deal of unnecessary concern about the reel, for the reel is the most important part of his plug-casting equipment. He should learn that the exact opposite holds true in fly casting. The reel is the least important; it is merely something to store line on when one isn't using it, and has nothing at all to do with casting.

However, some reels are much more convenient than

others. For instance, a reel with a small spool will get a line set into tight little corkscrews that will not "shoot" through the guides, and are maddening. Some prefer a single-action reel, some an automatic, and it is purely a matter of taste— I should suggest that, since neither costs a lot, a man have one of each, to find out which he likes. He may prefer, as many do, a single action under some conditions, an automatic under others. And there has lately been brought out a new type of reel, in which a pressure of the little finger works a ratchet and gives the spool several spins—pumping with the little finger of the hand holding the rod winds the line on. And a steady pressure of the little finger makes a drag of any weight one wishes against a running fish. This same reel may be used as a regular single-action without adjustments. I suspect that a good many fishermen will like this reel.

As most of us see it, there is another purpose for the reel: to balance the rod in one's hand. Some argue that partly filling the spool with sheet lead, as many of us do, is only adding unnecessary weight. Personally, if I do not weight my reel my wrist soon gets so tired that my timing suffers, and presently I cannot cast at all. A rod fitted with a heavily weighted reel may feel all wrong when one merely picks it up and hefts it; but after a couple of hours of fishing it may feel far lighter than an unbalanced one.

The ancient rule is that the reel should weigh one and a half times as much as the rod. This should be taken as no more than a rough guess for a beginning, in trying balances. Some give different points at which the rod, fitted with line and reel, should balance across one's finger. About the farthest point forward I have seen recommended is eight inches ahead of the cork grip, and some hold that the balance should be brought back right into one's hand. The balancing point that feels most pleasant will vary somewhat with the action of different rods; so, since it will cost but a few cents for sheet lead, a man should determine what feels best and least tiring to him, for that is all that matters.

In leaders, nylon has almost entirely supplanted natural gut for bass fishing. A level leader of six feet or even less is usually used, but I prefer one considerably longer; I suggest using one of such length that the knot tying it to the line will come just short of entering the tip guide when the fly is placed in the little fly ring down by the grip, for carrying the rod when not in use. But a leader of this length should be tapered somewhat, by knotting strands of nylon of different diameters together. To cast at all well, the part next the line must be almost as thick as the line itself—it really becomes part of the line. How much it should be stepped down depends on whether one catches one's bass in weeds, and has to pull pretty hard to get one in, and also on the size fly or bug being used; with a large fly, a long, thin point on the leader makes it inclined to tangle in casting. Since nylon leader material is cheap, a man should experiment a little to find what suits him, the conditions, and the fly in use. But for sport, and for the most fish possible, use the lightest leader point that is practical at the time.

There is much heated discussion as to the merits of the various flies, streamers, bass bugs and metal lures used on the fly rod for bass. But few fly-rod bass lures have any action except that given them in the retrieve. So to enter into a discussion of them would be pointless; a man will soon find out which seem best to suit him, and the bass in his neighborhood. To discuss proper retrieves for them would be pointless too, for they are just the same retrieves that one would use at the time with a casting outfit.

Since I have recommended fly-fishing for sunfish as a good way to learn real fly casting, as distinct from "bugging," I might add that I think most fly-anglers for sunfish use far too large a fly, considering that the sunfish has such a small mouth, and usually feeds on such tiny things. Personally, I practically never use larger than a size ten, and I sometimes get down to fourteens or even smaller. And I usually prefer rather skimpy hackle flies to those with wings, again considering the small mouth, and what will enter it easily. Any trout fly of suitable size will take sunfish, and sometimes they can be quite choosy and insist on a certain pattern, but the favorites of most men for them seem to be the black and the brown hackle. I have my own notions, right or wrong; the one I usually try first is the McGinty hackle—banded gold and black, and differing but slightly from the Bee—for me, at least, that has proved about the most consistent of all.*

In fly-rod fishing for bass, the matter of creels, waders, wading jackets and other accessories is much debated. So much so, in fact, that we can regard all these as purely matters of personal choice and what may best suit local conditions, and therefore not worth any space here.

In short, when it comes to giving advice on choosing a bass-fly outfit, about all I can say of value is: Get a good rod, and specify "bass action"; get a good but not necessarily expensive line that just brings out its action. All the rest are chiefly matters of preference, and you will soon find out for yourself what you like.

* See Chapter XXXI, Fly Fishing for Sunfish.

CHAPTER XXIII

Correct Fly Casting*

O N THE back cast:
  Do not let the rod go farther back than STRAIGHT UP.

Try to flip the line STRAIGHT UP *into the air over your head, not back behind you.*

This is one rule put in two ways, and in it lies the whole secret of true fly casting, as distinct from merely dobbing a fly out clumsily for a short distance. Hoping to impress it on the reader, hoping that he will remember it, I have placed it first here, where it logically doesn't belong. Obey it, and you can hardly help casting a fly pretty smoothly after but one evening's practice. Ignore it, and you might as well forget about fly casting and take up pinochle instead; you'll never learn to fly cast.

First, before going out for your first practice, dress your ine to make it float—and if it's dressed several hours before, so much the better. Use any good dressing, or plain paraffin wax will do, and rub it in well; then polish most of it off. Don't get a notion that leaving a lot of dressing smeared on will help; it will only gum things up.

Now we'll go out and begin by rigging up the rod.

The reel always hangs down—the opposite of a casting

* For demonstration photos, see Plates 9, 10, 11, 12, Photo Section.

reel. With a single-action, most of us keep the handle to the right. If a man is more ambidextrous than I and most others are, it's better to have the handle on the left, and to wind it with the left hand; that will save changing the rod back and forth in the hands. Some reels can be used either way, some can quickly be changed to left hand. Of course, a left-handed caster will usually want a left-hand reel—though he will not necessarily have to go hunting a left-hand reel wrench for it.

Put the rod together, always pushing the ferrules straight in (and remember not to twist the joints when taking it apart later). Naturally, one should sight along the guides and keep them in line—on the bottom of the rod. Then the line is run through them.

I have seen beginners put the line through that little loose ring down near the grip. That, of course, is a blunder; the ring is to hook the fly into when carrying the rod rigged up. If you are stringing the line on land, don't put the reel down where it can get sand or dirt in it; I've seen that done too, and oftener than one would think.

When rigging things up in a boat—well, I've watched men scrambling the length of the boat to run the line through, putting themselves in imminent danger of falling out of the boat. There's a much simpler and safer method, a little trick which surprisingly few seem to know: Just put on your reel and then run the line through all the guides before jointing up the rod, leaving long loops between the sections. Then fit the tip to the middle (as one always should do first anyway), and the middle to the butt, pulling loose line from the tip meanwhile. It can be done easily without moving from one's seat. Indeed, most of us sit down and rig a rod that way even on land.

Attach the leader to the line. You can do this the first time by using a plain jam knot, though splicing a little loop in the end of the line is better. If the leader is natural gut, it must be soaked thoroughly before using it, and kept wet at all times in fishing; otherwise it would undoubtedly break and there would be another "big one that got away." Nylon needs no soaking, but pull the ends of it to straighten it out.

Tie on the fly—and don't forget that the smaller and lighter it is, the easier you can cast, and the farther.

I strongly recommend that this first practicing be done on some pond where there is no chance of catching fish; then one will concentrate on form, which is absolutely necessary, but very soon comes unconsciously. Still more important, one will not be tempted to try for too long distance at first, and so perhaps injure one's style forever.

It is almost impossible to impress sufficiently on the plug caster the necessity for correct "form," or "style" in fly casting. He knows that one can slop a plug out any old way—it won't be real casting, but one can get it out. This just won't work in fly casting; it must be done correctly, or it can't be done at all.

When one is practicing where there are no fish (no use begging one to do this where there are!) always snip the hook off at the bend. There is a chance of getting it in one's clothes or ear on those first casts, or even in the eye of a spectator who thinks himself a safe distance away. Also, the hook might catch on something on the ground behind, which could mean a broken rod on the forward cast.

Some recommend beginning by casting on a lawn. I am strongly against this unless no suitable water is available, for the feel of the thing is quite different, and also the line will be picking up some dirt. However, it will do if there is no water handy. Wherever you are, see that there is behind you a level stretch free from bushes or such things, for you must expect your back cast to fall too low a few times at first. But after the beginning, I recommend having some fairly high obstructions behind, to guarantee your keeping the back cast up where it should be.

Pull off twenty-five feet or so of line from the reel, not running it through the guides. This should be held in the left hand, either doubled back and forth in the palm or in loose coils; you can figure out later which method you prefer.

"Should be held . . ."—but for the first few times it is better to drop it at one's feet, to simplify things. Of course, be careful not to step on it and ruin it. If it's a good line, it will lie there in large, limp coils, not tangle into corkscrews.

Now—and this is important—relax. Remember, easy does it, and the easier the better. I might not have to give this warning but for the belief held by many that fly casting is difficult. It isn't; if you'll just take things easy enough you should be laying a very fair line within a few minutes—in a small fraction of the time that it took you to learn to cast a plug reasonably well.

Hold the rod with the thumb stretched along the grip on top. Some advise having the thumb curled down around the grip, saying that this helps prevent a tendency to bring the rod back too far on the back cast. It does. But most men like to carry the rod forward mostly by a strong pressure of the thumb, stretched along the grip on top, and that may be regarded as the standard way.

Begin flicking the rod tip back and forth in a short arc straight above your head, letting a little line slip out through your fingers and through the guides on each forward movement. When you have something over twenty feet out, make the same forward movement as before, but let the rod go out some more, and stop. Your line should fall pretty straight out on the water before you.

"Should"—but there isn't a chance in hundreds that it will, this first time. So if the foregoing didn't work right for you, pay no attention to that. Just get some line out there any way you can, and as straight as you can. But not by snapping it hard or using force. Now for the real cast, which is all that matters. Two necessary tips first:

Tip one: Relax! The least stiffening of the arms or body ruins not only fly casting, but any sport or game calling for use of the muscles; it means that the muscles are pulling against each other inside your body, fighting each other. The only muscles that should be tensed are those in actual use, and they only while in use, and no more than is necessary. Have you ever watched a really good boxer dance around lightly on his toes, relaxed all over, saving his strength—but for that fraction of a second when his arm flexes to throw in that terrific punch? He's a good model to keep in mind. And try to be as graceful as possible; the thing done well is always done gracefully.

Tip two: Keep your right elbow hanging practically motionless and almost touching your side, just as in correct plug casting. As in plug casting, a stick or handkerchief held between the arm and the body will keep that elbow down where it belongs, but it may lead to some temporary stiffness—using such a thing is perhaps bad, but it is much better than swinging the whole arm. There should be no frozen rigidity anywhere in the body.

Now, let's cast:

Hold the rod pointing out along the line. If there is much loose line beyond the tip, pull some in with the left hand—the left hand always holds the line, away from the rod, while you cast.

Imagine the rod a clock-hand. With a gentle sweep, raise it to about "ten o'clock," to take up the remaining slack in the line out there. Do not bring it higher now, or there will be no room for the next movement to be done correctly.

Without pausing to let the line slacken again out there,

flip the tip of the rod quickly to a vertical position, straight above your head. No more! You are trying to toss the line straight up, not back behind you. Of course, it doesn't go straight up, but it keeps high, where it belongs; trying to toss it back and high would mean that it would go back and low, probably falling to the ground.

Pause to let the line almost straighten. A few trials, with the line flopping, will show you how long to pause—and nothing else will, so there is no use wasting time on the matter here.

Some, who have read other instructions, may ask why I don't advise the reader to wait, on the back cast, until he feels the pull of the line, as a signal for the forward cast. It's because he won't feel it, at first, and with such a short line; he might as well forget about it.

Now bring the rod forward again, easily, ending with the tip well above the horizontal. Aim your line not at the water but some distance above it; thus you can get a long cast, and not slap the line down on the water—it should straighten well over it, and then fall to the surface.

Theoretically, on the very first cast, the line should have straightened out beautifully in the air and sunk gracefully to the water. But the man who can make it do that the first time is more than human. If it goes out pretty well on the tenth attempt, that is doing well indeed. Keep practicing,, and it will keep on going out more and more nicely, and flopping to the ground less often. In a short time, you'll wonder why you were so clumsy as not to do it right at the first attempt, it seems so easy.

And when you feel that way, you're fly casting—really casting a fly as it should be cast. Now, if you don't forget about form, you'll be improving so rapidly that you'll surprise yourself. A little daily practice for two weeks—there's nothing like daily practice for anything—and you'll be casting a fly far better than some you've seen who've been at it for years but never learned the right way, or never got the right outfits.

That is all, as far as actual instructions go; but, as I did in the chapter on plug casting, I'll add a few remarks which might help things along:

Some anglers hold that the wrist should be perfectly stiff in fly casting. For me, at least, this does not work well; each of my main movements is accompanied by a very short, quick flip of my wrist, and with my thumb, extended along the top of the grip, coming into play on the forward sweep. Indeed, I am inclined to suspect that at least some of the advocates of the stiff wrist really use this little wrist movement unconsciously. None of us know exactly what we do, and it would take a slow-motion picture to show us—and some of us would be due for a surprise on seeing that picture. Perhaps others purposely advise a stiff wrist just to keep the beginner from overdoing the wrist action, and taking the rod tip too far back.

As previously mentioned, the line, of course, doesn't go straight up—not even on a "steeple cast," which is nothing but an exaggerated overhead cast to clear high brush behind. As a matter of fact, if the line keeps somewhat above the horizontal it is doing quite well. Then, with the rod straight up, it can pull the maximum bend in the tip; and this bend shoots the line out again—about the way the casting rod shoots the plug out. If the rod is much behind straight up, this maximum bend can't be pulled in it, and you will be trying to throw with your arm.

In tournament-distance casting, and in a method used by a few fishermen for steelheads in big rivers, the whole arm is used, with a form entirely different from that which I described. This has nothing whatever to do with the beginner; he should learn the standard method first—and only a few will ever want to learn the other, which is very tiring, and can also smash ordinary fly rods with surprising celerity. Really, it should be used only with special tournament-distance rods—which are quite expensive, and have an unbearably harsh feel to most of us for ordinary fishing. Which, of course, isn't saying a word against that method for those who like it for their special purposes.

I should perhaps also warn the reader who has heard of the "left-hand haul," or "double haul," that it goes only with that tournament-distance method of casting, and is also a rod-buster, unless one has the special rod built to stand it.

As I said, when you find the line going out nicely and easily, keep on doing it over and over until it seems childishly simple, which won't take long. Next, as the line goes forward, let some more of it slip through your fingers and out through the guides—only practice, a very little of it, will tell you just when to let it go. That is "shooting the line," and you can shoot more and more of it as you get the knack. But do not, as I warned before, try casting a longer line than you can handle easily and comfortably; if you do, you will start "fighting the rod," forcing it—and perhaps ruin your style forever.

The longer you can refrain from actual fishing, the better, for in the eagerness and excitement of fishing there is danger of forgetting correct form, until you have got it thoroughly set in your system; and there is danger of trying to cast too far. At least, when you do go fishing, remember this warning every second of the time you fish, and consider your casting more important than your fish-taking—it is, for you are forming habits, wrong or right, which you will probably have for life; you are determining whether you will be a good caster or a poor one the rest of your life.

I have heard some advise that the angler should always turn his head and watch his back cast, and then swing his eyes

front again to see his forward cast. This is all right for tournament casters, but I have yet to see an angler use that method
in fishing. And before I'd attempt it myself, I'd have my neck
equipped with alemite fittings, and carry a grease gun in my
pocket for occasional use. However, a beginner may find it
beneficial to turn his head and watch his back cast a few times
at first, and occasionally later on, to check up on what's happening back there. But don't get the habit of doing it.

Try to cast as straight a line as possible; practice will teach
you how more than anything I can say. This straight line is
necessary in wet-fly fishing, to hook your fish. If you get on to
dry-fly work in a current later on, you will learn about "slack
casts" and "hook casts," but they do not concern you now.

Of course, the rod shouldn't travel in the same plane going back and forth, or the line would tangle with it. Instinct
will make you keep the sweeps slightly separated. In a stiff
wind, it is best to bring the line back on the downwind side.
But the novice should not attempt to cast in a stiff wind; it
may lead him to force the rod, to fight it.

If your leader cracks like a whiplash behind you, you
didn't pause long enough, and you've probably whipped off
your fly. Still more haste, and the line comes down in a pile
around your neck. Too long a pause and, naturally, the line
flops to the ground behind; also, your rod tip has lost its tension, so your forward cast will be a complete failure.

If your rod whooshes noisily through the air, you're using
far too much force. In fly casting, you should never resemble a
man angrily whipping a mule.

Find out what length of line you can cast most easily with
your rod—it won't be the shortest. Stick to that for some time,
and only gradually attempt longer distances.

Never shoot line on the back cast, to take tension out of
your rod tip. (This, too, doesn't apply to a certain method

which has nothing to do with the beginner.) Instead, you may often pull in a little line with your left hand as you begin the forward cast, to get more tension in the rod tip. But don't overdo it, or you'll be running into ways of casting different from the standard.

When you change the position of your left hand on the line, clip the line under a finger or two of the right hand, against the grip of the rod, in any manner that comes easy to you.

As in plug casting, this overhead cast is the basic one; all others necessary, with one exception, are but variations of it which will come naturally to a man when he needs them. That one exception is the "roll cast," done when there is no room behind for a back cast. It is quite easy. Merely raise the rod tip high and bring it well back; then wait for the line to sag toward you about all it will. Now make a hard sweep forward and down with the rod, and the line rolls out in a great loop. A little practice and care will teach it faster than any amount of writing about it. The overhead cast is simple enough if one goes about it right, but the roll is still simpler.

As with plug casting, I could describe a dozen or more other casts, and it might look impressive, but nearly all of them will come to a man by themselves as needed. And there are more "trick" casts with the fly rod than with the casting rod, fine to impress novices but good for no other purpose. Such casts remind me of my cowboy days. I spent part of my life riding with some of the best real cowboys in the West, and never met a single one who could spin a rope or roll a cigarette with one hand—both purely showman stuff. One may, of course, be a good showman and also good at the practical end of a game, but the two have little in common.

Some day, when you're casting particularly well, try, just for practice, to keep the line in the air, a fair length of it, going back and forth. Drop it gently to the water in front; pick it up and wave it a few times more.

I'm tricking you, of course. What you were really doing was dry-fly casting, that thing supposed to be 'way over the head of an ordinary man. At least, you were using the main movement in which dry-fly casting differs from wet-fly— drying the line and the fly. Now you are ready to put on a double-taper line and a longer, finer leader, and start attempting slack casts—which, again, aren't nearly as hard as some would make them out to be. You won't be a crack dry-fly man in one season, but you should be able to pick up some fish, dry-fly, first time you try, and you'll be rapidly catching on to finer points of the game.

So, you ask, what is so hard about ordinary fly fishing? Just as I have said—nothing; it's much easier than good plug casting. If you have the right outfit and follow the correct form, which mainly means not letting the rod tip get too far back.

And here I'll tell you a little secret: Most good fly fishermen bring the rod a shade behind "twelve o'clock"—just a shade.* But it's better to try not to go farther back than straight up, or you'll be sure to go too far back and kill your cast, or to find yourself trying to throw a fly with your arm. Anyway, so long as you attempt consciously and painstakingly to throw the line *straight up* into the air, you should be getting along fine.

To save you time discovering it for yourself, I might mention that the more line you are casting, the longer will be the pause on the back cast. A big, bulky fly, and especially bass bugs of some types, will also slow it; you must find out for yourself how much.

* See Plates 9, 10, 11, Photo Section. Note that in Plate 11 the lower part of rod *points only to* "12:30 o'clock."

Nearly all fly fishermen play a smaller fish by stripping in line with the left hand, permitting it to drop on the bottom of the boat or into the water, or coiling it in the left hand. This does not work well with a large fish that makes long runs, and it is better to play one from the reel, to avoid tangles. Which method to use with a fish of any given size is up to you. In this, as in other matters, I am not trying to force my way on you. Beyond the actual cast, there is no set form in which one must do things, and whatever way you find most convenient is the right way for you, though perhaps not for the other fellow.

In working the lure there are two methods. Some double the line back and forth in the left hand; it shoots out nicely again when you open your hand. Perhaps this is the most convenient way when you get used to it, and the one least likely to bring tangles. But most fishermen carry the line in long loops in the left hand, working it in by jiggles and jerks with that hand. Try both and find out which one suits you. You can get exactly the same retrieve by one method as by the other.

When working the lure, always keep the rod tip low. This avoids a long sag in the line, which takes time to straighten in hooking a fish, and may cause a missed strike.

In wet-fly fishing and bass bugging, most fishermen set the hook with a short, quick sweep of the rod tip, which should never be overdone, to break a leader or the rod. If there is a heavy reel balancing the rod in one's hand, this sweep of the tip can be made faster and under better control.

A method which I personally prefer in many cases is to keep the rod so low that it points directly out along the line. Then, working the lure with my left hand, my fingers feel the strike instantly, and jerk backward almost as a reflex action, setting the hook. Since there is no spring of the rod here to take up a shock, one using this method should be very careful to hold the line lightly in the fingers, so that it will slip through them if one jerks back too hard; otherwise there would be a broken leader if the fish is of any size. And the instant the fish is hooked, one must raise the rod to vertical, letting line slip out through the guides to permit that.

In Chapter XX I gave instructions for playing a fish safely on a casting rod, with no possibility of breaking the rod. All that was said there can, with slight and obvious modifications, be applied to playing one on a fly rod.

CHAPTER XXIV

Rebuilding a Split Bamboo Rod

I HAVE a friend who is manager of a large tackle department. Last spring he complained to me that he could not find anybody to put a guide on a fly rod belonging to a good customer of his, a veteran angler. I casually offered to do it, to help out a brother fisherman. My friend looked skeptical, for he knew I was no professional craftsman; but he let me take the rod home, no doubt hoping that the messy, amateurish job I'd do would be better than nothing, and wouldn't damage the rod permanently. This poorly concealed attitude of his touched my vanity—of course I have some vanity; a man who has none is unlikely to do anything well.

A few days later I strolled into the store, and it chanced that the owner of the rod was there talking to the manager; I had not met him before. I showed them a new fly rod that I had with me. They went wild about it. The veteran was green with envy, and he offered me a hundred dollars for it—in a tone that hinted he'd pay more with a little bargaining. Perhaps you can imagine how he felt when I told him it was his own old rod, completely refinished; only then did he recognize the polished-up reel seat, the only thing on the rod not completely changed in appearance.

I've had such things happen before; I've been regarded as

a sort of genius for making a decrepit old rod look actually better than when it was purchased—I can do that, unless it was originally one of the most expensive; then I can only make it look like new. But the plain fact is that so can any other man, and at the first attempt, if he will only take a little care. There's nothing whatever to it, nothing except the fear most men have of tackling the job, thinking it calls for great skill.

Or that it calls for too much time. It doesn't; and there's no need to work long at a stretch on it—odd moments will soon get it done. The middle of winter, with long nights and the weather fit for nothing else, is the right time for it—and that lets the varnish get very hard, and the sections straighten perfectly when hung up, before it will be used. Here's how to go about it:

It's the winding that most men fear, goodness knows why. So before beginning on the rod, it is well to practice making winds, partly to gain confidence. And when a man has made three or four good practice windings, wild horses could hardly stop him from stripping his rod down and refinishing it.

I'll speak only of fly rods here, but obviously exactly the same methods are applicable to a bamboo casting rod.

First for materials. Get the following:

A *hexagonal lead pencil.* Have one of light-colored wood, or scrape the finish from a dark one. This, for practicing on, will look like a piece of bamboo rod, and so will show the final appearance of the winds.

A *spool or two of oo rod-winding silk or nylon.* Get this a trifle lighter in shade than you want the finished windings to be; even with color preservative, it will darken a little and look richer.

Another *spool of oo silk or nylon.* This to be of whatever color you have decided to use for the narrow trimming at the ends of the winds. Black trim looks best with most winds.

A bottle of color preservative. Without it, the varnish will darken your silk too much. If this is hard to obtain, clear nail polish is about the same thing—a celluloid lacquer—and has the advantage of having a little brush kept right in the bottle, so that it won't have to be cleaned with special lacquer thinner each time it is used. If you do use regular preservative, get thinner too—or acetone.

A small bottle of rod varnish. Do not use ordinary varnish; it's no good whatever for the purpose. Slow-drying spar varnish will do quite well—so far as I know, rod varnish is no more than a spar varnish of the very best quality.

A varnish brush. A little round five- or ten-cent one with soft hair, no bigger than a kitchen match, will do as well as any.

Emery cloth or paper. Just a small piece, very fine.

A reading glass. I know a man of ninety-four who winds rods perfectly without a magnifier, or even eyeglasses. But oo silk is pretty fine, and most of us find a magnifier of some sort necessary for a good job. A cheap reading glass, which can be had at a dime store or from a mail-order house, will do nicely. Some crude stand can be devised to hold it in place while working behind it.

Ferrule cement. This only if there is a loose ferrule.

Scotch tape. A small roll from the dime store.

All these things should cost no more than a dollar or so. Having got them together, we're ready for work. But first break off six or eight inches of silk, double it to form a small loop, and lay it where it will be handy; you'll soon see what it is for.

I will not confuse the reader with instructions about which hand to hold the rod in, and which the spool of thread, and just what to do with each finger. All that makes no difference; you'll soon hit on a convenient way.

Begin by laying the end of the silk along the pencil, and winding over it four or five times to hold it. Then tighten, seeing to it that the coils lie close together, and cut off the end near the last coil you've made (A, Fig. 1). Now continue winding for about the length of a wind on a guide. This is done by twirling the pencil, for of course when winding the middle of a rod section one cannot pass the spool around it— which would be too slow anyhow. Keep the incoming thread on top, with the spool away from you.

Do not have the spool straight out from where the thread comes on; keep it a little back over the part already wound and that will make the coils lie tightly against each other but without overlapping (B, Fig. 1). Keep a fair tension on the thread all the time, but there's no need to risk breaking it; it will be plenty tight without that. The tension can be kept more even by holding the spool a few inches from the rod, for the slight elasticity of the thread helps in this respect. It may be advisable, every few turns, to press the coil a little closer together with the thumb nail, doing it evenly all the way around.

If the thread should accidentally break when a long winding is nearly completed, it is not necessary to unwind all that's done. Merely undo four or five coils and wind over the end, as you began at first, seeing that the two ends do not come out together, to make a slight hump. This may sound sloppy, but actually the result can hardly be noticed on the finished wind.

The "whip finish" at the end of a wind is easy toc Reach for that little piece of doubled silk you'd laid by, and place it along the rod (A, D, Fig. 2). Continue winding for four or five turns, over it (B, Fig. 2). Then cut the thread you are winding with; pass the end (C) through the loop (A), and draw under the coils by pulling the ends (D). Tighten all up, using the thumbnail to smooth the last coil, and cut the thread close where it comes out.

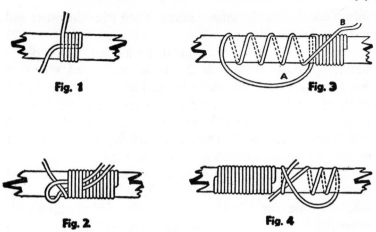

Fig. 1

Fig. 3

Fig. 2

Fig. 4

Rod Winding

In pulling a loop through, press it against the wood with a finger, so it won't twist and possibly break.

Some hold that this method of winding over a double thread, which is afterwards removed, leaves the last coils too loose. I do not find that so, especially since the color preservative or varnish tightens things up. However, I show another method of finishing, in Fig. 3, which avoids this. The loop, A, is shown short to have space; it should be much longer. Keep winding with it over the end, B, until a single long coil is left; then pull this through.

Now for the narrow trim at each end, which adds so greatly to the appearance of the windings:

Usually only three to five turns are used for this, so it is necessary for both ends to go all the way under. Make the same wind as for the second whip finish which I described, except that both ends are wound under all the coils. After tightening and cutting off the ends, press it neatly with the thumbnail into place against the long winding. Then trim the other end in the same way.

There is no reason why this first wind made on a pencil should not come out perfect, if a little care is used, though it will take more time than one will need after getting the knack of the thing. If it didn't come out perfect, try again. Anyway, three or four practice winds, before tackling the rod, will give you confidence. There's another reason for making the first winds on a pencil: to see how they look when varnished.

Now the color preservative is put on. Use several good coats, letting each one dry well, which takes only a short time —but be sure the last is completely dry before varnishing, otherwise it will soften the varnish. Remember, varnish can be used over dry lacquer, but lacquer cannot be used over any varnish, for it would ruin it.

Next, varnish the wind. The simplest way is to work a very little varnish on with a thumb and forefinger; this saves cleaning brushes. If the winding shows dark blotches when it dries, it means that you have made the beginner's common mistake of not using enough lacquer. Later, if you find this blotching on a rod wind, remove that wind and start it over— don't leave it looking messy.

My long and careful description of this winding process perhaps makes it sound difficult. It isn't; hardly more so than tying a necktie. A perfect wind—better than is usually done in a factory—can soon be made in less time than it took to read this.

And now we're ready for the rod. First, measure carefully the exact distance of each guide from the bottom of its section. Write the figures down and don't lose them, for they are very important; they will let you get the guides back exactly in their right places.

Sometimes black marks will be found where the feet of

the guides had stood. These marks show careless workmanship —that some bamboo was left exposed where water got at it. But if they're there, they may be used in replacing the guides, and measuring will be unnecessary.

Take off the guides, by cutting the threads at one end and unwinding them—and, of course, avoid scarring the bamboo. There is no need to keep track of which guide came from where; the largest goes toward the butt, and they gradually decrease in size.

Use your varnish remover on all the bamboo, following the instructions on the bottle; and be sure that every trace of old varnish is off, even if it calls for several coats of the remover. Then take the sections outdoors, where there is no danger of fire, and give them a thorough cleaning with plenty of gasoline and a rag. If a trace of remover is left, the new varnish won't stick permanently.

Are all the ferrules tight? If not, use your stick of ferrule cement—and never pay any attention to the man with some concoction of his own which he says is better. Remove each loose ferrule and place a little melted cement under it, then heat the ferrule and put it back on. An alcohol lamp is best for this, since it leaves no black stain on the metal; a match does, and it's hard to get off. But how many have alcohol lamps? My own method is to heat the ferrule a foot or so over a cook stove as I put it on. By using no more heat than the hands can bear, the rod won't be damaged. Be especially careful not to get a varnished rod too hot, to blister the varnish.

Is the rod straight? Heating it gently in the same way, and bending it with the hands, will help take out kinks. However, I'm suspicious of this method—perhaps unreasonably so—and use it only as a last resort; I prefer to hang the sections up for some time, with weights on them. I leave some of mine hanging thus all during the off season for fishing; and when that much time is given, weights are not generally needed. But do not tie the string by which you hang them to the ferrules; the steady tension, and the heat of a warm room, will finally pull the ferrules loose unless they are pinned. Tie it immediately below the metal.

It might be well to mention here that many men are entirely too concerned over slight sets in their rods. They do little or no harm, and the fact is that one practically never sees a rod which has been used even a few days that does not have some set in it. Still it is just as well to straighten the rod during the winter, if hanging sections by the ends will do it. Then, the set will have to begin all over next season, instead of growing greater.

Even on good rods, we still occasionally find one with a pin through the ferrule and the bamboo. Examine the rod carefully for this—it is sometimes not easy to see—and if there are pins, drive them partly out with a small nail or something of the sort, being very careful not to batter the ferrules; drive a short way, then pull them out with pliers. And leave the pins out; if the ferrules are not tight enough without them, they're not tight enough with them. Where the pin goes through but one side, drive it into the wood.

Before cementing the ferrule back on, wrap it to its open end, and the bamboo to exactly where it enters, with a little scotch tape. That will prevent smearing cement where it doesn't belong—and some cement will squirt out as the ferrule is shoved into place. The tape is easily removed; hardened cement isn't. Should some stickum from the scotch tape be left on the ferrule from the heating, it can be removed with gasoline and a rag.

If there's any old varnish on the guides—and there probably will be—soak it off with varnish remover. Clean the hand guide, or butt guide, with silver polish and a nail brush; or a good scrubbing with soap and water will likely be enough. And make sure that all varnish remover and polish are washed from the guides, either with gasoline or soap and water.

For a neat wind, see to it that the ends of the guide feet are thin, sharp edges; if they're not, make them that way with a stone—an ordinary file will not cut a hard guide. The beveled edge should be on top, the bottoms flat, not touched. Then, no break or ugly hump in the silk coils will appear at the beginning of the feet when the winding is done. The feet should lie flat on the rod, but if they are not perfectly so, it is of no great consequence. Do not try to bend good guides into shape, for they are very brittle and will likely break—they are not the common wire they look like.

We must decide whether to put the guides back in their original positions, or on the opposite side of the rod. The second method will help straighten any set in the tip, when one comes to use it again. But the six sections of bamboo are never exactly alike, and there is a correct side on which the guides are placed, if the rod was carefully made. If you want them back there, when you take them off make a mark on that strip, where it will later be hidden by a winding. However, so far as I can see, the benefits of having them on any certain side are, on many rods, more theoretical than real. Of course, the hand guide will have to go back in its old place on the butt section, because of the reel seat; and on a two-piece fly rod there will also be one or two snake guides there.

It would be wise, before proceeding further, to joint up the rod, with all sections in the same position in which you mean to use them, and to sight along it. Sometimes, especially on a cheaper rod, you will find that it is necessary to turn a section another way, or even to heat a ferrule and turn that, to have the rod as straight as possible. If the rod looks straightest with the ferrules in any certain position, mark the strips accordingly for the guides. Now we are ready for the winding and varnishing.

Lay the hand guide in its place, and wrap one leg (keeper, technically) with scotch tape to hold it while the other is being wound. Or if you wish, stick it on with plenty of quick-drying cement—"airplane glue." Color preservative applied later over this cannot harm it, for it is exactly the same stuff, only thicker.

Make the wind as you did your practice wind on the pencil. It should begin on the bamboo only, a little way before the sharp end of the guide. When you come to the guide, the thread may show an inclination to lie unevenly. If so, make several turns up out of place on the metal, letting the beginning of the foot show through; then, pulling the thread, press them gently into position with the thumbnail. Keep on until the winds are beginning to climb well up the slope, and then make your whip finish.

Remove the scotch tape and wind the other leg of the guide. Keep both windings of the same length; it's best to measure them. Then put on all the other guides in the same way. Sometimes guide windings decrease very gradually in length from butt to tip, to match the smaller guides and smaller rod diameter. Very long guide windings never look well.

Trim each winding as soon as it is made. A narrow trim should go at each end of every winding, no matter how short, but for some exceptions which I shall make. The first of these are the ends of a pair of guide windings which are toward each other. Each pair is supposed to represent a single winding divided in two; hence, no trim—a rod looks best when done that way.

Give the winding its first coat or two of color preservative.

This will prevent its becoming soiled, loosened or roughened as one works elsewhere on the section.

If the tip-top (top guide) was removed, only chance could get it back correctly before the other guides on the top section are in place. Now, with the snake guides on this top section, sight through them and turn the tip-top until it lines up—of course, heating it slightly to loosen the cement.

Next come the windings at the ferrules. If the ends of the ferrules are straight tubes, wind up to, but not onto, them.

Good rods have split ferrules, brought down to knife edges; this is because a stiff rim causes too sharp a bend in using the rod, increasing danger of breaking it. If a single winding is used here, the serrations will show through after varnishing and look very bad. Cover the slits with a preliminary winding, with two or three coils on the wood to avoid more step-down than is necessary in the final long winding over it. Make this first winding carefully, for flaws in it would show through the other.

Even with split ferrules, the bamboo has a sharper bend at the end of the metal than elsewhere. So we are always advised to keep the silk winding on the metal only; this because the winds and varnish will eventually break there, which looks unsightly. Nevertheless, my own practice, and the one which I strongly recommend, is contrary to this: I always wind down onto the wood for some distance—rather, I wind from the wood up onto the metal, for it is much easier to do a neat job going up a step than going down.

I have a purpose in thus opposing custom: Even plain varnish may crack there in time, and this crack probably will not be noticed if at the edge of a winding; therefore water will be getting in to the bamboo and weakening it, leading eventually to a broken rod. When I wind well over the wood, a crack in the winding is plainly seen; it is a warning to rewind immediately before damage is done—and that single winding is a negligible job for a man who has wound a whole rod and knows how simple it is. Be sure to save some of the thread, for such repairs; you might have difficulty matching it later.

A tip here: Such a repair may be needed during fishing season, on a rod in daily use. Then, it is only necessary to let the first coat of varnish get reasonably firm before taking the rod out, and the others can be added a day or two apart, using the rod all the time. Really, this airing, and the alternate wetting and drying, leads to a more durable finish than usual.

Before putting color preservative on a wind next to a ferrule, or a tip-top, or a winding check at the grip, wrap scotch tape on the metal exactly to where the winding ends. This avoids smearing preservative or varnish on the metal, where it would look bad—the procedure is, of course, nothing but the masking process used by car painters and such, to keep paint where it belongs.

Now for the windings that are purely ornamental. The first of these goes down against the grip, and is usually fairly long. Sometimes it covers the metal winding check and lies right against the cork grip—this looks especially well on a very light rod. And I think any wind here appears best when the lower part is left untrimmed.

The fly ring is put in this lowest winding. It is always a ring-and-keeper guide. (It is from this ancient and inefficient form of guide, long ago used the full length of a rod, that the feet of a modern guide are still generally, and inappropriately, called "keepers.")

One leg of this is wound on like that of a snake guide. Then a few turns must be worked in beneath the other foot and pressed into place, to fill the gap, after which winding is continued along the other foot and onto the wood. Since we have a step-down from this second foot, it should be extremely sharp and perfectly flat on the strip. Another way is first to make a short wind the length of the gap, and then wind toward it from both ends as on a regular guide; thus, there is no step-down, and smoothness is assured.

Personally, I dislike the ring-and-keeper for my fly, for it must be pried up with a fingernail to insert the hook—that, or scratch the varnish digging with the hook point. I prefer a small stand-up guide, which is like a snake guide except that the high part forms a solid ring. These are not easy to find, but one can soon be made from the hard brass of a safety pin, flattening the feet with a hammer and filing them sharp on top.

From the foregoing it will be seen that my methods are strictly home-tinkerer and non-professional. Therefore they should just suit the average fisherman. But these methods produce results as good as the best.

In case you didn't notice, in taking it off, where the fly ring came from, the usual place is on the left side, on the strip next to the bottom one, with the reel down.

There is generally another ornamental wind, of a quarter inch or more, about halfway between the grip and the hand guide; with, usually, a much narrower wind about its own width from it on each side—all three trimmed. Often three winds about like these are put on a little distance above the winding next to the grip.

Sometimes a short ornamental winding is used against the tip-top; sometimes not. I think it looks well if it is short enough, but a long one appears top-heavy and clumsy here. And I prefer it untrimmed on the upper end. If one is made here, it should never go up onto the metal.

All this matter of ornamentation is, of course, up to the man who is doing the job; he can copy some rod he likes, or use his own taste. It is well, however, to warn that an effect of plain elegance is far and away better than trying to pretty the rod up too much. Dragging in a third color, putting on too many ornamental windings, or the least sign of gaudiness, gives a dollar-ninety-eight effect.

If there were narrow windings all along the rod, be glad to have this chance to get rid of them. They, too, are nowadays in the dollar-ninety-eight class. They add nothing to the strength of the rod. If it was well made in the first place, it will hold together just as well without them; and if it wasn't, they won't materially delay its going bad.

For the benefit of those who have heard somebody sing the praises of a solid-wound rod, I'll put in a few words: Long ago, when I was a lot younger and piscatorially greener than I am now, I solid-wound a nine-foot fly rod with very fine silk. I spent evening after evening working tediously on the thing, and I used silk enough to reach from here to the moon—almost. When the last coat of varnish was dry, I proudly took the thing fishing.

Alas! Only half a dozen casts, and I trudged home with hanging head, to pull that swathing off. The rod, formerly a dandy, had all the lovely snap and action of a green willow switch; it was dead as a door nail. But on the other hand, if I had never solid-wound a rod I could not tell the reader, positively and from my own experience, how it works out—and I have a definite dread of peddling second-hand information without at least testing it thoroughly to be sure it's correct; so often it isn't, no matter how long or how frequently it has been repeated.

To get back to the matter at hand—now we give all the windings their final coats of color preservative. And I repeat, be sure there is enough of it on so that varnish can't get through to stain the silk and call for a rewind job.

Some prefer to varnish directly on the silk, without using

any preservative. Unquestionably this makes a more durable finish, for no color preservative will stand up as well as good varnish; but it limits one's selection of colors. Plain black winds are usually the preference of men who use this method; they are often used without trim. This makes a very dignified finish, one found mostly on better-class rods. However, a rod wound in black does not look quite as light and airy as one with more delicate tints.

This method can also be used by getting winding silk of some very pale pastel color, and letting the varnish darken it. There is no way of telling how such a shade will turn out without wrapping it on a pencil or stick and varnishing it, then letting the varnish dry—and it's well to use as many coats of varnish as you mean to use on the finished rod, since each additional coat obscures the color just a trifle. One of these pastels can be used, too, for trimming black windings—but I think the plain black looks best.

Still another method is to use white silk, and varnish directly over it. It then becomes transparent, hardly noticeable on the bamboo, and with the guide feet showing plainly through almost as though standing unattached to the wood. I rewound a rod thus last summer, but I heard so many remarks about "that ugly thing!" that I rewound it all over in another color—that's how little it takes to make a man rewind a rod once he finds how easy it is. And I'm not sure but that I agreed in the matter; the oiled-silk effect didn't look right to me—it seemed clumsy, somehow.

Now comes the varnishing. This may sound like the easiest part, but it is just where one is most likely to make a mess of one's rod—a badly varnished rod does look like the very devil, no matter how neatly the windings may have been done.

Originally, all rods except the more expensive ones are varnished by dipping. That is by far the fastest and cheapest.

way when production costs must be considered; it makes a good enough finish, but by no means the richest-looking or the most durable.

Fortunately, the very best way is also the simplest, and one that calls for no previous experience in painting. The usual mistake is to use a brush, which leaves streaks and waves; it is almost impossible for anybody but an expert professional painter to varnish a hexagonal rod properly with a brush.

The right way? No, not an air brush, which few would have anyway. Just take a little varnish between thumb and finger and rub it quickly the length of each section, using barely enough so that you can see it looking wet and shiny when one end of the section is held toward the light—to make sure you're covering all of it.

A little brush is, however, necessary to work under the guides. Put the varnish on as thinly as possible with it. With one exception: if some of the legs stand up from the bamboo, work plenty of it in under them. These little gobs of varnish in there may take months to dry hard, but that doesn't matter, for the outside surface will form a skin to hold the rest in until it does dry. And when this is done there is no danger of those black marks from the guide feet which I mentioned; there is no water being trapped in there to rust the guide and rot small patches of bamboo. The brush work under the guides should be done before the rest of the section, so that any surplus varnish will be spread the length of the stick.

Good varnishing must be done in a warm room, one of not less than seventy degrees, and preferably warmer. The bottle of varnish, too, should be of that temperature, and not just brought in out of the cold. The less dust flying around, the better, for each tiny speck of it leaves a noticeable little bump on the varnish. The thinner the coats, the harder they become. Five or six of these very light coats are necessary for a good job.

At least twenty-four hours is necessary for each coat to dry before the next is put on, and still longer is better; when I am in no hurry for a rod, I like to give each coat several days, to get very hard, before applying the next. No varnish that will dry in less than twenty-four hours is suitable for a fishing rod.

After the second or third coat, and again before the final one is applied, rub the varnish down, to remove any dust bumps or other blemishes—a little touch after each coat is still better. I do this with a piece of very fine emery cloth or emery paper held over the tip of my index finger; I do not use a small sanding block because the strips are somewhat rounded, and my finger conforms to their shape. I rub the sides mainly, for it takes very little to rub through the varnish on the corners. Probably this is not professional; perhaps I should use rotten-stone or pumice—but I get a good finish.

Never attempt to rub a coat of varnish that is not completely dry and hard, or it will roll and be ruined, so you may have to take off all the varnish and start over, perhaps having to do your winds all over too. Do not rub down the last coat. On a trout rod, however, I sometimes dull this final coat with pumice, so that it cannot flash in the sun to scare fish. That way it is a somewhat more efficient trout-getter, but it is far from as good-looking as when left shiny.

If you have accidentally got some varnish on the guides, where the line can touch it, it has to come off. This is most easily done with varnish remover, but be extremely careful not to get any of it elsewhere, to ruin the finish. It might be safer to scrape it off gently. Hardened varnish on guides not only hampers shooting the line, but it can damage it.

Where no color preservative is to be used, it is well to give the sticks a couple of coats of varnish before winding is begun. Then you know that you have left no exposed wood under the guide feet. But do not be tempted to try putting preservative on windings and keeping it away from varnish underneath; it can't be done—and it will ruin the varnish.

Nothing is left now but to furbish up the grip and the reel seat. If the metal parts down there are shiny, not oxidized, good silver polish is the thing—use nothing coarser. This—with a drop of oil rubbed in after it—will also make plastic look like new. Remember always to rub back and forth, one way, to get a good result. A wood reel seat should, naturally, be sanded down and revarnished; this can conveniently be done while you are varnishing the rest of the butt section.

Scrub the cork grip thoroughly with soap, warm water and a stiff brush. Then rub it down with fine sandpaper—using a somewhat coarser grade first if it is in bad shape.

Now there are two things that it is imperative for you to do: First, stand the rod against a wall, and get back a few feet and admire it; it's as it looked when new, or perhaps prettier. But the man who wouldn't do that without my telling him to isn't suited to be a fisherman. Next, you leave it in the living room for several days—as if it just happened to be forgotten there when you finished work on it—so you can sort of casually pick it up and show it to any friend who comes in. Yes, you did it all by yourself—sure, those windings and all. No, they're not enamel or colored cellophane, to look so even. There's nothing to it—it's easy when you know how!

Do I do that? I do. I'm not pretending to be any different from the rest of the fishermen tribe. But I'm philosopher enough to believe that there's nobody quite so big a fool as the man who's too sensible.

CHAPTER XXV

Hooks

WHAT really catches your fish? The hook! It is the sole completely indispensable part of an angler's equipment; with patience enough, one could unquestionably catch fish with a baited hook held under water in the fingers—but the hook must be there.

Hooks vary tremendously in efficiency, in the number of fish that one can catch with them. Still, the average angler will spend days, perhaps months, debating with himself what rod, reel or line to buy; and then, as a vague afterthought, "Oh—give me some hooks," with hardly a glance at what is handed to him.

I feel safe in saying that most anglers could double their catches, with no more time spent fishing, if they would use proper hooks. This is because wrongly shaped hooks, poor hooks, dull hooks, will easily cause a man to miss half or more of the striking fish that he should land.

Furthermore, he is misled by the fact that hooks of some of the most highly touted shapes, and therefore the most popular, are the worst possible, the least efficient—but his best friend hasn't told him. I shall try here to set him straight in this matter, to tell him what is a good hook. This though I'm afraid that I shall be treading on the toes of some hook makers—but they can make properly shaped hooks as easily as poor

273

ones if anglers demand them. It would be hard, though, on their publicity agents, who'd have nothing distinctive (though silly) to sing praises of.

SIZE NUMBER	WIRE DIAMETER IN 1000 THS. INCH
5/0	.051
4/0	.049
3/0	.047
2/0	.045
1/0	.043
1/2	.041
1	.039
2	.037
4	.033
6	.030
8	.027
10	.024
12	.021
14	.018
16	.016
18	.014
20	.012
22	.010

Size	Length
5/0	2 INCHES
4/0	1⅞ "
3/0	1¾ "
2/0	1⅝ "
1/0	1½ "
1½	1⅜ "
1	1¼ "
2	1⅛ "
4	¹⁵/₁₆THS"
6	¹³/₁₆ "
8	¹¹/₁₆ "
10	⁹/₁₆ "
12	⁷/₁₆ "
14	¹¹/₃₂NDS"
16	⁹/₃₂ "
18	⁷/₃₂ "
20	⁵/₃₂ "
22	³/₃₂ "

HOOK MEASURING CHART

HOOK WIRE SIZES

I should begin by saying that I am here, as elsewhere, but expressing my own opinions—and bluntly—for what they may be worth. At least they are opinions founded on more years of fishing than I care to think of, and on the catching of many thousands of fish. Still, it is almost never possible for an angling writer to say definitely, "This is so!" and prove that he is right, as though he were speaking of an algebraic equation.

Generally, any writing on fishing bourgeons with perplexities for its author, and no matter how conscientiously written it may strike the reader as in spots vague, possibly even evasive. Let us see why, so that I may not be unduly blamed when I cannot be minutely specific:

Nobody, least of all Massenet himself, could tell us how to put notes together so that they would result in another composition as beautiful as his *Élégie des Érinnyes*. Nobody can even explain why I like it so well, though it would only bore some others—for instance, the man who said that he could never tell *God Save the Weasel* from *Pop Goes the King*.

But in rifle shooting, everything can be reduced to precise figures—powder load, breech pressure, twist of rifling desirable, and all such. How fast a given bullet, at a given velocity, will drop in each hundred yards is mathematically demonstrable; I could quickly figure it out myself, after some hard thinking to recall the formula.

The difference lies in the fact that music, like painting, is an art; rifle shooting is purely a science. A science can be explained down to the last tiny detail. Art cannot, and any writing concerning it must necessarily be little more than saying, "This is my personal opinion, right or wrong—and even if I'm right there will be exceptions."

Fishing is an art, and therein lies a wide world of difference between it and shooting. The angling writer is too often trying to explain intangible, indefinite things; therefore rarely, if he is honest, can he make a statement without admitting, overtly or tacitly, that there is room for disagreement.

But remember that even the violinist—and to me violin playing is the highest art—must spend weary hours studying mechanical details of his playing if he is to be good; the painter must learn his pigments. And the fisherman, if he is to be really good at it, must learn the mechanics of the tackle he uses. These things might be called the basic strata of science which underlie all arts.

Having said all this, as a repeated warning to the reader that I make no pretence to piscatorial omniscience, I should add the following, that he may judge how much importance

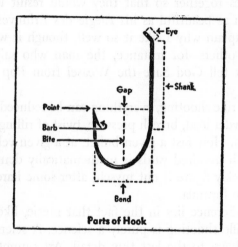

Parts of Hook

he may well place in what I am going to say here: When I first published these remarks on hooks, in a magazine, I was surprised to receive a letter from an official of the largest hook company in the country, saying that it was the soundest article on hooks that he had ever seen, and that he entirely agreed with all I said. Therefore these things may be considered as his opinions too.

Before beginning our analysis, it is well to explain some of the mysterious letters and figures which one may find on a box of hooks. Most of the symbols which I give are those sanctioned by the National Association of Angling and Casting Clubs, but there are some on which the Association does not seem to have made a decision.

FINISHES

Japanned—Hook covered with black enamel.

Bright—Polished hook covered with clear lacquer.

Chromium, Tinned, Cadmium, Etc.—Type of plating used on hook.

RP—Rust proof.

POINTS

Sp—Spear point. Inside of barb flat, not hollow ground.

Filed Point—Same as Sp.

N—Needle point. A special point put on with a machine like that used in making needles. Very good.

Sup—Superior grade. Point not hand filed.

HP—Hollow point. Point hand filed—maybe! If properly made, this is the best point for about all fresh-water fishing.

Rolled in Point, sometimes *RIP*—Point curved in toward shank. As will be seen, I would give my own translation of those initials as *Requiescat in pace*.

Out Point—Point (or sometimes front of bend) directed away from shank.

EYES

BE—Ball eye. Wire at eye same size as shank, and directly in line with it.

TE or *T*—Tapered eye. Wire thinner at eye than elsewhere. (This is used almost solely for dry flies.)

SE or *R*—Straight or ringed eye. Eye straight in line with shank. Unlike BE, wire of eye may occasionally be of smaller diameter than shank, but often these three terms are used indiscriminately.

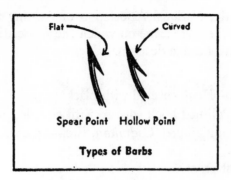

Flat — Curved

Spear Point   Hollow Point

Types of Barbs

TDE—Turned down eye. Eye bent slightly in direction of barb.

TUE—Turned up eye. Eye bent away from direction of barb.

LE—Looped eye. End of wire from eye, generally thinned a good deal, brought back down alongside shank.

SHANKS

Reg—Shank of regular length.

SS—Short shank. (See X.)

LS—Long shank. (See X.)

Sliced shank—Barbs on shank to hold soft live bait.

Humped shank—Hump bent into shank, to keep such lures as cork-bodied bass bugs from turning on hook.

Marked shank—No eye, but corrugations on shank to help hold gut wound on with silk or such. These rarely seen now, since snelled flies are about out of date.

X

The letter X means nothing by itself. It may refer either to the size wire used or to proportional length of shank, as follows:

X *Long*—A 4X Long hook, for instance (sometimes marked 4XL or 4XLS), is of a length that would be standard for one with a bend (and wire, unless otherwise specified) four sizes larger.

X *Short*—18-2XS (18-2XSS) does not mean, "One ate to excess." It means a length that would be regular for a hook two sizes smaller—a No. 20.

X *Fine*—In a 1X Fine (1XF), the wire is of a thickness commonly used for one a size smaller, and so on. Thus a No. 8-2XF will be of wire that would be regular for a No. 10.

X *Stout*—The opposite of X Fine. A 1/0-3X Stout (sometimes 1/0-3XSt) will have wire of standard thickness for a 3/0 Reg.

Miscellaneous

Oval—Hook made from oval wire, not from round.

Forged—Hook flattened along the sides, as on a properly made O'Shaughnessy.

Snood—A short loop of gut wound to a marked shank, to serve as an eye.

Rev—Reversed. Barb and part of bend twisted to one side, not parallel to the shank. Properly speaking, if twisted to the right it is reversed or snecked; if to the left, kirbed; but these terms are often interchanged. Do not confuse "snecked" and "kirbed" with "Sneck" and "Kirby," which denote specific types of bends—a hook of any shape may be snecked or kirbed.

Slight variations from these markings will cause no confusion.

In using the scale of regular hook sizes, always remember that the eye is not measured. To permit clearer figures, I show only even sizes for the smaller hooks; odd sizes come half way between the lines.

Unfortunately, some makers still insist on using irregular size numbering, the meaning of which is known only to themselves. So when buying hooks of a brand with which you are not familiar, it is well to measure them.

No. 22 is the smallest hook regularly made, and it is very difficult to obtain—a glance at the tiny space it would occupy on the chart will show why. A 5/0 is the largest commonly used in North American fresh-water fishing; it is occasionally used for muskellunge, large lake trout, and such.

There is great variation in the naming of bends; for instance, one maker's Limerick may be almost identical with another's Sproat. So great confusion exists in this that it would be pointless for me to describe or illustrate hooks called by different names. When you have finished this chapter, you can tell at a glance the shape hook you want, and what you wish to avoid; you will know which design is fundamentally sound, and which the creation of a publicity agent rather than of a fisherman.

Now, what shape is best—what will hook and land most fish for you?

Nearly all commercial fishermen—to whom efficient hooks are a matter of their bread and butter—and most veteran anglers hold that the most efficient hook is one with a plain round bend, such as the Model Perfect. But this has the least attractive appearance of any hook made; no living artist would give its shape as his ideal "curve of beauty." Not being pretty, it will probably never be a favorite of sportsmen; indeed, it is usually difficult to obtain hooks of this shape. However, the difference in hooking efficiency between this and some more easily obtainable is so slight that it is scarcely worth while to spend much time hunting those with perfectly round bends. But remember that the more nearly round the bend is, the better.

The Sneck, easily recognized by its square bend, was once extremely popular among live-bait fishermen, but it has come to be recognized as very poor, so it seems to be passing out of the picture. Just two of its faults are that it usually has a too-short bite and too-wide gap.

Perhaps the most popular hook at present is the Limerick, known, as usually made, by the rear part of the bend being greatly flattened, and the part running down from the barb being straight. It has quite graceful lines which appeal to the angler's eye. Among its several faults is the fact that often, when a fish takes it lightly in his lips, one jaw, pressing against that flat rear of the bend, will change the angle of the point to his other jaw so that it cannot penetrate easily. While it is much superior to some hooks of other types that are sold, more and more anglers are coming to realize that it is over-rated, that it should not be classed among the most efficient hooks.

Some hooks which have recently appeared on the market have far too narrow a gap. The front part of the bend is generally parallel to the shank, but far too close to it, giving an unnecessarily deep bite. A glance should show the inefficiency of such a hook, so there is no need to say more about it.

Is the straight or reversed (snecked—kirbed) bend the better? Those favoring the reversed say to place a hook of that type in a closed book and try to pull it out without its penetrating the paper. They hold that the same principle holds good when a fish takes a hook flat between his jaws.

The straight-bend advocate replies that the pull is always inefficiently sidewise against a reversed point. Also, that the straight one may be jerked out only on the rare occasions when one pulls from directly in front of and on a level with the fish —and to do it fairly consistently, even then, the inside of the fish's mouth would have to be as flat on each side as those pages of the book, which of course it isn't. A pull from on top, behind or one side—as most pulls do come, of course—will, they insist, instantly tip the point so that it cannot help but penetrate. This sounds like good logic to me.

Sifted out, the fact is that a very large majority of veteran users of artificial lures, fly or plug, much prefer the straight bend and use it exclusively. Many users of live bait seem to like the reversed; but the users of live bait are almost never as advanced anglers as those who stick to artificial, nor do they study the fine points of the game—with their cruder method of fishing, they don't have to. Also, when the live-bait user strikes, the hook is usually far down in the fish's gullet, so it stands a good chance of hanging on something or other on its long way out, even if it is a poor one.

Still, it is worth while to mention that a very few skillful users of flies (but almost never plug casters) consider a reversed bend the better. Oddly, I have found these reversed-bend men confined almost entirely to certain districts of the West. But it would be hard to convince most of us that these strong, silent fish of the West bite differently from others.

As one may gather from the foregoing, I invariably use straight-bend hooks, for I regard them as much superior to reversed. Indeed, the only experienced men whom I have seen, in any numbers, using reversed bends were professional eel-fishermen of Europe; they told me that their reason for doing so was that the reverse facilitates quick removal of a hook from one of these strong-jawed creatures while pulling in a set-line, before the others could twist themselves up with things in general—and then a razor-sharp knife is always kept at hand to cut the hook off if it does not come loose instantly; it is left for the fishmonger to remove. All of which has, of course, nothing to do with the sport-fishing which we are discussing, nor with commercial fishing of more usual types.

Most anglers seem to prefer a hook with the front of the bend, including the barb, about parallel to the shank. As the diagrams show, the angle here greatly influences the direction in which the point is pulled when one attempts to set the hook. For all North American fresh-water fishing, I much prefer a slight out-point. The term "out-point" is used both for a rolled-out point and for a hook the front bend of which has been turned out a trifle. I personally prefer the latter. Since hooks can rarely be purchased that way, I shape my own by a light pressure with a pliers on the front of the bend; all but the most highly tempered can stand this small reshaping.

There can be little question but that a hook shaped thus begins to penetrate more readily than any other. It will, however, be somewhat more difficult to make it keep penetrating —but once it has got that imperative start a series of jerks and jiggles will work it all the way in. Theoretically, a hook shaped thus is more easily broken at the front of the bend, but in fishing I practically never break one. Of course the story might be different if on the strike I should try, as some do, to toss the fish clear over the moon. I seem rarely to fail to hook a fish because of this slight out-point—and very frequently a hook of another type would not get that necessary little start; it would be another missed strike.

A glance at one of the diagrams will show that the tendency of an out-point is to penetrate deeply. But remember, if you change your hooks thus, that this outward deviation should be very *slight*. Bend it out a trifle more, and you have a hook that will probably break or straighten before the barb is driven home, even though you strike with reasonable force.

It might be argued that an out-point can be thrown more easily, by a leaping fish, than one of another type, because the bend is not curved so much around its grip as some others would be. The greater penetration makes up for that; it is

far more likely that his struggles will tear the hook through
a shallow grip on his jaw. In actual practice, I find that I lose
fewer fish, while playing them, from out-point hooks than

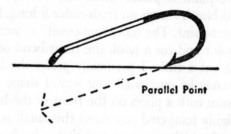

Parallel Point

from others. Once having driven my hook deeply in, I'll take
my chances on what happens afterwards.

I should suggest that here the reader might get some

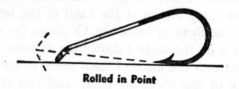

Rolled in Point

hooks and draw them along this page with the point and eye
of each touching it, the bend straight up. This is a simple and
interesting experiment for any angler, and it will fix in his

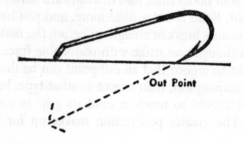

Out Point

mind things about penetration that he might never get quite straight otherwise.

One thing he will see is that a hook with a very long shank does not penetrate as readily as a regular; this because the eye, farther off, lessens the angle of the point to the paper. Therefore it would obviously be well to give the point of a long-shanked hook a little extra outward angle. Even then, a hook with an extremely long shank cannot be quite as efficient as a regular.

He will see, also, that when it comes to short-shanked hooks the converse is true; the greater angle of the point causes it to dig in too much. So a very short-shanked hook should be in-pointed a trifle; then it will have the same angle of penetration as a straight-point, or even a slight out-point, on a regular.

Curving the front of the bend slightly toward the shank, to produce an in-point effect, will have the exact opposite result to bending it out. If the point starts in at all—which it may not; drag an in-point hook along this page to see how it acts—it is likely to take but a shallow grip, easily torn loose, in the fish's mouth.

A salesman, demonstrating the supposedly great virtues of an in-point hook, will hold a sheet of paper and pull the point perpendicularly into it. His argument is that, since the point enters in line with the tip of the rod, it penetrates very readily. He is entirely correct—if one wants hooks to pull into sheets of paper rather than to catch fish.

Let's analyze the thing: Draw an in-point hook along a sheet of paper with the eye touching it. If it has much in-point it won't begin to penetrate at all. And what does it do in a fish's mouth? If it does start in, it penetrates readily for a short distance—and then that curved point immediately starts it back out again, instead of leading it in deeply. The result, of course, is a very shallow, short grip, easily pulled loose. Not that this always happens; if it does chance to wrap around something fairly solid, it has a very fine hold—but all too often it either fails to enter at all or gets but that light, shallow grip.

I should mention here that I am speaking strictly of fresh-water fishing. In certain types of sea fishing, a hook of this sort is highly desirable. That in-line pull is necessary to penetrate the extremely hard mouths of some sea fish; also, this point is less likely to be broken by the terrifically hard strike given by a heavy-tackle sea fisherman braced in a fishing chair and harnessed solidly to his huge reel.

We are sometimes told that a hook of this type is the very latest thing—an achievement of modern piscatorial science. As a matter of fact, bone hooks of identical shape were commonly used by cave men, as any paleontologist can tell you. They had a sound reason for using them; bone, being very brittle, needed the extra strength given by this shape; and the poor point that it would take made this in-line pull desirable —those paleolithic men were astonishingly scientific in designing a hook best suited to their material. And such hooks have been made regularly ever since, but were never popular until recent publicity gave them a large sale.

So I highly recommend hooks of this shape to any cave man who asks my advice about making bone hooks. To others, I do not recommend them.

In the foregoing, I have been considering front bend and point together. Some prefer a rolled-out point to the slight outward turn of the bend which I like. In actual fishing, the effect achieved by each is practically the same, so it is hardly worth while to discuss which is the better. Nor to argue whether a turned-in bend or a rolled-in point is the worse.

Now for points proper:

Be sure to note this, a trick which one must watch for

when one buys hooks: Very often the point of a spear-point hook is rolled in, and often the barb turned too far out. By an optical illusion, this may easily pass for a true hollow-point hook, which it most certainly isn't. And the abnormally wide barb makes this hook difficult to set in a fish's mouth, which of course causes many missed strikes.

A real needle point is the sharpest possible; it is, as I remark in the list of abbreviations, put on by a special machine. It might interest the reader to know that the secret of how this machine is made, and how it operates, is one of the most jealously guarded matters in all industry; some English companies, and Mustad of Norway, managed to preserve it for ages. Parts for a new machine would be ordered from widely separated places, and perhaps only two men in a factory, men who had spent their lives working there, would know the secret of assembling it; only old, trusted employees would be permitted to operate it, and even the most influential visitors would be strictly barred from its vicinity. Americans spent fortunes vainly trying to devise similar machines. With the almost totally ineffective patent laws, one can see that such precautions were no more than sound common sense—and we could wish that some of our military secrets were kept a tenth as well.

Though plug-casting hooks are about always quite soft—too soft, in my opinion—we find a wide variety of tempers in fly hooks, from very hard to quite soft. There is disagreement among anglers as to what is best here. In fly fishing, I prefer my hook quite hard, because it will take—and retain—the extremely sharp point needed to set it when one is using very fine leaders and so cannot strike with much force. There is one disadvantage of a very hard temper; the best of anglers will, with a long line out, sometimes permit his back cast to fall too low, when the slightest tick of the hook against a stone may break it. When this happens, one may not know about it until missing a good rise or two gets one to wondering what's wrong.

Until recently, some English companies made hooks with almost razor temper, very brittle; but I believe that now their hardest will bend slightly without breaking. The huge Mustad company of Norway makes chiefly hooks of a good medium temper; they will stand a considerable amount of bend without breaking. Hooks of different American companies vary greatly in temper; some American hooks are good, and some, I'm afraid, very poor indeed. At the time of writing this, Japanese hooks are not yet back on the American market, but any of them that I ever saw were pure trash.

When it comes to hook weight, one of standard thickness will be found best for most purposes, but of course there are uses for which it isn't. For instance, many prefer a 2X Stout for such battlers as big steelheads in a swift current.

There is disagreement as to what is the best weight hook for dry flies. I happen to like a 2X Fine, since it permits flies to be dressed with very light hackle and still float well enough —hardly any veteran angler will deny that a lightly hackled fly will take most trout. But some argue that a 2XF is too likely to break if hard, to bend if soft, so that a regular thickness is better. There is hardly a wrong or right here; it depends mainly on where one is fishing and what one is fishing for.

All this has little to do with the bass fisherman, since dry-fly fishing for bass is rarely practiced—though it is one of the grandest sports imaginable on the occasions when they rise reasonably well to dry flies. But bass dry flies are almost invariably very heavily hackled, so there is little objection to using hooks of standard thickness. Still, I prefer 2XF for my bass dry flies—when I can find them in bass sizes, which isn't often.

Some tie wet flies on Stout hooks, so that they will sink better. Others prefer to use hooks of standard thickness, and wrap thin strip lead on the shank before beginning to tie. This, too, seems chiefly a matter of taste—but one should remember that when using lead one can regulate the weight to suit the water in which one is going to fish. I dislike using split shot when I can avoid it.

If the hook is the all-important part of one's tackle, the point is the all-important part of the hook—if it doesn't penetrate, you don't catch your fish. But hardly an angler in a hundred thinks of watching his points, and resharpening them if necessary. Many use hooks so dull that sharpening them would alone probably double their catches; at least half of one's missed strikes are not the bad luck one thinks, but are caused by pure carelessness in using dull hooks.

Yes, I'll admit that sharpening hooks is a dull and tedious task for the man who has many flies, or a big box of plugs, but an hour spent at it occasionally will bring in more fish than many hours spent fishing with dull hooks.

Do I, you may ask, always keep my hook points absolutely perfect? Better, I think, not to get this discussion down to a personal basis. Anyhow, I have fished more in a year, and caught more fish then, than the average man does in a lifetime, so it's no serious thing for me if I miss an occasional fish —unless he's a really big one and I happen to see him, when I can feel as sick about it, and curse myself as much, as you would. And no clergyman living is so superhuman as to be able to live up to all he preaches, so why should a mere angling writer be expected to? I'm telling you how to catch fish, not how I foolishly miss them sometimes. But I do keep my points sharp a great majority of the time.

For sharpening hooks at home, except for the very hardest, a small half-round file is about the most convenient thing.

This would soon rust if taken fishing, so for that it is best to carry a good hook hone—and some cheap ones sold are certainly not good; they're too soft. One should absolutely never go fishing without this. Each time a fish is landed, and whenever there is the least chance that the point has been dulled by striking something, test it for sharpness; it takes but a second or two.

The best convenient test is to draw the hook, point forward, along the side of the hand and lying about flat on it, to see if it starts to dig in easily. And run your thumb gently up along all sides of the point, to find if there is a wire edge caused by a slight bend at the tip. A small, cheap magnifier is handy to examine hook points—I personally use a watchmaker's eye loupe for this purpose.

In sharpening, do not touch the outside of the point except to remove a wire edge there; file behind and at the sides of the barb. Indeed, in sharpening my own, I purposely make a very slight wire edge, pointing outward; drawing this against the hand, lightly, will show how quickly it begins to penetrate.

One should spare no pains to get the best hooks obtainable. Their additional cost is trifling; it is a small investment that will pay off many times over in fish landed. There is nothing more maddening to an angler than to lose a good fish because of a poor hook.

Before closing this chapter, it might be well to discuss the sportsmanship, or lack of it, in the use of triple hooks.

Occasionally somebody comes up to me waving his arms, a wild light in his eyes, to inform me that he (or she—the last one was a she, a she who probably doesn't fish twice a year) won't use triple hooks; he's too good a sportsman. The implication is that anybody who does shouldn't be shot at sunrise —because it's much better not to wait that long. And hanging, as more degrading, would be better anyhow; with, perhaps, drawing and quartering added.

Not only that, but every so often somebody starts a drive to have triple hooks legally barred, they're such terrible contraptions. Here's how I see the thing:

The use of single hooks on some of our most effective lures would render them practically useless, since they were designed for triples. This is particularly the case in fishing for bass, because of a bass's usual method of striking, taking a lure sidewise and quite gingerly in his lips. It holds true to a greater or less extent of all our fresh-water fish except pike and muskellunge, which frequently gulp a lure so deeply as to be hooked by the gills inside—but a single tail hook would be about as effective for these as a rule, because of their different manner of striking. And of course this tail hook would often hook a small one, which one wishes to liberate, so deeply that getting it out without injuring him would not be easy.

Any proponent of the single hook will tell you that a fish hooked on it is more likely to be landed than one on a triple. Often one hook of a triple cannot penetrate deeply so easily, because of the other two in the way. And the other two can be used as leverage to get that one out during the fight. And where there are more than one triple on a plug, the loose ones dangling outside will catch on weeds and things, to cause one to lose one's fish.

So here's a question that puzzles me: If it's harder to land bass on triples than on singles, why should singles be considered more sportsmanlike?

But, says our single-hook friend, as his great and final argument, those damned monstrosities of triple hooks get in his fingers! They're dangerous!

This strikes me as pretty nonsensical logic. Just because a man is unusually clumsy and cannot handle them safely, or because they don't appeal to his esthetic sensibilities, is hardly a sound reason for condemning their use by others. If he doesn't like their looks, or isn't safe around them, why, nobody's going to make him use them. The triple-hook man isn't trying to get laws prohibiting his singles just because they are more sure to land fish; so why should he take a prohibitionist attitude toward those who don't happen to have the same notions that he has?

Yes, I use triple hooks on bass plugs, and I shall continue to do so until somebody convinces me that there's the least thing unsportsmanlike in doing so. This though I like singles better when they can be used successfully—like them better solely because they're nicer to carry, to handle, and to remove from fish.

I have remarked elsewhere that I much prefer barbless hooks to barbed; I am not at all sure but that they will catch more fish, because of the very easy penetration of that slender, barbless point, to cause fewer missed strikes. I should probably use barbless hooks exclusively but for one thing: I receive a continuous stream of plugs from manufacturers and inventors, who ask me to test them in fishing and give them my opinions; and I do not always go to the trouble of filing off or pressing down the barbs before using them.

Nobody could be a stronger proponent of sportsmanlike practices than I—but I want to be very sure that the use of any certain tackle or method is poor sportsmanship before I condemn it. I have a horror of acquiring the name of being a "crank" or "screwball" in piscatorial or any other matters.

CHAPTER XXVI

Storing Tackle in Winter

EVEN in the extreme northern parts of the country, the man really bitten by the angling bug will be fishing through the first part of November, and almost certainly getting the finest and largest fish of the year. But as the month advances there will be a wave, spreading south, of men sadly putting their tackle away, until we reach those happy subtropical regions where one can fish comfortably all winter.

Too, too often, when the fisherman digs out his tackle again in spring, he finds himself gazing at a woeful mess of ruined stuff which has to be replaced, at some cost—if he can find things to replace those now useless. His pet bamboo rod may have disintegrated hopelessly; his casting lines and landing net may be rotted and weak, his fly lines stuck together irreparably; the hooks on his flies and plugs may be badly rusted, and the lures themselves discolored by lying so long against rusty steel. A woeful mess indeed, and there is no use in kicking himself for letting it happen; too late for that. A little trouble at the close of fishing season will let him avoid the catastrophe and find the things, in spring, just as good as when he put them away.

We'll take the bamboo rod first, for of all the more expensive items it needs the most care. Damp storage is its greatest enemy, and particularly storage in a place that is both warm and damp; it means a practical certainty of the strips of bamboo coming unglued from each other, though this may not happen until one begins to fish with it again, bending it. When it does happen, the rod may well be called beyond satisfactory repair; a good rod maker could perhaps take it all apart and put it together again, but he'd prefer to make a rod from new materials, and would probably charge less for doing that. And even the average "dry" basement is much damper than one might suspect, so leaving the rod in it all winter is about equivalent to tossing it into the hot furnace. Don't risk it!

Many houses, especially in parts of the country with severe climates, are kept quite hot and dry during the winter. Dry heat will eventually cause the bamboo of any rod to shrink so much that the ferrules become loose. This should be avoided, but it isn't nearly so serious a matter as basement storage, though it necessitates recementing the ferrules into place, perhaps with a wind of fine silk under each. I do not think that any reasonable amount of dry heat damages bamboo, since I have kept all my rods, and for long periods at a stretch, in the extremely dry climate of the Southwest, and I could not see that they were any the worse for it. But there is no use in begging for an unnecessary repair job by storing them in excessive dry heat.

Any bamboo rod that has been used much will be sure to show at least a slight set. This does no harm. Neither is there any harm in trying, by gentle methods, to remove that set, for appearance at least—and so it will not get just that much greater from next year's fishing.

Nearly always, hanging a rod by the tip all winter will remove these sets completely. A casting rod may be hung in one piece, but it is usually more convenient to hang a fly rod in sections. If the set is severe, a fairly heavy weight dangling from the lower end will pull it straight.

There is a precaution to be observed here. If a weight is used, especially, do not tie the string to the tip guide or to a ferrule, for the sustained strain may eventually pull the bamboo from the metal. Suspend it by a lashing just below the tip guide; and fasten the weight from above the ferrule. ·

Do not hang by a knot with both ends of the string coming out on one side, for this, especially with a slender tip, may cause a slight, sharp set of its own. Personally, I use a clove hitch, quick to make, secure, and easy to loosen again, but any good knot will do as well. The thing is, after it's made, to throw some half hitches around the rod until one string comes out opposite the other; the necessary number of half hitches will vary acording to the diameter of that particular part of the rod. Then tie the loose ends of string together, leaving a smooth loop which will slide on the nail until the pull is equalized on both sides, and so prevent sidewise strain.

If the rod is left in a case all winter, be sure that it—and especially the frail tip—is perfectly straight in it, and will stay that way. And it might be well to leave a metal case open, at least at first, so that any moisture in there will dry out. But hanging is the best way, for straightness, and the driest way.

Before storing either a bamboo or a steel rod, it is a very good plan to give it a coating of floor or auto wax, to help keep out moisture. Indeed, an occasional such coating (and polishing, of course) through the fishing season not only helps preserve the rod but keeps it looking its best. Before waxing, any slime, particles of weed or other dirt should be washed off, and the rod dried thoroughly before the waxing is done.

It is well to clean reels too before storing, for discoloring may occur under dirt left on for a long time, and there is some danger of rust on steel parts. For cleaning, a reel must be taken completely apart, a simple thing—see the chapter on reels. And putting one back together is also simple enough to trouble nobody but the most unmechanical man; the chief thing he has to remember is never to force anything in the least, for if something seems to require force he's putting it in the wrong place, or backwards in the right place. And screws on reels should be turned in barely snug, for they are generally made of soft metal which can easily be twisted in two.

Carbon tetrachloride, being noninflammable, is fine to clean a reel; gasoline is as good, but it should be used outdoors, for safety. An old toothbrush is just the thing to clean the gears and such, and a pipe cleaner is handy for getting into smaller holes. Be sure that all steel parts are well oiled before putting the reel away; in a damp climate, light grease such as petroleum jelly is safer—but it should be removed with tetrachloride or gasoline in spring, from all but the gears, or one will do soggy casting until oil, water and use finally remove most of it. Even when it is greased thus, it is of course best to leave the reel in a dry place for the winter.

A silk casting line should be dried very thoroughly before storing, or it will soon go to pieces. Again, dry storage is required—and for everything but a bamboo rod, the drier the better. The silk line should be left in no place which a careful housekeeper wouldn't consider safe for storing good clothes. One of the advantages of nylon lines is that they can be tossed, sopping wet, into almost any corner, left there all winter, and come out entirely undamaged—there seems to be no point to drying a nylon line.

Remember that water will have penetrated the coating of a silk fly line, so it, too, needs drying; and it takes much longer to dry thoroughly all through than a casting line. For proper drying it must, naturally, be removed from the reel and hung up. And it should not be stored on the reel, for there is some danger of its getting set into spirals, though some of the best modern fly lines give very little trouble in this respect. About the handiest thing is to coil it loosely around a large breakfast-food box or such (remembering to turn the box, spooling the line onto it, to avoid twisting); then slip the coils off, tie them, and hang them to dry.

It is much safer, however, to dress the line before storing —use any good mineral dressing; then polish it, and it is ready for fishing in spring. This will make it less likely that the coils will stick to each other if they should accidentally become somewhat too hot during storage; if they do stick much, the line is ruined—its maker would not like the individual job of redressing an old line, and would probably charge more for doing it than for a new one.

Melted grease can quickly be coated over hooks and such by using a small, round paint brush costing only a few cents, and then they are safe from rust. Some use wax for this, painting plugs all over with it to keep them from discoloring and —the wooden ones—from drying too much, to crack the enamel on them. Not many will want to bother with this, but it does preserve the finish and keep them looking well.

Moths, with their morbid and inordinate craving for the things that constitute our best flies, are not present in winter, so any dry place suitable for silk lines will do for them.

Landing nets, live nets, stringers and such things should of course be dried and kept dry, or they will very soon rot, especially if made of cotton. And when one does rot, it may mean calamity. As a warning of what may happen, I'll tell of something that happened to me:

Last fall, when I was ready to trek southward for a winter of trout fishing, the men in the editorial offices of Sports Afield decided to give me a farewell party at Ted Kesting's farm, across a large lake from where I then lived. They told me they'd drive by and pick me up. And—oh, by the way!—I might dash out and get my limit of big bass, and a few wall-eyes and pike and such, so we could have a nice fish fry under the big oaks. Just as casual as that—and the lake within ten miles or so of a big city and very badly overfished. Those fellows seemed to think their angling editor a magician when it came to catching fish—maybe one should be, but I'm not.

I hated to shake their sublime confidence in my piscatorial skill—the trouble with a reputation like that is that a man will try to live up to it or bust something. (This was the day I busted something!) I decided to do myself proud, if possible.

So out there I was at dawn in the morning, tossing plugs and flies to all sides. Fortunately, the fish were striking very well. I kept catching them on barbless hooks and dropping them into the live net alongside my boat until I had my limit of bass, a walleye or two, some good pike, and an exceptionally large crappie to round out my limit. No, I have no compunctions about bringing in my limit on rare occasions like that, though generally I bring no fish in unless I happen to get an unusually large one and want to show it, or to get its picture —the result is that, the season through, I kill scarcely a tenth of the fish that I catch and could legally retain.

Still I kept on fishing. When I'd get a large one, I'd drop him into the live net and release a smaller one—seeing to it, of course, that he had no more damage than the slight pin-prick of a barbless hook in his lip. Larger and larger grew the average size of those fish in the live net, until I had a collection of really splendid ones. I kept at it until noon, though they were striking but slowly during the last hour or so.

Was I proud of myself! And why shouldn't a man feel proud of himself with a string like that?—he's no fisherman if he doesn't. I was whistling like a somewhat off-tune lark; I think I was even singing—I've never quite succeeded in breaking myself of that bad habit, though I'm under no illusions about my voice, or my "vice," as an Irish friend pronounces it. Oozing cheeriness over the gunwales, I started the motor and headed for home and lunch. Those fellows from the office —I'd show 'em fish!

But—I'd forgotten to pull in the live net, which was several years old. I saw the cord holding it stretch, and I grabbed to stop the motor. Too late! The bottom burst from the net, and there went my grand fish, swimming merrily in all directions.

How long I sat there, I don't know. Only another vat-dyed angler can understand my quick tumble from joy to the black bottom of dejection. Bottom, nothing—I'd burst clean through the bottom, like the fish through the bottom of that rotten net. A man of six foot, one inch can't very well cry— somebody might be watching him from shore with a telescope. Finally I went home, ate a flavorless lunch, and started out again.

Yes, I got my limit. But they were far from resembling those beauties I'd lost. And I, injudiciously, told what had happened, though I knew those fellows from our office to be inveterate kidders; they can, and do, dish it out, and, more important, they can take it and enjoy it—Ted's the chief one to hand out or take. So all evening I heard about the Big Netful That Got Away. Now I look back at it as one of the funniest things that ever happened to me, but then it was not funny.

The moral of this is obvious, so I need only remark on how to make use of it. Test your nets before storing, by pulling hard against two or three strands of each, not against the whole net. If one gives way, burn it up, so you'll have to find a new one next spring, and not be tempted to use it just once more. Man, you might catch *anything* that first time out! And stand on one end of your cotton stringer and pull on the other with both hands, hard; if it can't bear that, you don't want it any longer.

But, for that matter, any uncared-for equipment can easily cost you the prize fish of your life, for the big one will naturally break something plenty strong for smaller ones. And proper storage in winter is a great part of taking care of tackle.

Apart from actual tackle, there are other things used in fishing that must have proper storage, but reasonable judgment on the owner's part will tell him what to do with them. However, it might be well to say a few words about waders and other articles of rubber.

We have always been told to keep waders hanging upside down all the time, open, to dry out. That is unquestionably the best way for fishing season, when they are used off and on.

But the other day I received a pair of new breast-high waders of high quality, tailored especially for my long legs and rather small feet; it is impossible for me to get a reasonably comfortable pair ready-made. The instructions with them said *not* to leave them hanging up when they are not to be used for some time—to wrap them well, put them in a light-tight box, and store them in a cool place. That sounds logical, for we all know that light has a deleterious effect on rubber, even on the rubber of a tire, immensely thick by comparison. And don't forget, in a *cool* place, for heat is more injurious to rubber than light.

But worst of all is grease or oil; they rot rubber very quickly. So if there is the slightest trace of either, wash it off thoroughly with soap and water, and then rinse away the last trace of soap. There is some oil in perspiration, so it is well to wash away any that may be in waders, before storing them. If they are of the stocking-foot type, it is easy to turn them inside out and wash thoroughly with soap and a brush. And strong soapy water may be swished around in boot feet, and let stand a short time in them. Be sure to use several clear rinsings after that—or shove a hose down inside to the toes and let it run for some time. Then dry them bone dry before wrapping up. Stuffing with loosely crumpled newspapers is one way of keeping them open and letting air circulate; hanging upside down is another—the method doesn't matter.

Anyhow, fix up your fishing gear at the end of fishing season, before you forget it, and store it properly for the winter.

PART III
Miscellaneous

CHAPTER XXVII

The Thermocline

THIS can happen in summer only: Out in a lake—in an average lake—there will be a hole which is the ideal fishing spot, full of big fellows feeding lustily. An observer could see no change, chemical analysis would show no poison, but presently the last fish has fled there for his life. To remain would mean the same quick, sure and painful death as if he had been thrown on the hot shore. Now, no fish can live there, no plant, nothing but some worms of a lowly type. How they can do so baffles science, for it seems against the laws of biology.

This spot may remain barren of life, but for those worms, until fall. Or an hour later it may again be the most suitable part of the lake for fish. All this happens because of an everyday but curious scientific phenomenon called the thermocline.

We are dealing here with lake thermodynamics. That sounds like a formidable subject, as though one might need a college course to understand it. But all that an angler needs to know of it is simple. A knowledge of it will clear up some points about midsummer fishing that have always discouraged and mystified him; it will keep him from fishing where no fish can possibly exist; he will have a better idea of where and when summer fishing is most likely to be profitable. At the worst, it will show him why he should not expect good fishing during the summer in the lake available to him.

There are but three technical terms connected with the thing which it is well, but not necessary, to remember. We shall begin by defining them, dictionary style:

epilimnion (eppy-*limb*-knee-on) Upper layer of warm water.

hypolimnion (high-po-*limb*-knee-on) Lower layer of cold water.

thermocline (*ther*-mo-kline) Where these two meet.

Briefly, the whole matter hinges upon the fact that, in most lakes, a thermocline forms during the summer at, generally, a depth of from thirty to forty-five feet. One has never been observed to form in a lake less than twenty-five feet deep, but for the fisherman's purposes all the water in a shallow lake may be regarded as constituting an epilimnion.

This thermocline, though really nothing at all, acts very much as though it were a thin sheet of rubber spread under water across a whole lake, for it prevents any mixing of the warm and the cold layers. Strong winds may drive a greater part of the warm layer to one side of the lake, but still the thermocline does not break; it is forced deeper at that side—and so must rise nearer the surface at the opposite shore, as if it were that imaginary sheet of rubber holding the same volume of water above and below.

How does this affect fish? Of course fish, like ourselves, must constantly breathe oxygen or die promptly.

A lake receives oxygen in two ways: From water plants and from the air. Most of it comes from plants, which release it as a by-product of the photosynthesis by which they take in carbon dioxide and make starch for their own food This process—this release of oxygen—can take place only during sunshine. On a very sunny day, one can frequently see little streams of bubbles rising steadily from underwater plants, many of these being completely absorbed by the water before reaching the surface. These bubbles are pure oxygen.

But, except in an unusually clear lake, few or no plants will be found deeper than twenty-five feet or so; enough sunshine to permit their growth does not get down farther. Therefore there is little or no oxygen production below that level. Some oxygen is also whipped into the surface water from the air by the action of waves, but the thermocline keeps it from reaching the hypolimnion.

In winter, a lake has complete circulation of water from top to bottom, so there will be plenty of oxygen all through it. But in summer, when a thermocline stops the circulation, the decomposition of organic matter on the bottom quickly exhausts the remaining oxygen down below.

The result is as one would expect. Lower some fish in a cage to just above this thermocline, and they can be left there all day and brought up lively as ever. Lower them again, just a shade farther, and what happens? They actually die faster than if thrown on shore, for on shore, so long as their gills are moist, they will be picking up some oxygen from the air, but the hypolimnion may contain no oxygen whatever. So the man who fishes below the thermocline—which may be only twenty-five feet deep—might as well be dragging his lure across desert sand and expecting to catch fish.

Since all fishing must be done in the epilimnion, in what part of it are we most likely to find fish at a given time?

While there is more or less constant circulation through this epilimnion, the upper part of it will be warmest during the day, because of the sun beating on it. All our game fish prefer cool water, principally, it seems, because cool water can hold much more dissolved oxygen than warm, and game fish need a good deal of oxygen—most rough fish don't, and can thrive where game fish would either die or become unhealthy and languid.

So, very naturally, on a hot day a game fish will leave the warm surface water, with its deficient supply of oxygen, and go down seeking a cool spot until the thermocline stops him abruptly; to go a shade deeper would be to die. Logically, then, on a hot day the place to seek fish is just above the thermocline.

How does one find the level of the thermocline? A stream thermometer very quickly brought up and read would show temperatures for various depths fairly accurately, though it would change its reading a little on the way up. A better reading could be had by sinking the thermometer in a jar which had a lid that could be opened and closed by means of a line, to trap some water at the desired depth.

Few anglers would want to bother with this, and since the level of a thermocline shifts up and down because of winds, one might have to find it anew each time one went to the spot. Then, one would have no assurance that there were fish at the place tested. So fishing deep—but always remembering the thermocline and the futility of fishing too deep—seems the most practical way of discovering what's there.

However, many creatures upon which our game fish feed multiply best in water considerably too warm for the game fish. The result is a high concentration of desirable food in shallower water; and this shallow water, easily penetrated by sunshine, will contain the most weeds to furnish both food and shelter for these smaller creatures.

Toward evening, these shallows begin to cool, the sun not being so hot, and the air in contact with them cooler. Also, the slow currents are gradually mixing the top and bottom of the epilimnion, bringing it to a more even temperature all through, and equalizing its oxygen-carrying capacity. Result? All game fish, naturally, begin to work in toward that abundant supply of food which was not available to them during the day.

In very hot weather, that inshore water may not feel comfortable to game fish until well into the night. They will usually find things most to their liking just before sunrise in the morning, when the shallows are coldest.

Therefore, as experienced anglers knew long before they had heard of thermoclines, very early morning, from dawn on, is generally by far the best time of the day to catch fish during hot weather. This is particularly true of bass, which seem to require more oxygen than most lake fish. Further, large bass, to judge by habits, seem to need more oxygen than smaller ones, for they commonly avoid warm shallows when small ones are fairly plentiful there.

It would seem, too, that the matter is affected by the comparative abundance of food in proportion to the number of game fish. Where game fish are plentiful, they will rush in early, each trying to get there before others have diminished the supply of food. In a hard-fished lake there will be the same amount of inshore food, but fewer mouths to eat it; therefore the game fish can take their time about going in, knowing that there will be more than enough to go round. So it is in a hard-fished lake that early morning fishing is almost certain to be far and away the most productive in summer, especially for big bass.

As the sun gets well up, these fish retire to their deep holes, generally about as deep as the thermocline will allow them to go. If they had found an abundance of food and are stuffed full, naturally they will not feel at all hungry again until toward evening. One will take a lure, but only if it is dragged close to him, with an especially enticing action. Even then, he will look at it pretty languidly first, very much as a man stuffed full of Thanksgiving turkey looks at the piece of pumpkin pie which comes on last. There's the problem of deciding whether the darned thing is worth bothering with or not.

This means that in a wild lake, fish are likely to feed avidly all day, if the lure is sent down to them. In hard-fished water, with food plentiful, daytime fishing during hot weather will generally prove comparatively unproductive, though some greedy ones may be caught if one works hard enough.

The same amount of mixing will not take place in the thermocline on all nights; the matter will be influenced by winds and by how currents happen to form. On some nights, the water may remain practically stagnant, then one would look for quite poor fishing in the shallows next morning.

During a protracted period of gloomy, calm weather, there will be little new oxygen added to the water in the epilimnion. Because of the lack of sunshine, weeds are not exuding it, and there is none being whipped in by waves. This can possibly result in so great an oxygen depletion that the fish become listless and do not feed well at any time, which, of course, means poor fishing.

In a very shallow lake, all the water will become so warm that the fish in it will feel uncomfortable, will even become unhealthy. It is useless to expect good midsummer fishing in such a place. But in a deep lake the epilimnion can retain a comparatively low temperature throughout the summer. Though the thermocline precludes transfusion of cold water from the hypolimnion upward, heat is constantly being dissipated downward by radiation—as it would pass through the solid metal of a radiator.

This tendency to equalization of temperature is accelerated by the fact that both epilimnion and hypolimnion have rolling currents within themselves, which are constantly sliding across each other. The result of this is that a very deep lake may produce comparatively good fishing all summer, though never as good as in spring or fall, before the thermocline forms, or after it has dissipated.

A full thermocline cannot form in a lake of more than several miles across, for the winds on such large stretches cause strong currents which keep the water mixing from top to bottom. But small thermoclines may form here and there in such a lake, especially during calm weather, and in sheltered bays.

The formation of a thermocline does not stop suddenly with lakes of a given size. The matter will depend on windiness and mean average summer temperature of the region. Also, in a certain lake, a thermocline may form during a hot, calm summer, but not during a cool, windy one. A lake with no thermocline may hold good fishing all summer.

There is but one kind of lake in which fish can thrive below a thermocline. It will be very deep, with almost no organic matter on its bottom to deplete the oxygen—in other words, it will be an extremely barren, infertile lake, such as is rarely found except in parts of the northern border country. The hypolimnion of such a lake may hold a plentiful supply of oxygen all summer, stored since before formation of the thermocline. In such a lake, fish may be found to great depths in the hottest weather.

To show how deep fresh-water fish may go, I might mention that in Lake Superior—too large to form a thermocline—lake trout known as siscowet, or "fat trout," are regularly taken at depths of several hundred feet; I have even heard apparently authentic instances of their being taken at a thousand feet.

But it should be remarked that a lake with a barren bottom can never support many fish of any kind. The number of game fish in a lake is almost entirely dependent on the amount of vegetation there; successively larger creatures feed on it and on each other until we reach those large enough to be food for game fish. Therefore a glance at the countryside around will usually show how many game fish a lake can support; rich, fertile country means a fertile lake bottom; barren country, a barren lake, one that cannot stand hard fishing. One should, however, be careful in applying this rule. In parts of the West, the soil may have great natural fertility, but scanty rainfall will permit but sparse land vegetation. So a highly fertile lake may exist in a desert, and a rocky, barren lake will sometimes be found in fertile country.

Likewise, other conditions being equal, a comparatively shallow lake can carry far more fish than a deep one of equal area, for much more of its bottom receives a sufficient amount of sunshine to permit luxuriant growth of weeds. And a lake with a very long shoreline for its area—a lake with many points and coves and islands—will provide far better fishing than a round one of equal size and maximum depth, for there is much more shallow inshore water in which weeds thrive.

In short, a crystal-clear, rock-bound lake is a beautiful thing to see, to write poetry about, even to fish in. But the less pellucid lake to which most men have access will produce many times the number of fish.

CHAPTER XXVIII

Muskellunge

AFTER a lifetime spent in closely observing such things, I have reached the conclusion that if a man, for some reason best known to himself, wants to be made a complete fool, there are but two quick, sure and convenient methods of going about it. One is to fall in love with the wrong woman. The other is to fish for muskellunge. I am not prepared to say, without further study, which method is the more efficacious.

One trouble with muskies is that they are pretty scarce even in the best of waters. Some hold that musky fishing isn't what it used to be. After twenty-five years of fishing for them off and on, I suspect that it never was. I doubt if there ever was a time when one could be fairly sure of getting muskies on a two-week trip, for they are so large, fierce and voracious that no water could hold many of them. Savagely cannibalistic too—why, the female will sometimes swallow her smaller husband the moment spawning is done, behavior which Emily Post would never condone as even passable table manners. How *could* such diabolical creatures ever have been plentiful?

This probably will be controverted by the old-timer who remembers the highlights of his musky fishing long ago, but forgets the many, many weary days of futile trolling or casting.

Indeed, I have a notion that muskellunge fishing is actually improving in many districts. since conservation authorities have pursued an unusually wise policy regarding them. After all, we must give the devil his due, and admit that Fish and Game Department men sometimes are wise, and sometimes have policies, in spite of what the dub angler says of them when fish won't jump into his boat after his crude offering.

For one thing, a few years ago they discovered the secret of propagating muskellunge artificially, which long had baffled them, and since then they've been pouring almost countless numbers of fry and fingerlings into suitable water. I haven't the latest figures, but in Wisconsin alone the number planted must now run close to 200,000,000. Two hundred million is an awful lot of muskies! Even supposing a high rate of infantile mortality among them, there must be a powerful lot of big muskies in the waters.

Another thing these conservation men have done about everywhere is to set a size limit of 30 inches on those to be retained. The joyful tidings in this is that a 30-inch muskellunge (he'll be about six years old) will usually have spawned at least once, so no musky may be legally taken until he's left a lot of posterity. Muskies are good at leaving posterity. A pair of thirty-inchers may supply a lake with as many as 100,000 little posterities at one time.

Of course the perfect little devils immediately start, at a furious rate, to devour each other and everything else in sight. But a lot of the strongest ones, those with the largest appetites and the most evil dispositions, must survive, simply because there's nothing bigger or more savage to eat them, or swift enough to catch them—they make greased lightning seem slow.

What's the result of all this solicitude toward them? This: While we might now be finding large muskellunge only in the yellowed pages of some old book, more 60-pound muskies have been taken lately than ever before, and each season turns up quite a few 50-pounders. And I'll bet my pet casting rod that new world's records, far larger than these, are hooked each season but not landed, for when it comes to wrecking tackle and getting away, a big musky's the undisputed heavyweight champion.

Plenty of muskies left—big ones! Then why is fishing for them so conducive to acute melancholia? It's a sad story, mate. Only the Ancient Mariner could tell it with proper quavers and doleful inflections, but here goes for a try—and, Lord knows, how they've often done me should help me with my task:

Even where muskies are found in comparatively large numbers, for muskies, they have a temperament that makes them the world's most maddening fish. When they won't strike, they won't strike, and that's that; and I've yet to see the angler skillful enough to do anything about it.

Day after long day, we'll cast or troll, the backs of our laps aching, in what we're told is good musky water—you couldn't prove it by us, for we haven't seen hide nor scale of a muskellunge, and we suspect that if there ever were any here they've all died of some mysterious disease. No other fishing can be so disheartening. But the worst is yet to come.

Suddenly muskies become plentiful—for muskies. A dozen times or more in a day, some great monster will follow the lure in, his nose not three inches from it, until we can almost reach out and touch him. We see him perfectly, just under the surface; we could almost count scales on him. He's the sort of fish we have happy dreams about.

And then he's turned and he's gone. And another—and still another—does the same thing. In the somber shades of dusk, angler after angler comes in with the same dreary tale, the same desperate, hopeless look in his eyes. The stronger ones sit in their cabins and brood; the weaker get plastered, hoping to forget. As if one could! Why, that one over by the rushy point was 65 pounds, if he was an ounce!

But, brother, the worst is still to come. It's called giving us the Third Degree. Here's how it's done:

The next day muskies are hitting. Oh, sure—they're *hitting!* You receive a ferocious strike that almost tears the rod from your hand; it would seem that the brute had poised under the boat and charged the lure head on, at full speed. Either that or you've hooked a flying diesel train down there, which doesn't seem likely.

There is a terrific run or two, straining your rod and your arms. You're more excited than if you'd won the jackpot on a dollar slot machine—merely winning a jackpot wouldn't make you tremble that way.

And then your line goes slack; you're reeling in your lure. There isn't any musky on there any more. He's calmly swimming back to his favorite spot in the woods, or by the log; and if a musky's face could show expression, his would have a diabolical grin at what he's done to you.

About the sixth time that happens in one day, you're ready to give the Apache war whoop with no previous training. You're ready to bite hunks out of the anchor. That, or you've sunken into a state of profound gloom which should have psychiatric attention—it's a matter of a man's disposition.

What happened? What did you do wrong? You did nothing wrong, and there's a lot of argument among experienced musky men as to what happened. Some hold that he grabbed the extreme rear end of the bucktail, behind the hooks, and made those savage runs just out of pure fiendishness, to taunt you—it was his gruesome idea of fun. Others say that he took the hooks into his mouth, but clamped down so hard on them with his powerful jaws that they could not be moved, to set the barbs; so when he opened his mouth the hooks just dropped out. Still others insist that he'd struck the spoon so far forward as to miss the hooks completely.

Me, I don't know, and I don't pretend to. I've been around women and muskies a lot in my life, but when anybody asks me what I really know about either, I can only shake my head and sigh. All I know is that muskies love to make a jibbering idiot of a man when they get the chance, and that they're sure good at doing it. This being about fishing, we won't discuss what some women will or won't do to a fellow.

Add to all of this the fact that most really large muskies hooked aren't landed—they wreck things in general and get away—and what have you? Musky fishing!

All the foregoing is to warn the prospective muskellunge angler that he will often need patience that would make Job seem jittery. Really, the best thing a man can do, if he hasn't the sweetly philosophic disposition of a Spinoza, is to keep studiously away from water that may hold muskies.

To be pitied is the impatient man who strikes hot musky fishing on his first trip and gets some good ones. For, after having caught two or three, never again can he take a musky or leave it alone—he's sunk for life, always hoping that history will repeat itself. Of course it will repeat itself, sooner or later; but often, as the governor of Wisconsin said to the governor of Michigan, it's a long time between muskies.

Yes, there sometimes is hot musky fishing. And, brother —oh, brother!—short of the atomic bomb, it's the hottest thing known to mankind.

That terrific smash at your lure. That irresistible run, with your rod bending and your reel screaming. Your thumb on the spool burning as you try futilely at least to slow him down. That nerve-jangling quiver of the rod as he lies sulking on the bottom, savagely shaking his great head, with every movement coming plainly up to your hands.

And then, that wild leap! We sometimes read arguments that his smaller cousin, the pike, will leap. Sure he will—but rarely, in my experience, and I've caught thousands of pike; and I've yet to see one much more than clear the water, and it isn't often that he'll even come up and splash on the surface.

Nobody has to argue that a musky will leap. He does! Not every musky, of course; like the heavyweight boxing champs, each has his own individual way of fighting. But often one will shoot high and clean into the air like a tarpon—and do it two or three times during one battle. He comes out with an explosion of flying water; he's up there, silvery, quivering. And then he falls back with a crash that just does something to a fellow.

Cool indeed is the angler who can keep his head and manage everything just right while all that is going on! Too cool, perhaps, to get the maximum kick out of fishing.

Yes, there are deep-sea fish that are much larger, and even faster, that leap higher. But there will be no snags or weeds around for one to tangle in and escape, so all the fisherman has to do (some of my sea-fishing friends will murder me for saying this!) is to set the star drag on his reel, and yawn as the fish runs, and then reel in again, knowing that the drag handle will absorb the shock of a sudden whirl. (Yes, indeed, some of my sea-fishing friends are going to have things to say to me next time they meet me after reading this.)

Supposing that, knowing what one is up against, one still decides to try musky fishing, how does one go about it? It would seem that a great deal of special knowledge and skill must be necessary to take such a rare prize as a large musky.

That's the helluvit!—pardon my irate exclamation; I used to be a cowboy. What I mean is, some of us, snootily fancying ourselves somewhat more piscatorially erudite than the angling hoi polloi, are severely provoked by the fact that a rank tyro, a pure dub, not we, will invariably catch the largest musky. That, really, is the principal reason why the true musky addict regards a straitjacket as standard fishing equipment.

If you know how to fish for pike—real pike, not walleyes—you know how to fish for muskellunge; it's the same thing. Or fish for them just as you would for bass, and you'll probably do as well as the next fellow. But if you've never fished before in your life, that's when you're about sure to land the season's record. However, if you do that, green at the game, don't let a veteran angler catch you out alone in the woods for two or three days; thus you can avoid being brutally murdered.

Solely to keep the green angler from catching more and larger muskies than I do, if we chance to be fishing the same lake, I'll give the following tips:

Most muskellunge are caught in July and August, simply because that's when nearly all the fishing for them is done. They're usually striking much better before and after that—and late fall's the time for the big ones.

They're late sleepers; they generally don't seem to get up until around ten o'clock. Then they'll strike for a couple of hours, and take a siesta until later afternoon, when they get going more and more until nearly dark; that's when they're really on the rampage if they're going to feed at all. So, sad to relate, the lazy, stay-abed angler is more likely to get them than the energetic, enthusiastic one, who has worn himself all out before evening.

The musky, in spite of his size, is a shallow-water fish, and he'll be found hanging out in pretty much the same place that a bass will. He likes clear, clean water, not roily. And, for some reason, he does not seem to like large bodies of water, so he's much more likely to be found in sheltered bays than out in the main part of a big lake.

Almost everybody agrees that he likes a faster-running lure than does a bass, or even a pike. But I have caught good ones on slow lures—slow lures with good action—when they seemed to take no interest in fast ones. So if nothing else is doing any good, there's at least no harm in trying a slow lure.

I believe that more muskies can be taken on spoons, shiny ones of natural metal finish, than on plugs. I know that some won't agree with that, and certainly a lot of fine ones are taken on plugs. The matter isn't worth much discussion, for anybody should have both plugs and spoons along—it's merely a question of which one will use most.

Indeed, some hold that it makes little difference what one uses, that if a musky is feeding, the ferocious brute will grab anything moving of appropriate size. I do not hold with that; I maintain that a plug or spoon with attractive appearance and action will invariably get more muskies than just any old thing.

Yes, there's the classic story of the Chicago dentist who caught a great muskellunge on a set of false teeth fitted with spinners and hooks. But how many muskies have been caught on false teeth? All that incident proved was that the dentist had a strong sense of humor, and would get along on fewer muskies for the sake of a good story to tell the rest of his life.

The venerable fluted spoon with feathered hooks still takes a lot of muskies. But it seems that a great majority of experienced men now prefer bucktail back there—I'm staying out of the hot argument as to whether natural, white, black or some-other-color bucktail is usually best. Just now, in looking over a long list of muskies caught in a certain district, I find that nearly half of them were caught on spoons with bucktails —it doesn't say what colors.

Here's one thing worth noting about that list I mention: not a single one of those muskies was caught on live bait.

Experts pretty well agree that casting is better than trolling. But far more are taken by trolling, for the simple reason that most people fish for them that way—they do it because they find it hard to cast heavy lures, or haven't the outfits to do it.

Are large lures necessary? Well, personally I almost never use anything heavier than a ⅞ oz. casting spoon—plain nickel, copper or brass. This because I don't like casting things of flatiron weight, and much trolling bores me. Somehow I seemingly manage to get about my share of muskies—that is, allowing for my great handicap in being an experienced fisherman. I've a suspicion that I'd get more, or more large ones anyhow, if I'd use bigger lures. But I won't; I fish for fun, not to see what weight of dead fish I can bring in.

In tackle, the expert will generally be found using no more than a fairly heavy bass outfit, with an 18 lb. line. He's out for maximum sport with the average musky that he'll hook, which may run 10 or 12 lbs. He knows darned well that a really big brute is likely either to tangle in something or to smash him up, but he's risking it.

Fly-rod fishing for muskies? Oh, sure, it can be done— I've landed some that way myself, and will guarantee to do it again. But a fly-rod lure is far too small to appeal to many muskellunge of any size, and that outfit isn't right to handle them anyhow. As I see it, it's just stunting.

At the other extreme, we sometimes see a man using a two-hand sea rod with a small star-drag reel, for trolling. An old-timer may grin sarcastically at sight of this rig, but pin him down and he'll have to admit that an inexperienced angler may need it. He may even go so far as to say that he wished he'd had it himself, when that big one tagged on.

However, for the man with some, but none too extensive, experience in fishing, here's a nice outfit: A good solid-steel rod of 4½ ft., and a bass reel of the regular, larger size—not one of the smaller ones now rapidly coming into favor for bass, and fine for them. By removing the arbor, if there is one, and filling the reel with line, there should be plenty of line for any emergency that may arise—in spite of all his hell-raising propensities, a musky rarely makes long runs.

It's puzzling to know what line to recommend, without knowing what the prospective user's skill is, how big the muskies will run, and how many snags and such there will be where he fishes. One trouble is that the heavier the line, the harder it will be to cast with it—trolling, of course, it makes no difference. Perhaps a line of 25 lbs. test would be a good bet for average conditions. But if your guide says to use heavier, use it; then you can't blame me if something untoward happens.

Yes, it's well to get a guide if you can afford it. Big muskies, especially, have a habit of hanging out in favorite spots more than almost any other fish, and a guide will know these places. That is, if he's a good guide; some hire out as guides merely because they consider it easier than digging post holes in the hot sun.

I do hope the reader carefully rereads and studies and memorizes the latter—the instructive—part of all this. Then, if I should run across him on some lake, he isn't so likely to show me up at musky fishing as he'd be if he hadn't the first notion of what it's all about.

That's musky fishing. And I still maintain that the best thing to do about those big brutes is to stay strictly away from them. After all, there's a limit to what any man's mind can stand without popping like—like a line with a musky on the end of it.

CHAPTER XXIX

Pike

Let me begin by saying that by pike I, oddly enough, mean pike, not walleyes—which are large perch, fine to eat but comparatively poor scrappers. The true pike is about the only fish found native to both Europe and North America; he is almost identical on both sides except that he seems to grow larger in Europe. He has been known as a pike since there was an English language, and it is plain as a pikestaff that that should be the thing to call him. The erroneous name, "pickerel," belonging to a much smaller related fish, is rapidly dropping out of use for him. "Northern pike" is unnecessary, for there's but one pike. "Great Northern Pike" is still worse—the Great Northern's a railroad, not a fish, but the confusion is so confounded that even the capitals are usually retained when the term is applied to *Esox lucius*.

Sportsmen get almost all their pike in midsummer, because they rarely fish for them at any other time. But, except in the extreme North, where the water never warms up very much, that is the very worst time for them. To me, the pike is peculiarly a fish of the late fall.

Some time in September, pike fishing begins to get really good, and as the season advances that adjective can gradually be changed to "fine," "grand," and—I'd say "stupendous" but

323

that Hollywood has got that term down to where it means that something smells but may possibly get by, with luck.

Rarely indeed are worth-while pike taken before September, and I've got practically all my really large ones still later. Through spring and summer, one will be catching mostly two-pounders—if one is lucky—with a pike of five pounds thought excellent. In fall, ten-pounders are not uncommon, and occasionally somebody will be bringing in one of double that. Where all these big fellows keep themselves the rest of the season seems to puzzle most anglers.

As we know, pike feed actively all winter. Spearing them through the ice (and wounding a good many, so that they get away to die later) is a common northern "sport." I have always opposed this. That swift, stealthy blow of a barbed spear doesn't give this great fish a chance, and of course he cannot put up any fight when stricken thus. So these very big ones that run in winter are not available for real sport with rod and line in summer. That the consensus of opinion seems to be swinging rapidly to this point of view is proved by the fact that each year more and more lakes and rivers are being closed to winter spearing, so that soon, it seems, spearing will be a thing of the past.

Practically all winter spearing is done by residents of resort districts, men who are mainly dependent for their living upon money spent by sportsmen in summer. So in ruining the sport of their summer visitors, these year-round residents are neatly and effectively cutting their own throats, sending sportsmen elsewhere. Shakespeare had the words for it—"What fools these mortals be."

How high should the pike rate as a game fish, when taken on reasonably light rod and line? Three years ago, in an article in a magazine, I expressed the belief that the pike is gamer than the bass. Ever since I have felt somewhat uneasy about that article—sometimes I'd think it right; at other times, wrong.

The criterion I used was the comparative ability of each, weight for weight, to break similar tackle. By that standard, certainly, the article was correct, for it is quite safe to say that no other fresh-water fish in the country is responsible for a third as many broken rods as is the pike. This with the possible exception of the steelhead, which uses a swift current to help him break the rods—and it is utterly unfair to compare the fight of a fish in swift water with that of one in still. As I have remarked elsewhere, an old shoe on one's hook would give a fine battle in a strong current, and could easily break a rod if one got half as excited "playing" it as many men do handling a large fish. Just imagine hooking a hard, healthy ten-pound pike in the fast water frequented by steelheads!

The thing that makes the pike such a rod-buster is his manner of fighting. Often, but by no means always, when first hooked he will come in almost limply until he is close to the boat. Then, if one is using the common slightly modified whale line, he is yanked unceremoniously aboard, where he flops and thrashes and leaps around at a terrific rate, upsetting tackle boxes, getting slime all over everybody, and making a pretty menacing thing to have rampaging around at such close quarters.

If the angler is using a light line, the pike takes one look—with his evil, crocodilian eyes—at the boat and the man in it. Then, fast as lightning and as unpredictable, he has swapped ends and is headed like a rocket for somewhere out there. That is when the rod goes smash—it takes an expectation of the thing, and quick wits, to give him line in time.

He is powerful, considerably more powerful than a bass of equal weight—of that, I think, there can be little question. He is much faster too; no bass can make a reel scream as he does. At last when he is apparently exhausted, and led quietly up to the boat—he makes another of those lightning-fast, powerful whirls, and off he goes. He won't go far this time, but plenty far enough to break a rod.

Mixed up with this there will be periods of sulking, of swimming around slowly, of permitting himself to be led quietly—periods when he is doing practically nothing at all—depending on his mere weight to keep one from landing him promptly. The bass never does this; from the moment one hooks him until he is in the boat, it is swift action; in the boat, exhausted, he lies comparatively still—which the pike certainly doesn't!

I have always regarded the bass as about the cleverest fish, the most intelligent, and recent investigations by scientists bear me out—the carp, formerly reputed to be the genius of the tribe, turned out to be a complete numbskull by comparison, a nitwit. Frankly, I regard the pike as a stupid brute, with an I.Q. close to zero; so far as I know, scientists have not yet got around to investigating his mentality. For instance, he will frequently strike over and over at the same lure, until finally he succeeds in getting himself hooked—apparently his burning ambition. He will sometimes, indeed, break a line and escape —only to smash immediately into a perhaps similar lure, with the old one dangling from his lip.

Or possibly it isn't sheer stupidity that makes him do such things; it may be his demon disposition, for a savage brute he certainly is—that, nobody who knows him will controvert. He seems to hold one continuous grudge against things in general.

While I was writing this, a friend walked past my window with a good pike which he had caught, and of course I had to rush out and begin the usual angler's jabberfest. He is one of the keenest pike fishermen in the country—and if he ever gets a notion that his wife will stay at home and cook his dinner when pike may be striking, she'll quickly set him right on the matter; she's going after 'em too, and that's that.

Now Roy comes close to being my ideal of the fisherman —a big, brown man, quiet, but very friendly, and he always badly underestimates the weight of a large fish which he has caught; perhaps he does it to be conservative. The hoary old jokes about all fishermen being exaggerators, or just plain liars, become wearisome to a lot of us.

Having caught so many pike, he did not judge the one he held as big enough to be weighed and he had removed its insides. I guessed it at eleven pounds, as caught. He said no— nine. So I got my scales, and it turned out to be just ten as it was. And by the way, the weight of pike is very hard to guess correctly, for they vary greatly in girth compared to length.

He told me that his wife had just lost one that probably would have been over twenty pounds, lost it by the totally uncalled-for snapping of a new wire leader, when the fish was exhausted and near the boat. The battle with it, as he described it, shows another great difference between pike and bass.

A two-pound pike can give a very nice tussle for his size, though he's but a callow youth. An immature bass, even on the lightest tackle, comes in weakly, with little attempt to make a fuss about it.

The pike puts up his maximum fight at a weight of per- haps between six and eight pounds—then, he is really fast, a hell-raiser. At around ten pounds or so he begins to slow down. Over fifteen, landing him is little more than a lot of slow, patient pulling, with pauses between pulls—there is nothing exciting about it; one has only the satisfaction of returning to camp with a very large fish. Satisfaction enough for most of us! Of course a man is much longer boating him than one half his size, but it is slow-motion stuff, and a rod is very unlikely to be broken unless one just refuses to give an inch of line, to let him run. Most men, hooked onto a big one, do refuse to give an inch of line, and so the big one usually does get away, trailing broken tackle behind him.

Does the lunker bass slow up? Ask anybody who's landed one, and watch his eyes glow reminiscently. The bigger they come, the harder they——fight. For wild gymnastics, a lot of them out of the water, it's hard to imagine anything that will beat an old granddaddy bass ready to die of old age, and he is solidly hooked indeed if he doesn't throw the plug far during one of these eruptions.

My friend Roy is a specialist at pike fishing; it is almost a mania with him. In pike country, to him, bass, trout and all the rest are little more than nuisances. Year by year I meet more anglers like him—and none too long ago the pike was a "dirty brute," a "snake," despised by all. I am glad indeed to see this really great game fish at last get the recognition he deserves.

I have heard men say that pike never fight—and I have heard the same said of bass, that one could not fight nearly as much as a catfish. Needless to say, these men have never caught a healthy specimen of either in cold water; when one of them has his first experience he is due for a great and pleasant surprise, and he will indeed find his hands full.

Though pike are great game fish, I will confess that I prefer to fish for bass. Fishing for them can be more artistic, and I like their fast, flashy fights, their wild, explosive leaps. Certainly I fish for pike too, and frequently. I have fished for about everything except Aunt Martha's goldfish—and I'm afraid that spinster lady feels decidedly uneasy about those when I'm in her house; at least she seems to keep a cold and suspicious eye on me when I'm around them. But of the lot, bass and trout are my favorites. This is no more than a casual statement of my own personal preferences, with no shadow of a hint that they are the "right" preferences. In this northern district where I now am, I happen to prefer to fish for bass, Roy for pike—and what of it?

So, all things considered—the pike's tackle-smashing abilities, the bass's flashy fight, his leaps, his knack of throwing lures—which is the gamer? I now can see but one broad-minded answer: whichever one prefers to fish for.

Roy—who certainly knows his pike—remarked that he has found them striking badly indeed, and running very small, as he'd expect at this time of year, early August. He gave this explanation: He opened the mouth of the one he'd brought in and showed that it had almost no teeth—just a few short, dull ones far back. Pike, he said, have now shed their teeth and not yet grown new ones.

This has always been the theory of "ignorant natives," of "moss-backs." Scientists have smiled tolerantly at it, holding that pike never lose all or most of their teeth at once, but that some are always dropping out and being replaced by new —and I have been inclined to go along with the scientists, thinking that they should know what they are talking about. Indeed, the word scientist comes from the Latin scire, to know, and it literally means "one who knows." But quite frequently they don't, and a true scientist is the first to admit it. Maybe they don't in this case.

Now, how do we fish for pike? Trolling for them is much more common than trolling for bass, and more effective. This because pike are more likely to be found lying just outside the weed beds, where this method is really practicable—too many completely weedless lures are about completely fishless too.

There is the debated question of whether it is better to troll by rowing or by motor. Some hold for rowing quietly, not to alarm them; others insist that the low, motononous throb of an idling motor stirs them up and makes them strike—and recent experiments seem to prove that an idling motor passing over them does alarm fish less than even quiet rowing. In my own experience, trolling with a motor is often—not always—more effective than rowing.

But I completely fail to see that this superiority is great enough to warrant the banning of trolling by motor in certain states—I know of no other reason for it, for the quiet power troller certainly disturbs no other angler. If laws against outboards are wanted, let them be aimed at the adolescent nitwit—of any age—who tears madly around in a speedboat with open muffler, driving everybody frantic afloat and ashore as he shows off, wildly shattering the peace for which one comes to the lakes. Unfortunately, we are forbidden to shoot him.

Yes, power trolling for pike is efficient at most times. And few nowadays like to row along slowly, hour after hour, staring straight at a perfectly good outboard on the transom of the boat. Even to me—and I am accused of having too much restless energy, rather than of laziness—that seems a senseless procedure, especially since all modern fishing boats, being made for outboards, row very hard; the true rowboat, with its small, high transom, is a thing of the past, since it operates badly, and dangerously, with even the smallest outboard.

What speed is best in trolling for pike? That is often discussed, and it is commonly said that it is best to go considerably faster than for bass. Frequently it is—but don't overdo it. And sometimes I have found them to strike freely at a lure barely moving, but to refuse one going faster.

A common mistake is to troll both fast and slow with the same lure. This is a very poor way, since each lure has a limited range of speed within which it has most attractive action. Also, many lures will, if run too fast, revolve and twist one's line badly. Another great error is to think that a good swivel will prevent this; it will not, without a heavy keel sinker ahead of it, for a long line in water will turn before any swivel will.

The thing to do is to drag a lure alongside the boat, without moving the rod tip, and adjust the idling speed of the motor until one gets the right action—and then allow for whether one is trolling with or against the wind. From this it will be seen that running depth should not be regulated by altering the speed of the motor, but by changing lures, or by adding sinkers. Or, with many lures, it can be done by letting out or taking in line.

About a hundred feet of line seems to be generally regarded as best for trolling. But I have found times when pike appeared to strike better with less line out—which seems to substantiate the theory that the sound of the motor sometimes makes them strike. And with over a hundred feet out, it is difficult to set the hooks, owing to the stretch of the long line, and the wide bow it makes in turning. Also, a fish hooked far off is much more likely to tangle badly in weeds, and be lost, than one hooked closer. For the same reason, unnecessarily long casts should be avoided where there are weeds—as there generally are in pike fishing.

I have never owned a special trolling rod, and never want to. I troll with my most delicate bamboo casting rods, and often even with light fly rods. Doesn't it put bad sets in them, as we hear it will? No—because I always point the tip back along the line, so that there is little or no bend in it.

This method not only saves the rod but it has another great advantage: There generally is quite a long line out in trolling. And a long line, especially if of nylon, has a good deal of elasticity to it. Add to this the spring of a rod stuck out sidewise, also the inevitable turning of one's relaxed wrist when a fish strikes unexpectedly, and a sharp, sudden jerk to set the hooks immediately becomes impossible.

All of this will lead to the unnecessary loss of well over half the fish that strike. With the tip pointed back, a solid setting of the hooks becomes easy—indeed, then, one usually hooks himself when he strikes, though an added yank or two will help make sure of things. The elasticity of the long line averts any danger of its breaking while one does this—that is, of course, if one merely jerks moderately hard, all that is necessary, and doesn't try to yank the fish's head off, as some do.

Nearly all experienced fishermen have noted that pike, and especially large ones, seem to strike best in weather that is windy, even quite stormy. The other day, a thoughtful and analytical friend of mine suggested that this might be because the tossing, swerving boat gives the lure an attractive action. I do not believe this has much to do with it, since I find the same superiority of windy weather when I cast, and in casting I always give my lure sufficient action.

And sometimes just at the approach of a storm, especially of one accompanied by lightning, pike strike madly. (A warning here; do not stay out in a boat when lightning is close, for you are a perfect lightning rod out there.) Some believe that a sudden rise of barometric pressure, often accompanying the beginning of a storm, explains it. However, this seems discounted by the fact that I have always found large pike to strike far better on a windward shore, among tossing waves, than on a comparatively calm lee shore, where barometric pressure is of course the same. So all we can say is that pike often seem to develop great activity—and ravenous appetites—when waves are tossing high.

The strength of line to use in a certain place must be determined by the size pike around there, and the angler's skill in playing fish. An eighteen-pound test line seems fairly well standard in most places, though some experienced men use much lighter. If the pike run large, and the angler has had little experience in playing such tricky fish, it would be well to use a considerably heavier line.

A veteran angler can land very large pike on a frail rod, but it is best for the average man to use a strong one—strong, but not too heavy or stiff to be used comfortably, or to cast the necessary lures pleasantly. I should recommend a first-class rod of solid steel for most men; some of the newer ones of this type are really nice fishing rods, with good feel and balance and action, unlike the top-heavy, clumsy things that solid steel rods were not long ago. These newer ones cast very well indeed, but they demand considerably slower wrist movement than most rods of other types—be sure to remember this, and don't try to hurry a solid steel casting rod, or you will get neither distance nor ease of casting with it; time it correctly and you will find it working pleasantly for you.

Four and a half feet was the longest advisable with older solid rods, for beyond that they became too top-heavy and slow. The same length in the newer ones would suit many best, but some in five-foot length now work very well indeed, and will suit those who like a slow-action rod—it's purely a matter of taste here.

What lures? Very few use heavier than the larger bass lures. A pike will strike anything that a bass will, but he generally seems to have more preference for spoons than a bass. And he is not nearly as temperamental, as changeable in his notions. Three or four good lures will be found sufficient for pike under all conditions—for bass, one never has enough to suit all their moods.

The old-fashioned revolving-blade spoon with a feathered treble hook behind is still excellent for pike, but it is usually trolled, being very hard to cast without tangling in the line.

A wobbling, rocking casting spoon is more popular now, and there is much debate as to whether it is best in plain nickel or copper or with red-and-white stripes—it certainly is a good idea to have all three along to try in turn.

But watch out for these casting spoons, for most of them, especially if worked too fast, will revolve and twist your line badly—some of them do it if not worked fast enough. Don't pay too much attention to a maker's guarantee that his spoon won't revolve and twist your line. Most makers seem to have forgotten to tell their spoons to read these guarantees and live up to them.

A pike-scale plug also seems very good at times, and on the whole I think a jointed one considerably more efficient than a solid. All this of course does not mean that there are not a lot of other lures that will take pike well. As I've said, if a pike is feeding, he is not nearly so finicky as the bass; he's likely to smash head-on into almost anything of suitable size that he sees moving. Still, he can take decided notions at times about what he wants. Last year, in a river near me, it seemed that the pike had all made a solemn covenant not to strike anything that didn't have a pork rind dangling behind it, and the individualists who wouldn't abide by the agreement were few.

Watch out in using pork rinds for pike! Even very large ones will frequently follow along behind for some distance, nipping at the end of the rind—though it's generally crappies or big sunfish that are doing the nipping which you feel. And very often a pike will seize only the rind savagely and make one or two strong runs before just opening his mouth and letting it go. The language of many fishermen when this happens can, as the old novelists used to say, be better imagined than described—anyhow, this book must go through the mails.

The cure for this is a trail hook attached to the end of the rind. But the trouble is that if it's large or heavy it may ruin the attractive action of the rind, and if it's small and light it takes a very experienced fisherman to handle a big pike on it —and even he may lose him in weeds. So each angler must judge for himself whether it is desirable to use pork rind at a given time.

Indeed, a pike, unlike a bass, is nearly always taken on the tail hooks—hooks farther forward are practically needless on a pike lure. He often follows the lure some distance, looking it over before taking it, as a bass almost never does, and then he just puts on speed a little, opens his mouth, and takes it from the rear—or takes part of it. A bass more commonly strikes from below and from the side. And a bass, in spite of all his dash and splash, generally begins by plucking gently at a lure, and so is lightly hooked, in the lips. In spite of his occasional tail-plucking habits, a pike generally gulps a lure, and so he is usually very solidly hooked, often through the gills from inside.

Though the pike is but rarely as notional as the bass about what he wants and doesn't want, he can at times be just as capricious. Here is an example: Last year I saw a good pike— about nine pounds—rush at my large plug only to whirl back, refusing it, at the last moment, leaving the surface of the water boiling. I had seen him plainly, and wanted him—and I knew that pike, unlike bass, will nearly always strike again under such circumstances, and after only a brief rest. So I touched the lever and eased my anchor quietly down—I have reached the point where I will hardly go fishing in a boat without a good anchor lift operated from the seat by a crank; it not only adds greatly to the pleasure of fishing, but it will lead to a lot more fish, in cases like this.

I was in a little cove with a stream running into it, in moderately deep water, fairly free from weeds, but with dense weeds all around—it seemed an ideal place to pick up some nice pike. And there I sat for perhaps an hour, throwing almost everything in my huge tackle box at that pike. He charged the lure half a dozen times, coming right to the surface, in plain sight, only to whirl back leaving the water swirling. That, as any angler knows, is maddening—one can't catch him, and one can't make up one's mind to go off and leave him there.

Often, while resting him briefly, I'd cast in a circle about me, to see if there were others nearby. I thought there should be, but no sign of one did I see.

At last, in desperation, I started rummaging through the contents of my tackle box, and wondering. Frequently when fish thus follow large lures, but refuse to strike them, I can get them on smaller ones—but even quarter-ounce plugs did not seem to interest this fellow enough. It appeared that he just wanted to taunt me, to keep me sitting there all day, wasting my time.

On an impulse, I decided to see what going to extremes with the thing would do. I picked up a tiny fly-rod lure, nothing but a flat piece of metal attached along a hook—a fly-rod Trix-Oreno, to be specific. I'd caught a lot of crappies on it, and even some sunfish, but the great mouth of that brute down there could easily take in several dozen such things at a bite—offering it to him just did not seem sensible. But, I thought, sensible things having failed, why not try the silly? I put it on the snap of my leader, with a small dipsey sinker to give casting weight, and laid it in the spot where I well knew him to be.

It was what he'd wanted all the time! He smashed into it like a streak, and I had him solidly hooked. After a battle that churned up the water, I landed him.

Nor was that all of it. Right there, without once moving my anchor, I picked up my limit of very nice pike about as fast as I could play them and get them in—all on that silly little fly-rod thing, and after I'd been dragging big, enticing plugs over their heads for a full hour, without a sign of one except that first. Since then, I've used the little gadget often for pike, with surprisingly productive results—and I'd probably have got a lot more on it if I could have gained more confidence in it for such large fish, and used it oftener; but it just doesn't seem logical to me. I fully believe that one can get more of these savage brutes, especially of the larger ones, by offering them a pretty fair mouthful.

I still think, perhaps wrongly, that the pike has some shortcomings, both as a game fish and as an intellectual, but I would be about the last to deny that he is a really terrific fighter, holding, with his slightly larger and much rarer brother, the muskellunge, the fresh-water heavyweight championship of the world for rod-busting. Really, I think he's just roughneck enough to enjoy breaking rods; there's nothing whatever gentlemanly about the way he acts when you hook him.

In conclusion, let us try to clear up the difficulty which most have in distinguishing pike, pickerel and muskellunge.

Size, or girth compared to length, is of no use whatever in identifying them. No matter how small or scrawny a pike may be, he is still a pike, not a pickerel. Nor is color at all reliable as a means of identification. Still, we will give usual coloring here, for what it may be worth:

If the fish in question has small, oval, cream-colored spots on his sides, I think he may safely be called a pike—but it is not, as I shall soon show, safe to say he isn't if he hasn't.

A young pike has *light* bars on a *dark* background, and this marking is sometimes retained until he is a foot long or more.

Curved *dark* bars on a *light* background mean the barred pickerel of the East, which rarely weighs a pound or is a foot long.

Of the same small size is the mud pickerel of the Middle West, which has dark, wormlike, wavy bars on a lighter background.

The chain pickerel, an Eastern fish rarely weighing ten pounds or more, and usually much smaller, has dark, chain-like markings.

Muskellunge vary greatly in coloring. I have caught them pure silvery, with no markings, and sometimes they may even be brown. But the usual thing is a silvery background with shadowy darker markings, none too distinct, as in the tiger muskellunge (vertical stripes), the leopard muskellunge (spots), and the Chautauqua muskellunge (crossbars).

Here is the most definite way for the man without scientific training to tell them apart:

Pickerel—Gill covers and cheeks completely scaled.

Pike—Lower half of gill covers without scales, but cheeks in front of them completely scaled.

Muskellunge—Lower half of gill covers (as in the pike), and lower half of cheeks, without scales. (Rarely, muskellunge show scales on the lower cheeks, but they are generally badly developed.)

Some confusion is caused by the fact that muskellunge and pike in the wild state occasionally interbreed, and such hybrids are now sometimes bred artificially and liberated. These seem always to have the fully scaled cheeks of the pike, but may have muskellunge markings.

Within the past twenty years, a very strange thing seems to have happened among pike. Mutants, creatures different from their parents but breeding true among themselves, are extremely rare in nature, but a mutant of the pike is now fairly common in Minnesota. He has come to be erroneously called the "silver muskellunge," though he is not a muskellunge at all, nor even a hybrid; he is a true pike, with his cheeks entirely scaled.

He has a plain silver color, sometimes flecked with gold, without the usual pike markings—he is a very beautiful fish. In the wild state, he does not interbreed with ordinary pike, or with the muskellunge—but he has been artificially crossed with the common pike, producing a fish with odd black mottlings. This silver pike is gaining a great reputation as a battler, and his progress is being watched with keen interest by sportsmen. Such a mutant—a brand-new game fish—occurring in our generation is an almost incredible thing; we might have to stick around a few thousand years if we want to fish for the next one.

CHAPTER XXX

Walleyes

WALLEYES strike well in spring, but there are few places— these mostly in the wilderness—where they can be taken in any numbers during the hot weather. For that reason, many think that when the early fishing is done walleye fishing is over for the year, so they don't try it again. This certainly is a mistake, for late fall brings by far the best walleye fishing of the season, both for numbers and for size of those caught. So let's discuss them a little.

In the first place, I do wish that everybody would decide to call a walleye a walleye—only that and nothing more. He's not a pike of any kind, nor distantly related to the pike family; he probably hates all pike. Still, we hear him called a walleyed pike, yellow pike, blue pike and, for all I know, a pike of a few other colors.

In places, he's a jackfish. And in parts of Canada—goodness knows why—he's called a pickerel. Down South, he's often known as a jack salmon, to the amusement of anybody who ever saw a real salmon, even canned. But, then, down there they will insist that a bass is a trout, and that a sunfish is a bream—the real bream is a European fish whose nearest but still distant American relative is the little golden shiner.

Scientists agree that he's a perch pure and simple. Still,

340

it's they who are most unkind to this poor fish; they call him *Stizostedion vitreum*. No wonder his eyes bulge and look glazed. So would mine if I'd been named Stizostedion Lucas; nor would I have much fight in me as I went through life.

We'll admit that the man who likes to think of himself as an angler, or something highfaluting that way, rather than as a mere fisherman, isn't much interested in walleyes. Not, that is, until evening brings that aching void in his middle which one gets outdoors. Then, you'll probably see him dropping his lure toward a deep, gravelly bottom, licking his lips, and hoping.

For wherever one puts the walleye's fighting ability, there's no least argument about his palatability; he's certainly among the best food fishes of our fresh water, and he retains his good flavor through the hot months when some others may get a slightly queer taste. This undoubtedly is because he prefers clear, cool water with a stony bottom free from weeds.

When you're out with a guide in the North, your day's catch may include fish of every species there, but when supper-time comes, what does the guide cook? Walleyes—every time! He wants 'em; you want 'em; everybody wants 'em, meal after meal. And, owing to some law of nature imperfectly under-stood, nobody else can cook a walleye even half as tastily as a Northwoods guide can do it over an open campfire. How he can make one taste! It's yummier than a radio drooler says some of those crunchy things are, as he blats along until you're so upset at the stomach that you couldn't face even guide-cooked walleye.

Largely for his table qualities, in some sections of the country the walleye is prime favorite with sort of run-of-the-mill fishermen, even if he doesn't put up an exciting battle. There's also the fact that when one is caught there's likely to be a school of them down there, so a man can sit right where he is and fill his stringer. In a lake, that is; in a river, he's inclined to be more solitary in his habits.

No, the walleye is no mighty battler, no aerial acrobat, and not too fast. Some walleyes fight hardly at all. But when one of them does take a notion to put up a scrap, he can be among the strongest fish of his size in fresh water, while he lasts.

All this refers to the usual way of fishing for walleyes, with heavy, crude casting tackle, or a beam-like cane pole and tuna line. But some fine sport indeed can be had with them if one knows how to go about it. Just try 'em once with a fly rod, or with really light casting tackle, evenings, when they come into the shallows to feed. I know some men and women both who have gone practically nuts over this form of fishing.

Does it work well? You bet! It's the very most successful way of taking them then, and often one after another will tag on about as fast as you can chuck the lure back to them. Then, it's exciting enough to suit even the most blasé angler.

One can work it from a boat, and sometimes from the bank, but, somehow, it's ten times as much fun to wade. And the wader will generally get more fish, his head being so low to the water that a walleye can't see him far, to become suspicious.

For the fly rod, a streamer fly works well; so does a shiny metal fly-rod lure. And don't forget to try some little wooden or plastic plugs of fly-rod size; they often murder 'em. When you're looking for walleyes feeding in the shallows, don't expect the splashing and commotion that bass would make there; walleyes can pick flies off the surface very quietly. And they won't be in until dusk; as his eyes show, the walleye is largely a nocturnal feeder.

If you don't use a fly rod, casting-rod plugs will do the trick; it's nearly always best to stick to small ones. Work them slowly, for in spite of his ferocious dental array the walleye is a timid feeder. However, the man who sticks to either the long or short rod exclusively is cheating himself out of about half the fun that he could have in his fishing. And this evening stuff, wading for walleyes, is a fine way to learn to use a fly rod, since long or delicate casts are rarely needed, nor does one have to know much about fly-rod lures. If trout were feeding thus on natural flies, they'd want artificials pretty much like them. The walleye isn't so finical; he seems happy about it when something larger spats down to make him a bigger bite.

Daytime fishing for walleyes is a completely different matter. Then, they're down deep. But while they're probably not seeking food, they're not likely to overlook anything suitable that comes by close enough, and slow enough, to seem an easy snack. The disadvantage of daytime fishing is the difficulty of finding them far out in a big lake; while we're often told to fish for them off sharp drop-offs, I can't see that they're more likely to be found there than in deep water farther out—if more are caught at those inshore holes, I think it's merely because so many fish for them there. On the other hand, when you do catch one far out you're nearly sure to get more right there, and perhaps your limit.

Owing to the open water which they frequent, trolling is much more successful for walleyes than for bass; really, it's about the best way of locating a school. But most fishermen seem to go about it in a completely wrong way; not knowing the walleye's daytime nature, they troll too fast, and run their lures too far from the bottom.

So troll very slowly, barely fast enough to get a shade of action into your lure. And let the thing sink frequently until you feel it touch bottom; near the bottom is about the only place you'll get them in daytime. An exception to this may sometimes be found on an extremely dark, gloomy day, especially if it is raining; then, you may find a school of them about where you'd look for bass—but they're not at all likely to come to or near the surface for a lure.

Most men unfamiliar with walleyes make another very grave mistake, a mistake that will absolutely prevent their getting more than a very occasional walleye. They'll catch one, and either keep on going or lose the exact spot. Or they may think they're trolling back over where they caught him, when really they're far from it, and getting farther off with each circle of the boat.

There's but one satisfactory way of working things here: Have a little buoy of some sort along, and drop it overboard— if there's the least wind, do it immediately when you hook one, not waiting to land him. Excellent and convenient markers may be bought already made up. In a pinch, an empty can or bottle will do; but have it rigged up and ready beside you, with some old line and with a large sinker or a stone to anchor it. A child's rubber balloon makes a conspicuous mark, but it's well to keep it inflated and ready to go overboard.

When you drop out this buoy, immediately upon hooking one, be sure to note about how much line you had out behind, and toward what mark on shore your lure was running. The school won't be under where your boat was but back there, and you've got to return and fish right through the school, for a few feet away will be completely useless. The inexperienced angler is sure to forget about all this in the excitement of hooking a fish; he'll remain a green and inexperienced angler until he can remember to do it.

Trolling back and forth over that spot is the usual way of working things next. I much prefer to go back, anchor, and start casting in a wide circle from about where I judged that I hooked that first one--always, of course, letting my lure sink clear to the bottom before starting the retrieve, and always retrieving so slowly that I'm really dancing the lure along close to the bottom, often letting it drop to touch it. Trolling in circles, one wastes too much time on water where they aren't.

This is one of the very few places where being able to make a long cast comes in useful; it lets one cover a large circle from the anchored boat. If you hook one far off, move the boat closer to there, partly for more comfortable casting, and partly because they may be moving off slowly and might get out of range. Do this quietly, shuffling feet or other commotion in a boat never helps fishing, since fish are very sensitive to slight vibrations going through the water. Personally, both for quietness and convenience, I always use one of those crank-type lifts; too, it keeps the bottom free of wet rope in which one may tangle one's feet, to fall overboard. In fact I don't see why anybody sticks to the messy, dangerous way of standing up to pull an anchor in over the side by hand.

Far more than the bass angler, the man out for walleyes should be able to return infallibly and quickly to anchor in a small, definite spot, even if it's a mile or two out in the lake. And, of course, leaving a buoy there is an invitation to everybody who comes along to try the place and see why it was worth marking, which won't help your fishing next time you go there. Chapter XI gives full instructions for returning to these spots, so be sure to study it thoroughly if you expect to have much luck with walleyes.

Any lure that will take a bass will take a walleye, but it's generally best to use small ones. Here, again, a shiny spoon will often do the work nicely, but some insist that plugs are better—I've generally had best luck when using one with a natural pike finish.

When all other lures fail completely, there's one that

often produces fine results, but most anglers can't be persuaded to use it because it looks too small for such a large fish. And that's a plain fly, trolled down there, with a sinker to keep it near the bottom. I've frequently picked up many nice walleyes on flies as small as number eight when they didn't seem at all interested in larger things.

In trolling, I think it best as a rule to keep the sinker a couple of feet or so ahead of the fly. Casting, too, this would probably be best, but I dislike casting that rig, so I place the sinker directly against the fly or very near it. Sometimes a spinner ahead of the fly helps; again, the plain fly seems better.

Another thing that has often produced fine results for me is a rather small spinner—say, one an inch long or so—with a pork rind on a plain hook behind it. For this kind of fishing, I'm inclined to favor a spinner of the june-bug type. It may be just my notion, but I think that a dash of bright vermilion toward the head of this june-bug, on the inside, is very important, so if it isn't there, or has got partly knocked off, I paint it on again with quick-drying enamel.

River fishing for walleyes is more sport than getting them in still water; any fish seems to fight much better in a current. Of course the true fact is that the current is doing most of the "fighting," but that doesn't matter; the man holding the rod is having plenty of fun, and that's what he's out for, not to go analyzing things in a cold-blooded manner. A fly-rod or small casting lure cast across the stream, and then danced around just a little as it swings down, seems to appeal strongly to a walleye, and it's an interesting way of fishing too. As in a lake, they'll usually be found deep in daytime, but they come to the surface late evenings and at night.

Can as many walleyes be taken on artificial as on live bait? A few who have specialized on walleyes loudly yell, "Yes!" Frankly, I'm no walleye specialist, though I've caught plenty of them, and I can't catch as many on my artificials as others do with live bait—except in that late-evening inshore fishing, when artificials will nearly always take more. But I'm out for fun, not for fish, so I stick to my artificials.

However, many anglers who would think it a lifelong disgrace even to be suspected of using live bait for bass, trout or pike will sometimes condescend to use minnows for the walleye, not regarding him as a game fish—they just want him to eat. Others insist that he's game-fish enough to be honored by offering him artificial lures exclusively. I will give no advice in this matter; let your conscience be your guide. Here, as in all other live-bait fishing, detailed instructions are of little value, since no particular skill is required—the live-baiter just jabs a hook through a minnow, drops him overboard, and sits waiting, or moves his boat slowly around.

What tackle should one use? For the man who doesn't insist on just freezing to the reel handle and pulling, the very lightest bass tackle will do. This because the walleye is generally found in such open water that one can play him as long and as lightly as one wishes. And when he gives up, he usually gives up all at once. He never pulls that trick that a pike does near a boat: whirling like lightning, throwing water all over you, and, somehow, being 'way out there instantly—with you, unless you know the pike's tricks, sitting holding a broken rod and wondering what happened so fast.

But there's one thing that a large walleye often does, and if you're not looking for it things may go smash: from beside the boat, he'll sound clear to the bottom. He won't do it rapidly, but he certainly can put a lot of strength into it. So be ready to loose your left thumb a little on the spool and let him go down. It's his swan song, and he seldom repeats the trick—at least not very forcefully. But once is enough if you're not looking for it and have reasonably light tackle.

Landing a big walleye is a pretty ticklish problem. You can't take him by the lower jaw and lift him in as you would a bass—rather, it's inadvisable unless you want some mangled fingers, to dodge a draft board or something of the sort. Nor can you slip a thumb and forefinger behind his gill covers as some experienced anglers do with pike, for those sharp stickers on his back are always stiffly erect when he comes in.

A net is much the safest and most convenient thing. But be sure to use it properly; don't start jabbing with it. Hold it under the surface, still, and quietly lead him into it head first. And be darned careful who you let net your fish for you, walleye or any other kind. Nine times in ten, your friend, if he isn't a very experienced angler, will start dipping wildly with the net and lose your fish for you—of course you can't say anything, and you look away so he can't see the desire to commit brutal murder dancing in your eyes. Best to remark quietly but firmly, "I like to net my own fish," or something that way.

Another good way is to have a priest along. I don't mean a Roman Catholic or Episcopalian clergyman, though I've fished with some of both that were fine to have along, fishing, "Priest" is the standard name for a small club kept handy in the tackle box, to kill fish—and I've always wondered if the name wasn't originally given because it administers the last rites. Don't start swinging wildly with it, to knock him loose; a firm, well-aimed tap behind the eyes gives him a ten-count that will let you lift him in at leisure.

One friend of mine goes about it more artistically: he has a cute little hammer about eight inches long, metal handle and all chromium plated, and he taps with it on an exact spot —I believe there's some certain scale on which he takes his sharpshooter aim. Neat, but it's getting things down a shade too fine for me; I manage with my old piece of half-inch water pipe. Oh, yes—I've another friend who carries one of those miniature baseball bats about a foot long used as ornaments; it works well, and he enjoys the amusement caused by his carrying a baseball bat to swat fish.

A walleye having such strong, sharp teeth, one must use a wire leader for the occasions when he takes the lure deeply; because of his timid feeding habits and rather small mouth, he generally doesn't. Either cable-type or solid wire will do, and I see no need for it to be over six inches long.

Remember what I said: walleye fishing is at its best in fall, and it doesn't reach its height until after the first hard frost. So go out and try your luck with them. If you hit a school, you'll have lots of fun catching them, and meanwhile you'll be smacking your lips and thinking of how delicious they'll be fried or baked—they have their best flavor, too, at this time of year.

And don't forget to try them, late evenings, on a fly rod!

CHAPTER XXXI

Fly Fishing for Sunfish

THERE are two reasons why I am inserting a chapter on fly fishing for sunfish:

The first is that bass-bugging is but a crude method of using a fly rod; he who has never cast anything but bass bugs has no right whatever to call himself a fly fisherman—he knows nothing about real fly casting. Nevertheless, bass-bugging is often difficult for the beginner with the fly rod to learn, since proper timing with bugs is somewhat tricky; so, to a lesser extent, is timing with the large flies proper generally used for bass.

The smaller and lighter the fly with which one begins, the more easily can one learn true, artistic fly casting—and very small, light flies are used for sunfish. So I strongly suggest that the beginner with the fly rod confine himself strictly to sunfish, for if he should use bass bugs before becoming fairly adept with the little flies, he may set up bad habits of technique which he will later find hard to break.

The other reason is that bass fishing, even in the best of places, and for the best of us, can often be so slow that we wonder whether we should call it sport or pure hard work. But sunfish are found practically anywhere that bass are found, and they can be caught in numbers during almost any time of the season or of the day. So when bass fishing becomes too discouraging, one can always change to a fly rod and have plenty of sport with those little fellows.

I feel little sympathy for the man who moans that he can't get to fish except during a short and costly vacation each year. He nearly always has, if he'd wake up and see it, a fascinating kind of fishing so close that he could reach it quickly any evening. And that is catching sunfish on a fly.

Before going further, the reader may want to ask three questions: Is this a successful method of getting them? Is it easy to learn? Is the sunfish game enough to be sport?

One day not long ago I ran across three friends in a boat; they were using worms and grasshoppers for sunfish. We began joking each other about our methods, and it ended by their challenging me to prove what I said about mine. I anchored so close that I could cast past each end of their boat, and I caught fifty-nine bluegills, most of them large, while the three of them got—two small ones!

Luck was with me, of course, for conditions were exceptional that day; presently, I'll point out why. But in no other form of angling is the superiority of artificial lures so extremely marked; one can perhaps invariably get more sunfish, and certainly more large ones, on flies than on live bait. And have at least twenty times the fun!

Fly casting—fly casting good enough to catch plenty of sunfish—is easier to learn than plug casting; a little practice each evening for a week should have one doing very nicely indeed at it. Few people annoy me more than those fly-fisher-men who pretend that theirs is an esoteric art suited only to exceptionally clever fellows like themselves; they've been getting by far too long with this egotistic faking.

There's a slight catch here: One can manage to chuck a plug out anyhow, clumsily, with anything. That won't work in fly-fishing; one must have a reasonably good rod with proper action, a line to fit it exactly, and must learn the correct but simple technique of the cast.

Is the sunfish game? I've had bass, big trout, even muskellunge put up listless, disappointing fights, but never a sunfish. And I'm thoroughly tired of having men explain gravely to me how the sunfish turns his flat side to one when he fights —I'd shoot the man who started the yarn but that he undoubtedly died of old age fifty years ago or more.

How could a sunfish make you pull against his side when he's hooked about at his nose—unless you had another hook and leader to his tail? And if he's wide, he's short; I doubt if the area of his side is greater than that of a trout of equal weight.

Sure, he's small; in most places, if a day's catch brings you two or three over a pound each you're doing well. But he'll probably average larger than the trout caught in most streams nowadays. He's got to be taken on suitably light tackle to afford sport. So has a bass; an experienced angler snorts with mixed pity and contempt when he sees some dub fishing for bass with tackle suitable for muskies. So let's be honest and give Brother Sunfish credit as, ounce for ounce, about the gamest fish in the water, for that he is.

Incidentally, most connoisseurs hold that he's about the daintiest eating of any fish except a trout from a cold mountain stream—better than trout from the average stream, especially if they are fresh from a hatchery and liver fed. This, and the fact that one can catch a mess of sunfish almost any day, is worth considering. And it's entirely ethical to consider it; alone of our game fishes, the sunfish in most places need thinning out, so that those remaining can find more food and grow larger.

Any fly rod with proper action will do for sunfish. Even

a heavy bass rod will serve, for it's only the strength of the leader that counts so far as sport and sportsmanship are concerned. But a light trout rod will prove much more pleasant to use, less tiring.

Remember that if a rod won't lay a fly out properly for a trout it won't lay one out well for sunfish—fly casting is fly casting. Nor, with a poor rod, can you develop casting skill. Fancy hook casts and such are rarely necessary for sunfish, but it's a good thing to practice them, to be able to show your friends some nice work with a dry fly when you get on a tricky trout stream.

Most use level lines for sunfish. Of course one will do, and will get lots of them. But why not use a good three-diameter? A line of this type does cost considerably more, but it will permit much greater distance without extra effort, and it handles better at any range except the shortest.

It was because of a good rod and a three-diameter line that I was able to get those fifty-nine sunfish while my three friends caught hardly any on live bait; it happened to be one of those days when a very long cast was absolutely necessary for sunfish; they would take neither flies nor live bait near a boat. And, nearly always, one can get far more big fellows by making casts of at least moderate distance; it's mostly the little ones that hang around under a boat.

A six-foot leader is generally used, but there's no harm in using one longer; at times, it will get you a good many more, especially in very clear, still water. To straighten one's cast properly, the butt of the leader must be about two thirds the size of the line it joins. But that's too big to get most sunfish, or to have sport with them.

This means that a tapered leader is advisable for either wet or dry flies. One can, of course, buy tapered leaders ready-made; or one can get them to suit oneself by tying one's own.

Next to the fly, about the smallest gut that one can find will generally be best; it should be under one-pound test.

One of the chief reasons why so many claim that they can't hook sunfish on flies is that they use flies far too large; I find most men trying to catch them on number eights or even larger. Remember that a sunfish has a far smaller mouth than a trout of equal size. For them, I never use a fly larger than a ten; I often use twelves, and sometimes get down to much smaller—indeed, my main reason for not using very small ones exclusively is that they take too many small sunfish which I have the trouble of releasing. The exact size fly you'll need will depend on the weight sunfish you're getting; if you are missing many strikes, you need smaller flies.

We have all seen the brilliant, beautiful colors that a male sunfish develops during spawning season. He's dolling up, of course, to attract a lady sunfish—and he wouldn't do it if her eyes weren't sensitive to color; Mother Nature wouldn't adorn him that way without reason.

Fishing experience proves this still further, for the sunfish can sometimes be extremely choosy about what shade fly he wants. But as a beginning one can get along quite well, and catch them at most times, with flies of black, white, brown and gray. And it's as well to start out with hackle flies only—large wings seem to keep sunfish from taking flies best into their small mouths.

So this gives us, as a beginning, hackle flies in the four colors mentioned, in sizes not larger than ten. Nor should the flies be too fuzzy and large; scantily dressed flies are almost invariably best for either trout or sunfish. If a fly is overdressed, a little judicious clipping with manicure scissors will often make it much more effective. Bivisible flies in those four colors are good, since generally they are not too bulky; they may be fished either wet or dry.

Of course it makes the game more interesting to have some more flies to start with, so here are a few others that I've had good luck with:

One of my old favorites is the McGinty, which is the striped color of a bumblebee but has a small red tail. And there's the Bee, exactly like it but without the tail—generally, I prefer the McGinty; I've got a lot of sunfish on it!

The Coachman has taken a lot too for me; a Coachman hackle looks like a juicy, dark-greenish housefly. And for most fish, the Royal Coachman is one of the old reliables; it's quite different from the regular Coachman, and looks like no natural fly known to man or fish. A king's coachman in England devised it 'way back.

Only last year I got to using a tiny white streamer fly for bluegills; it's just some hackles with a very few short strands of white hair running back over the bend of the hook. I found days when it just murdered the big bluegills.

Some anglers swear by rubber bugs of various sorts. Try 'em—half the fun of fly-fishing is trying things, and very soon you'll find the preferences of the sunfish in your neighborhood, which will depend to a great extent on the natural flies on which they feed mostly. Anyhow, even when they're taking fairly well, keep changing flies pretty often to see what happens.

Spinners? I nearly always get more sunfish with plain flies, but there are times when a spinner does help. When you use one, keep it tiny, and shiny. You'll soon find that you can cast much better and more pleasantly without even the smallest spinner.

One of the greatest mistakes that most beginners make is to think that flies must be used on or near the surface. Nearly always except late evenings, one can do best by fishing the fly well down, often near the bottom in water of six feet or more.

Sometimes one can get most fish by using no lead, by just making a long cast and then sitting patiently smoking while the fly sinks. Then, one can give it more natural action down there. I have fished the bottom thus in fifteen feet of water and made grand catches.

I'll frankly admit that I'm too restless to like all that sitting around waiting for it to go down; I use this method only when I'm not having much success with any other. Generally, one can get about as many by using a little weight to hurry things; what one loses in attractive action, one makes up for by more casts. But never use larger shot than BB.

Sometimes I place the split shot or lead strip right against the eye of the hook. More often, and I think this gives the fly much better action, I put it just above the first knot on the leader. There's still another way which some use with split shot: In tying on a fly, they don't cut off that little loose end of gut; they leave it to clamp the shot onto, close to the hook —thus, one can't damage one's leader when removing it.

Besides using too-large flies, there's another reason for failing to hook one's sunfish, and that is trying to set the hook with the rod tip. The sunfish is a confirmed hit-and-runner; generally, he's hardly whacked the fly before he's found that it's a fraud and released it—his brain must work fast. It takes a moment for one to note the strike and move the rod tip. And then, if one flips quickly, the first movement of the tip is downward, toward the fish—after which it flies back hard and perhaps breaks a fine leader if the fish is large.

I land practically every sunfish that touches my fly—except those little fellows, for which I've purposely used a hook too large. So can you, if you'll do this:

Point the rod straight down the line, its tip close to the water, and work the fly by stripping in line through the guides with your left hand. I nearly always have best success by doing this in quick little jerks of an inch or two, with quite long pauses between—sometimes I give two or three little jerks in a row between pauses. Much of the time, the fish is watching the fly while it is stationary, and hits it just as it begins to move, so he is automatically hooked by the jerk. (I feel that I didn't express myself well there—it sounds like the sunfish's opinion of anybody who'd do him that way.)

The instant you've hooked him, raise the rod to the vertical, letting loose line slip through the fingers and out through the guides. Play him by stripping in with the left hand, and letting line slip through the fingers when he runs.

Very often, one lands far more than one's legal limit, or more than one wants to take home. Nobody with more humanity or sporting instincts than a hyena wants to throw injured fish back to die slowly. So have a small trout-style disgorger slung from a button of your jacket to remove the hook without doing damage.

Barbless hooks are nice to use for sunfish, since it's so easy to remove them; the barb of an ordinary hook can either be filed off or pressed down with pliers. By keeping the tension which the long spring of a fly rod allows, one can land them as well on barbless hooks as on barbed. Unless a big one can't be held away from weeds; if one on a barbless hook tangles in weeds, he's gone. But what of it? You're out primarily for fun, not for fish, and that little extra gamble will add to your sport.

In conclusion, I'll give a simple method of distinguishing bluegills from punkinseeds—these two are our largest sunfish, and the ones commonly stocked. Don't pay any attention to general color, which varies with both in different waters. Raise the back fin; if there's a large, shadowy, dark spot near its rear, its a bluegill. If the "ear"—that little rear tip of the gill cover —is a bright orange, it's a punkinseed.

They're both great scrappers, and certainly among our very finest table fish. Fishing for them with live bait and bobber is, we'll admit, kid stuff—an angler of the least experience feels sheepish if caught at it. But I've yet to find the angler who, once he'd tried it, didn't admit that fly-fishing for sunfish is sport really too good for some of the kings and ex-kings that one finds running around nowadays.

CHAPTER XXXII

Spinning—Crappies

W HEN I published my first wild-animal story, the airedale was at the height of his popularity—which is about telling my age. Remember?—"the dog that could do anything any other dog could do, and do it better." He was especially boosted as a bear fighter, to hold a bear trailed by hounds—especially a grizzly, which can't climb a tree, and probably wouldn't anyhow—until the hunter can catch up, to shoot him.

I was a professional bear and lion hunter then, and in that story I called the airedale the most useless dog known. I said that if he could be particularly useless for any one thing, it was for bear fighting, being too pig-headed and stupid to be trained, and having little courage. I'd tried 'em, plenty.

Wow! The letters that poured in from airedale lovers!

The editor who published it happened to be going West, and he questioned about every good bear hunter in Idaho on the matter. None of them could understand how I'd stuck to such mild language in speaking of airedales as bear dogs—but of course my manuscript had had to go through the mails. And they all agreed with me that there's but one bear fighter, the fox terrier. That little bundle of grit, intelligence, docility and steel springs is too small and active to get himself killed as would a larger dog, and it's funny to see half a dozen of the little beggars holding a furious grizzly backed against a boulder, their sharp voices telling him their opinion—it isn't high—of such a big, awkward wallapus. When he runs out to squash one flat, it isn't there—but five more are nipping at his heels. Thinking of it, I can never see a fox terrier on the street without grinning. Little, but oh, my!

So the editor wrote to me that it seemed that I was right, and he'd take more of my animal stories, after all. But he warned me sternly never, never again to say a word against any dog or anything else that was popular at the moment.

It taught me a lesson, and I quote my old remarks now only because since then many Wonder Dogs have come and gone. They seem to lose their miraculous qualities when they become so common that one can get a pup for nothing instead of having to pay a stiff price for him. To me, a good dog's a good dog, latest model or not.

So now, when spinning is being called the method of fishing that will do all that any other method will, and do it better, what am I to say? Dare I hint that, just possibly, it may not be qui-i-ite that good, so perhaps we shouldn't burn up all our fly and casting rods without thinking it over a day or two?

This, of course, isn't saying that spinning hasn't its uses. I'll give here a few tips for those who, having tried it, find themselves dissatisfied:

In England, where it was invented a generation or two ago—and of course it has been used to a certain extent on this side ever since, but failed to catch on—it is known as thread-line fishing. There, it has long been recognized that it will not work satisfactorily with lines testing over five pounds or so, lines too light to hold a heavy fish from weeds or snags in which he'd be lost. And such things are far more common here than in carefully manicured British rivers. But many Americans will insist on trying to spin with very heavy lines.

This method was originally intended for lures of about an eighth ounce, and I fail to see how it can equal regular casting tackle for heavy lures. The backlashless feature of spinning makes no impression on experienced anglers. If one has a backlash complex, he's merely admitting right out that he's too bull-headed to learn to cast right, as he could in a day or so, with a gentle wrist movement instead of the old muscular heave-ho.

Some complain that few real spinning lures are available, and that most of what they do find are crude things; they say that those who hold otherwise must be counting in all casting plugs, and perhaps all flies, which too, with weights, can be used for spinning—or for the casting rod. I'll admit that I've found no great variety of good ones; but there are enough to catch fish.

One source of dissatisfaction is that it's impossible to cast properly with a standard spinning reel unless one has a true spinning rod to go with it; but most insist on trying to. This rod, generally of seven feet, will have parabolic action—that is, the bend nearly all comes near the hand, and the stiff, heavy tip remains almost straight during the cast. The thin line comes off the reel gyrating centrifugally, and a large "gathering guide" straightens it only partly, therefore it will foul against a whippy tip and won't go out properly. So if you want to use a regular spinning reel, get the right rod to go with it.

The underhand toss sometimes recommended for spinning is nothing but the dub caster's side-swipe. Years of practice might give one a sort of rough accuracy with it, but the average man using it has no vague notion of where his lure is going. Why not use the accurate, easily learned overhand? It works perfectly with a spinning outfit, and gives far more accuracy.

So if you want to spin, don't try to marry your spinning

reel to a rod or line incompatible with it—it doesn't hybridize well.

Now for an example of a purpose to which spinning is peculiarly adapted:

Crappies

There are thousands of men who would rather fish for crappies than for anything else. This chiefly because in the earlier part of the season they run in large schools, so when one finds a "bed" of them one can often sit right there, with no further work for the head or the muscles, and pull them in pretty rapidly.

Practically always, they are taken on small live minnows. But this thing of holding a cane pole and watching a bobber doesn't appeal to the sportsman, the angler with some skill, especially since the crappie generally puts up much less fight than his smaller relative the sunfish. So what does one do to make better sport of it?

I have, of course, taken plenty of crappies on a fly rod—it's sort of fun, in a mild way, when you know that there are dozens of them around and that they'll stay there. But the man with live minnows almost always beat me badly at the game; any lure that will work well on a fly rod seems just too small to appeal to many crappies.

How about the casting rod? Plugs of even a quarter ounce seemed too big for most of them—I'd get a few, of course, but the live-baiters were still beating me badly.

But I can catch them very successfully on little plugs of an eighth of an ounce. These have to be used with a long, light flexible rod, a fast, free-spool reel with no level-wind, and a soft line of no more than five pounds test—the same sort of line used in spinning as a rule. The trouble is that few anglers possess this sort of casting outfit, or would have practice enough to use it successfully if they had it. And that's where the spinning rod comes in.

I recall one day last year when bass weren't doing much in the lake where I was fishing. I saw half a dozen boats anchored close to each other. That meant a crappie bed. It is not bad manners for crappie fishermen to anchor near each other—a group of boats helps the fishing, in fact, for if the school moves slowly off, one can see what boat on the outskirts is taking them and move outside it.

I drifted slowly among those boats. I'd catch one at a certain spot, and pick up perhaps a couple more there. Then two or three blank casts would show that I'd got all there at the moment. So I'd cast around me in a circle until I struck another one or two. Presently I'd try a couple of casts in that first spot again, and more would probably have moved into it —there might be a little patch of invisible weeds which sheltered food for crappies.

What was I using? A little round brass spinner about as big as a penny, with perhaps an inch of thin pork rind behind it on a bare hook. This with the lightest weight that would carry it out a reasonable distance, for a heavier would sink too deep unless retrieved much too fast for best results with crappies. I have never found anything else that would get me so many crappies.

What luck did I have? Well, I caught more crappies than all the men in all those boats put together. This wasn't from any skill that I was using. One of the others would have to wait patiently until a crappie chanced to come along and find his minnow, while I was covering the whole area of a large circle, finding them, not wasting time on where they weren't at the moment. And I've often repeated the trick since.

Here are some tips on spinning for crappies:

Much the fastest way to find a bed of them is to troll an

eighth-ounce lure. Troll it very slowly indeed; keep the spinner barely spinning—and be sure that you have one that will spin at this low speed. I have not used an outboard motor that would idle down low enough, but since one is doing only gentle, lazy dipping of the oars, it's no exertion.

Lay the reel on the boat seat beside you, with the rod tip pointing back, resting on the transom of the boat. You'll hear the reel, or see the tip jerk, when one strikes—and a crappie, with his soft mouth, will generally hook himself. Let out different lengths of line, to try various depths, but it's usually best to avoid trolling too shallow—to keep the lure six feet down or more. A crappie can be very finicky about the depth at which he will strike.

When you catch one, back up and anchor near the spot where he struck. Start casting in a circle, to find the main bed of them. And be sure to let your lure sink to the proper depth before you retrieve. Of course there's a chance that it was a lone one, so don't waste much time there if you're not getting strikes; keep on trolling. And in the later part of the season, when the big schools have broken up, you'll probably keep trolling all the time.

If a crappie strikes and misses, cast back to him, and you're practically sure to get him unless you're using too large a hook—I never use larger than a number two regular. A crappie seems to be pretty stupid, for he'll almost invariably keep striking over and over, every cast, until he succeeds in getting hooked.

Be sure to keep a net ready. Crappies have the softest mouths of any of our fish, and you may lose half of them if you try to lift them in by the line. For the same reason, don't strike hard, and play one very, very gently and carefully, not to tear the hook loose if it has a poor hold.

This method really works. So try it next time you're going

out for crappies, and you'll have some fun, even if it isn't quite as exciting sport as catching muskies.

Still, I'll have to do further research before admitting that spinning is quite the complete answer to a maiden's prayer that its proponents hold it to be. Some like it, but some don't.

CHAPTER XXXIII

Odds and Ends

Fishermen's Knots

THE plug caster does not have to know many knots. To attach his line to a wire leader or to a snap, he can use the Double O, shown in Fig. 1; or a stronger and safer one for that is the Figure Eight, shown in Fig. 2. The loop is run through the eye of his leader or snap to form Joined Permanent Loops, as in Fig. 3.

To fasten his line to a nylon leader, there is probably nothing safer, smaller or easier to tie than the Water Knot shown in Fig. 4. When this is drawn tight, it is well to throw an extra half hitch of the line around the leader. It is doubtful if this adds strength, but it avoids a short end of line fraying out rapidly and slipping back through the leader material; if this is not done, at least the loose end of line should be left quite long. It should be remembered that all knots on nylon show some inclination to slip, so they should be inspected and tested often in fishing.

A fly caster should know all the following:

The knot shown in Fig. 5 is used to attach line to leader loop. This is the Combination Overhand Kafoozelum Knot with Retroflex Hypotenuse. Of course nobody ever called it

366

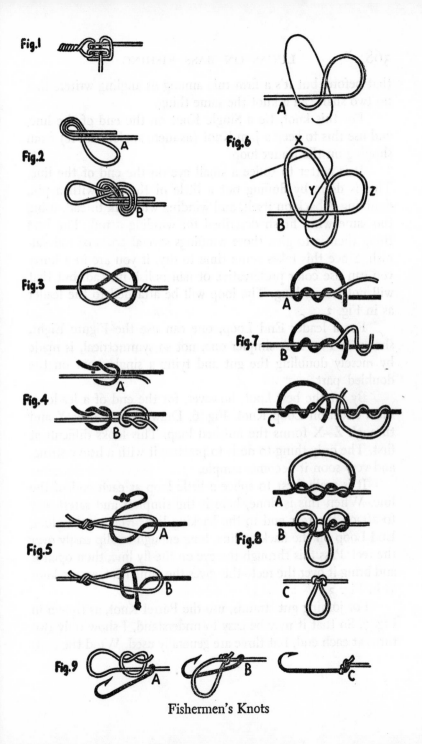

Fig.1

Fig.2
A
B

Fig.6
X
Y
Z
B

Fig.3

Fig.7
A
B

Fig.4
A
B

Fig.7
C

Fig.5
A
B

Fig.8
A
B
C

Fig.9
A
B
C

Fishermen's Knots

that before, but it's a firm rule among us angling writers that no two shall call a knot the same thing.

For this knot, tie a Single Knot on the end of the line, and use this to keep a Jam Knot (as mere anglers call it) from slipping on the leader loop.

It is better to splice a small eye on the end of the line. This is done by fluffing out a little of the end with a pin, doubling it back on itself, and winding with silk thread, using the same whip finish described for winding a rod. The best thing then is to give those windings several coats of rod varnish. Since this takes some time to dry, if you are in a hurry you can use color preservative or nail polish instead, but that will not last as long. The loop will be attached to the leader as in Fig. 3.

For a leader End Loop, one can use the Figure Eight, shown in Fig. 2. A simpler one, not so symmetrical, is made by merely doubling the gut and tying a single knot on the doubled part.

By far the best knot, however, for the end of a leader is the Perfection Loop Knot, Fig. 6. Draw loop X over Y and through Z—X forms the finished loop. This looks difficult at first. The only thing to do is to practice it with a heavy string, and very soon it becomes simple.

It is really best to splice a little loop at each end of the line. When this is done, here is the simplest and safest way to attach the rear end to the backing line: Make a very long End Loop on the backing line, long enough to slip easily over the reel. Pass this through the eye on the fly line; then open it and bring it over the reel—this gives the same neat, secure knot as in Fig. 3.

For joining gut strands, use the Barrel Knot, as shown in Fig. 7. So that it may be easy to understand, I show only two turns at each end, but three are generally used. Wind the ends in opposite directions, for by winding them the same way one gets a Blood Knot, not quite so secure.

When using this knot—and many others—on nylon, it is a good idea to steam the finished knot at the spout of a boiling tea kettle, pulling the strands meanwhile, before cutting off the ends. This sets it and makes it much more firm. In tightening knots on nylon, never jerk them—pull steadily. With natural gut, the exact opposite—a slight jerk—is best.

To tie gut strands in a hurry when fishing, the Water Knot shown in Fig. 4 is quite reliable. A variation of this is the Double Water Knot, made by bringing the ends around a second time, following the first strands of the single knots.

When casting with more than one wet fly (dry flies are practically always used singly, and most anglers now prefer single wet flies), use the dropper loop shown in Fig. 8. It begins with a Single Knot, and one merely keeps going through and through with the end. Go through four times, though, for simplicity, I show only two turns in the illustration. You must run your finger, or something such as a pencil, through the lower loop shown in 8-B, to hold it while tightening the knot.

For attaching ringed (straight) eyed flies to the leader, a Double O, as shown in Fig. 1, works well.

With the usual turned-down eyes, one can hardly beat the old Turle Knot for safety and simplicity, and for keeping the leader in line with the shank of the hook. Note that the name is not Turtle Knot, though many incorrectly call it so; it was named for Major Turle. The confusion comes from the trick of some Americans of dropping their t's, as some uneducated English drop their h's.

For the Turle Knot (Fig. 9), pass the leader through the eye; then double it back on itself and tie a Single Knot around it. Tighten this to form a loop, which you bring back over the fly and draw snug on the shank.

There are numerous other knots for all these purposes— some are weird and wonderful in their intricacy. The only advantage I see in them is to impress others with one's cleverness in being able to tie them. These I have given are about all that a fisherman will ever need.

After the manuscript of this book had been mailed to the publisher, I received information of some very careful and scientific tests of fishing knots which have just been conducted in England, using a machine especially adapted to testing gut. These seem to prove conclusively that by far the strongest and safest leader knot is the Blood Knot, always made with three turns on one side and three and a half on the other.

The Blood Knot is made exactly like the Barrel Knot (Fig. 7) except that both ends are twisted in the same direction. That is, if one begins by bringing the first end over the top, one must bring the second over the top too. Because both are going the same way, one side will always have a half turn more than the other, so that the ends may come out opposite, not side by side.*

A rough-and-ready method of comparing the strength of two knots is to make both side by side in the middle of a strand of gut, then pull on the ends to see which breaks. The test should always be made with gut that is well soaked, as in fishing, for tests with dry natural gut will vary widely. This test

---

* A last-minute footnote before publication: I have just completed thorough dynamometer tests, with nylon leader material, of all the knots described here, and of many others. I found the blood knot of 3 and 3½ turns but slightly superior to the barrel knot; however, this slight added strength makes it advisable to use it, since it is as easy to tie as the other. I discovered the water knot to be much weaker than I had suspected; therefore I do not recommend it even for a hurried stream-side knot. For joining leader material to a casting line, I now recommend perfection knots on each, to form joined permanent loops; though this looks clumsy, it is the most reliable by far and it casts well through the guides. I found all the other knots described here to be reliable for their purposes.

will not show the tensile strength in pounds of each knot, but it will show definitely which is the stronger, and that is what we are interested in.

It should be remembered that even the best knot has a far lower tensile strength than a straight strand, and some are unbelievably weak. Therefore the angler should be extremely careful to use the proper knots, and to make them correctly.

I might add that while we hear a great deal about the tendency of knots on nylon to slip, I have no trouble at all with them so long as they are leader-material to leader-material, and so long as I make them with even reasonable care, testing them by pulling when finished. Indeed, I rarely bother to steam them, as they seem to hold about as well for me without that. The case is different when it comes to attaching nylon leader material to something else, even to nylon fishing line. I have never found knots which I could depend on very much for that; the best need constant inspection and testing while I fish—and even then will occasionally fail me.

Wire Leaders—Snaps—Swivels

Where there are no sharp-toothed fish, a wire leader is not advisable, for some plugs have better action without one. But for convenience in changing lures, a snap should be attached to the end of the line. This should be about as small as one can easily operate; a large one will spoil the action of some lures. Not only that, but a large snap, especially if shiny, will appear part of the lure, and sometimes cause a bass to strike too far forward, missing the hooks.

With a few of the smallest lures, best action of all can be had by using not even a snap. In this case, a long end loop is usually made on the end of the line, passed through the eye, and back around the lure.

Where sharp-toothed fish are present, a wire leader is necessary. This seldom, if ever, needs to be more than eight inches long, and where there are only pickerel, smaller pike or such, four inches or so is often enough.

I long ago discovered a peculiar thing about wire leaders which I never saw commented upon before. During my first years of bass fishing, I was much puzzled by the fact that on some days I would get a great many fairly hard strikes and fail to hook a single bass. Experimenting, I even tried, on such days, hanging small and very sharp hooks all over the plug, until it would seem impossible for a bass so much as to touch one without getting hooked. And still it went on. Until then, I had used mostly leaders of twisted or braided bronze wire.

I changed to leaders of light, solid steel wire. And then, on days when I could not hook my strikes, I noticed something odd: after each missed strike, there would be a slight, sharp bend in my leader.

That solved it. The bass were striking at the shiny wire leader! Why they should do so, with a juicy-looking plug immediately behind, I have not the slightest notion. And it is a still deeper mystery to me why on certain comparatively rare days almost all of them do that. Perhaps at other times it accounts for some of our missed strikes.

The answer, of course, is a dull leader, and the least bulky or showy one possible. This dulling could probably be done quickly with chemicals, but I just remove all oil from the leaders with gasoline or soap and water, and then hang them out where they will rust—this, I think, is about the dullest finish one can get.

My reason for abandoning the use of twisted or braided leaders was not only their bulk, but the fact that most of them are almost impossible to straighten when they become bent all over; they look clumsy, and must be very visible to a fish. Now, I always use a single strand of quite light steel wire. It is easy to straighten, and when properly rusted should be least likely to be noticed by a fish.

One always finds leaders fitted with one or two swivels. A swivel is completely useless here; unless a heavy keel sinker is used ahead of it, the wet line will twist before it turns. This is something which nobody seems to realize. However, the swivel does no harm unless it is large, or shiny, making an occasional bass strike too far forward and miss the hooks, or unless used with certain very small lures the action of which it might affect.

Anyone who objects to a swivel can easily snip one off with his cutting pliers. It will not be necessary to make a new loop on the wire for the snap; with a snap of the ordinary type, the flat metal part can be pushed down, allowing the eye of the leader to be slipped on, and then that flat part worked back into place again.

One who wishes to make his own leaders can easily do so by buying a coil of suitable wire and a few snaps. The eyes can be formed by twisting the wire around a small nail or something of the sort, using pliers. It will be found neatest and most convenient to form eyes at both ends, then open the tops of the snaps and slip them through.

For sharp-toothed fish, one can use a long nylon leader with a short wire one at its end.

Glass-Plastic Rods

When I wrote Part II of this book, I was still reserving judgment on the latest development in fishing rods, those of glass-plastic, although I had used some of them during the several months that they had then been on the market. Now, after having used rods of this type steadily for more than two years, I will venture my opinion for what it may be worth:

I like them. In action, weight, balance and feel I find them comparable to bamboo rods—not to steel rods.

Since these are so new, I find some tendency among less experienced anglers to take for granted that all "glass" rods must be alike. That is not the case, for different companies make them by entirely different processes—and it would be possible to make a bad rod of this material, as of any other.

Some methods of manufacture seem to produce more uniformity of action than others, but in no case have I found the wide variance of action found in cheaper bamboos. Not only that, but a given maker's eight-foot glass fly rod may have action much superior to his rod of six inches longer—or vice versa.

There are some glass-plastic casting rods which I consider too stiff for good action; that is, to bring out action one must use a very heavy plug. But this same action might suit one who wants extreme distance with little delicacy.

I have heard a few men complain of the surfaces of their glass rods becoming damaged. I suspect that this may have been caused by the owners, accustomed to heavy steel rods, subjecting them to unwarranted rough usage, such as allowing the rod to rub against some hard edge during a long automobile trip. Mine have not given me the slightest trouble in this respect and show no sign of doing so; all, after much use, still have the appearance of new.

Somewhere a yarn got started that glass rods would break in cold weather. I have used mine in November on the Canadian border, when I had to stop fishing because my line was freezing stiff. Not only did they not break, but I could notice no change in the action; and at least one maker is now guaranteeing his glass rods to be undamaged by sub-zero weather—in which, of course, nobody uses a rod.

It is sometimes held that these rods will not stand heat. I have used mine on Lake Mead, in the desert between Arizona and Nevada, when the daily temperatures were such that we considered a mere one hundred degrees a cool wave, when I dared not touch metal with my bare hand. It made not the slightest change in their action, and had no deleterious effect on them. Pilots of fishing boats there, whom I questioned, told me that they had never heard of heat having any bad effect on these rods.

I know of split-bamboo fly rods which have been in constant use for fifty years and more, but still seem to be about as good as new. These were expensive rods in the first place, and had been given very exceptional care—a drop of two of water through a crack in the varnish would have ruined their careers before they had well begun. Whether glass rods will stand up that long, nobody yet knows, since artificial ageing cannot exactly simulate natural. But their being apparently waterproof all through should prevent the disintegration due to moisture which so often ruins bamboos; this is an important point, and it leads me to suspect that a glass rod may give longer service than would the average bamboo. Another good feature is that a glass rod, at least under ordinary circumstances, does not seem to take a set which would have to be removed.

The man who knows what real casting is will be happy to know that at last he is being given some consideration, for he can now purchase from stock a glass casting rod up to six feet long. One six-footer which I have been using for some time is powerful enough to handle plugs of five eighths ounce easily, and strong enough to be safe in the hands of a man of very moderate skill; still, owing to some peculiarity of its action, it will cast in a satisfactory manner a much wider range of weights than will most casting rods—I have used plugs as light as a quarter ounce on it with good results. Since this rod is very light for its length and strength, it can be used easily by one who might find a six-foot tubular steel so tiring that his casting would become poor after an hour or two of using it.

Not long ago I received a glass casting rod of six feet with extra light action, accompanied by a warning from its maker that it should never be used with plugs of over one-fourth ounce. However, I found it about ideal for those of three-eighths ounce when I wished the utmost in accuracy and ease at no more than good moderate ranges; a slight twitch of my wrist, and the plug seemed to sail out all by itself.

The maker told me that he is afraid to place these rods on the market, for their falling into wrong hands would mean a continuous stream of them being returned to him for replacement—this, of course, is what has always kept makers from putting out long, light rods for more advanced casters. I suggested that he put them out, by all means, but to attach to each a tag saying that it is not subject to his usual guarantee; that it is intended only for a skilled angler accustomed to playing fish on light tackle, one who knows better than to strain a rod by attempting a long cast with a plug too heavy for it; that it would be replaced only if inspection at the factory clearly showed some defect in workmanship—a thing, I should add, which seems unlikely in a rod of this type. I believe he is going to do this.

There is but one thing which I consider unfortunate in connection with this light rod: it is available at present only with sunken reel seat, and nearly all the top-notch anglers of my acquaintance prefer a straight reel seat and handle such as is usually found on a bamboo. For one thing, a handle and reel seat of this type can be lighter than any other; also, many hold that they can do better and more accurate casting with them. Since writing the earlier parts of this book, I have been using sunken reel seats a good deal, and I cannot bring myself to like them quite as well as the straight—which, as I have said elsewhere, is no reason why one who does like them, and can cast best with them, should not use them. I have been trying to persuade the maker of this rod to furnish it with light, straight handle and reel seat optional for those of us who prefer that, and I think I have him almost talked into the notion of doing it. If he does, the man accustomed to long, light bamboos could switch to this rod without confusion.

All the foregoing does not mean that I am calling glass-plastic superior to bamboo as rod material—and I should add that at last some light six-foot bamboos are coming somewhat hesitantly on the market in stock models. It means that at present I have no choice between glass rods and good bamboos; when I find one with balance and action to suit me, I do not care which of these materials it is made of.

Live Bait

For many years our leading angling writers have been growing more and more apologetic in writing about methods of using live bait for game fish, more and more anxious to let their readers know that they themselves rarely use it. I think it is high time we came right out with the truth, and risk a few irate letters from readers, high time men calling themselves sportsmen stopped using methods which they feel call for explanations and apologies.

To put it bluntly, taking game fish on live bait can hardly be regarded as either sport or sportsmanship. Not sport, because anything else called by that name implies the acquisition of skill. It takes no skill to jab a hook through an unfortunate frog or minnow, drop him overboard or let him wash downstream, and wait for some poor fish to swallow him so deeply that he cannot put up a fight when hooked—naturally, a fish being hauled by some sensitive and vital internal part cannot fight.

Not sportsmanship, because it means destruction of undersize fish. Too many caught on live bait are hooked so deeply that they die when released. Year after year I am disgusted, when passing live-bait fishermen, to see dying fish struggling feebly on the surface of the water. The matter would not be so bad if all live-bait men were careful in removing the hook, and would use disgorgers of some sort. The undeniable fact is that what happens at least half the time is that the man is provoked because a small fish has ruined his bait, and so yanks the hook out roughly, perhaps bringing part of the fish's gullet or gills with it. Then, about as often as not, in his exasperation he dashes the injured fish as hard as he can against the surface of the water. Multiply this instance by thousands of cases, and we can see one thing that is happening to our fishing—how can there be many large ones for next season?

The two principal American fresh-water game fishes are bass and trout. Fortunately, the times are rare indeed when artificial lures cannot take far more bass than live bait. If one will learn to use artificial lures properly, and develop the skill that should go with anything deserving the name of sport; and it takes very little practice and study to be able to catch more bass, at nearly all times, on artificial lures.

The case with trout is somewhat different. Few question that in clear water artificial lures, if used with any skill at all, will take more trout than live bait. But it is about agreed that live bait or salmon eggs will catch more trout in a muddy river. So, some argue, one is compelled to use live bait in a muddy river, or catch few trout. But if trout are taken by crude and unsportsmanlike methods when the water is muddy, that inevitably means that those trout are not there to be caught by sportsmanlike methods when the water clears. All this applies, too, to bass on the comparatively rare occasions when live bait is most productive for them.

Does a player of pocket billiards, on days when he is off his game, insist on pulling the balls into the pocket with a garden rake? Does the beginner insist on doing it so that he can get as many balls in as a skilled player? Certainly not— because there is more sportsmanship in pocket billiards than a great many apply to fishing; there is more sportsmanship in marbles, where "fudging" is not permitted. There are too many fishing who have not even a rudimentary knowledge of what the word sportsmanship means, who never can understand it, and it should be unnecessary to say what these are doing to the game for the rest of us.

The thing to do is obvious: either refrain from fishing or be satisfied with few fish on the days when live bait would be the more successful—and these times, as I said, are quite rare with bass, though more frequent in trout fishing. This also applies to pike, muskellunge and other fresh-water game fish which strike freely on artificial lures.

With the walleye it is different again: often, for long periods, he will not strike artificial lures well but can be taken readily on live bait. Because of this, and the comparatively poor fight he puts up, he is regarded as no more than a semi-game fish, and the really advanced sportsman will rarely bother with walleyes unless he wants one to eat—the walleye is one of our best food fishes. Matters being thus, I give no advice about the use of live bait for walleyes; let the angler use his own judgment.

I know of one lake up in the Quetico country, on the Ontario border, where the resort owners banded together to enforce certain rules. Their guides saw to it that nobody carried live bait onto the lake; a man who brought it and tried to rent a boat was ordered to dump it up on the hillside before going out. And these guides were instructed that, when they saw a man remove a hook roughly from a small fish before liberating it, they were immediately to bring him back to the resort, where he would be told to pack and get out—his kind wasn't wanted there. Fishing in that lake remained superlative, season after season.

Some of the resorts changed hands, and the new owners would not "play ball" with the rest; they were too anxious to grab every penny they could from guests. They permitted fishing with live bait, and they did not care how undersized fish were liberated. Result? Within a few seasons that lake was ruined, sportsmen and fish-hogs alike going elsewhere— and the formerly prosperous resort owners were going broke, their cabins shabby and needing repairs.

If that could happen on a wilderness lake, how much more quickly could the ordinary hard-fished lake be ruined by live bait and unsportsmanlike methods?

From the foregoing, it will be seen why this book contains no instructions whatever on the use of live bait for bass. I know that what I say here will bring me a few hostile, invective-packed letters—I know it because I've said the same thing before in print. But I believe that the man who makes no enemies in a good cause makes no real friends: he's too wishy-washy. I can only hope that my attitude in this matter will make me more friends than enemies; but I say it regardless. Anyway, I want no friends who are not sportsmen, and by that I certainly don't mean merely hunters and anglers; sportsmanship is as possible in an office or shop as on the water or in the field—it merely means being a "good sport" in one's dealings with one's associates, or with a stray dog. The man who is that will be a good sportsman when he goes hunting or fishing; he who isn't, won't, and the rest of us can only wish that he'd stay off the water, and not ruin our sport.

And so I conclude this book, sincerely hoping that it will be of some use to those who are already sportsmen, and also to the many fishermen who are good sports in their hearts but haven't yet learned how to apply sportsmanship to angling. Yes, as Izaac Walton pointed out three hundred years ago, there's a lot more to fishing than just killing fish.

So—good fishing, brother!